Praise for *Electronic Legal Deposit*

'*Electronic Legal Deposit: Shaping the Library Collections of the Future* brings together different voices, UK and international, to capture the joint endeavour between libraries and publishers to systematically collect and preserve the national collection of electronic publications, from websites to e-books. Critically, the editors use those contrasting voices to challenge the current model, resulting in a volume that both records the story so far and issues a call for policy change in the future evolution of e-legal deposit; a future shaped more clearly by the needs of research and access.'
Dr Jessica Gardner, University Librarian & Director of Library Services, Cambridge University Libraries

'If collecting and preserving all human records has been the greatest dream of all libraries since the Library of Alexandria, building an ark of digital knowledge is the remaining hope for modern librarianship. At the onset of this pandemic tragedy, this book is rich in thoughts and cutting-edge practices to show you how far we are from a possible future reconstruction of our human digital civilization.'
Wei (Keven) Liu, Deputy Director, Shanghai Library

'Taking a global view, and presenting the thoughts, critical reflections and commentaries of a number of eminent researchers, scholars, archivists and technologists, editors Gooding and Terras make a valuable contribution to knowledge, and produce essential reading for everyone interested in the past, present and future of electronic legal deposit.'
Gobinda Chowdhury, Professor of Information Science, University of Strathclyde

'This solid overview of the trends and commonalities between various approaches on e-legal deposit is useful for all of us who need to understand the basics. But what makes this a great read is that Melissa and Paul dare to go beyond the obvious and interrogate how libraries can remain relevant in an era where the likes of Google represent the first port of call for millions of individuals.'
Harry Verwayen, Executive Director, Europeana Foundation

'These thoughtful essays, focusing on digital deposit in the UK, but with contributions from both hemispheres, offer a history of digital deposit over the last 20 years. They consider the structures and capabilities that enable and inhibit efforts in this space, and balance a necessary focus on deficits – work that has to be done! – with the potential affordances of digital legal deposit collections. A must read for those of us that know that legal deposit is at the heart of every national library's mission.'
Dr Marie-Louise Ayres, Director-General, National Library of Australia

Electronic Legal Deposit

Electronic Legal Deposit

Shaping the Library Collections of the Future

Edited by
Paul Gooding and
Melissa Terras

facet publishing

Published by Facet Publishing,
7 Ridgmount Street, London WC1E 7AE
www.facetpublishing.co.uk

Facet Publishing is wholly owned by CILIP: the Library and Information Association.

British Library Cataloguing in Publication Data
A catalogue record for this book is available from the British Library.

ISBN 978-1-78330-377-9 (hardback)
ISBN 978-1-78330-378-6 (e-book)
First published 2020

Text printed on FSC accredited material.

MIX
Paper from responsible sources
FSC® C013604

Typeset from editors' files by Flagholme Publishing Services in
10/13 pt Palatino Linotype and Open Sans.
Printed and made in Great Britain by CPI Group (UK) Ltd, Croydon, CR0 4YY.

For Sian

For Os, Anthony, Edward and Fergusson

Contents

Figures and tables

Figures

Tables

Contributors

Linda Arnold-Stratford has worked for the six UK legal deposit libraries since 2014. Working closely with colleagues across all disciplines and libraries, along with publishers and the UK government, she has paved the way for a smooth transition from print to digital legal deposit. Prior to that Linda held curatorial roles in STM and Business and Management Studies at the British Library following a career in academic publishing. She was educated at the University of Leeds, where she obtained her PhD in Microbiology (2000). She is a member of CILIP.

Linda Berube is currently an AHRC Collaborative Doctoral Programme student, working with the British Library and the Human-Computer Interaction Design (HCID) Centre at City University of London. Her research is based on a mixed-methods and interdisciplinary approach to understanding the UK digital comics creation-to-consumption cycle. This work follows on from her role as Senior Research Associate at the University of East Anglia for the AHRC-funded Digital Library Futures project. She is also a digital programme management consultant whose career focus has been leading projects and services in the areas of information management, e-books and web services, and the legal deposit of digital publications. After a career in the USA in academic, law and public libraries, she came to the UK as a Fulbright Fellow and has since worked with the Legal Deposit Advisory Panel, as well as the Foreign and Commonwealth Office, the Bill and Melinda Gates Foundation and Amnesty International.

Blessing Chiparausha is the Deputy Librarian at the Bindura University of Science Education (BUSE) in Zimbabwe. He is also an active member of local and international library associations. His areas of interest include professional growth in LIS, resource sharing and digital libraries.

Chiparausha is a holder of a Master of Science in LIS, an Honours Degree in LIS, and is currently completing a PhD in LIS.

Collence Takaingenhamo Chisita is a Principal Lecturer and Research Fellow based at the University of South Africa's College of Human Sciences, Department of Information Sciences. Chisita is a holder of a PhD in Information Sciences and Master of Science in LIS. His doctoral research thesis explores the concept of resource sharing in the digital age and it also analyses the challenges and opportunities of the new trajectory of open access models. Chisita has served as a resource and focal person in Zimbabwe for the IFLA Global Vision.

Paul Cunnea is Head of the Acquisitions & Description Division at the National Library of Scotland, where he oversees the Library's acquisition of print and digital content through legal deposit, purchase, donation and web archiving, management of the Library's collections metadata and the Library's hidden collections programme. Paul is Chair of the Cataloguing and Indexing Group in Scotland and has worked on various projects and sub-groups of the Legal Deposit Libraries Implementation Group, the Joint Committee on Legal Deposit and the Legal Deposit Advisory Panel.

Isabel Galina Russell is currently a researcher at the Instituto de Investigaciones Bibliográficas at the Universidad Nacional Autónoma de México (UNAM). The institute is part of the Biblioteca Nacional, Mexico's national library. She works mainly on new modes of scholarship and digital projects within the humanities, as well as digital preservation and bibliographic heritage.

Paul Gooding is Senior Lecturer in Information Studies at the University of Glasgow. His research focuses on the impact of digital library collections on institutions and users. He was Principal Investigator on Digital Library Futures (2017–19), an AHRC-funded project to analyse the impact of non-print legal deposit on UK academic libraries. Paul holds an MA in Library and Information Studies (2007) and a PhD in Digital Humanities (2014) from University College London. From 2014 to 2018 he was Research Fellow in Digital Humanities at the University of East Anglia, where he founded and led the UEA Digital Humanities incubator, and before undertaking his PhD worked as a librarian for BBC Sport.

Eva-Lis Green has been Director of the Digital Collection Department at the National Library of Sweden since February 2017. She has a background at the Swedish public service broadcaster (Sveriges Television) as Strategic Media

Quality Controller, Head of Archives and Transmission, Information System Co-ordinator at the Engineering Department and also project manager for different IT and Media Management systems. She is a member of the Executive Council of FIAT/IFTA. She has studied Swedish language, literature and music at Lund University and is also a qualified Librarian.

Gill Hamilton is Digital Access Manager at the National Library of Scotland, where she leads on access to the Library's extensive digital collections and oversees resource discovery, library systems and the website. She also co-ordinates initiatives to share the Library's collections with services such as WikiCommons, WikiData, Flickr and YouTube. Gill is co-author of the book *Open Licensing for Cultural Heritage* (2017).

Graeme Hawley is Head of General Collections at the National Library of Scotland, where he is responsible for 20th- and 21st-century publications. A collection of over 14 million printed items, this collection has grown extensively since 2013, with the further addition of 5 million published collection items and 10 million archived websites. His team of curators are responsible for curating this collection, from selection of collection content to interpretation activities, research collaborations, and audience engagement. He is on various sub-groups of the Legal Deposit Libraries Implementation Group.

William Kilbride is Executive Director of the Digital Preservation Coalition, a global not-for-profit organisation providing community engagement, advocacy, workforce development, capacity, good practice and standards in digital preservation. William started his career in the 1990s, when enthusiasm for new technology outstripped the capacity to manage the resulting data. He joined the DPC from Glasgow Museums, where he was Research Manager, and before that was Assistant Director of the Archaeology Data Service at the University of York. He was previously a Lecturer in Archaeology at the University of Glasgow, where he completed his PhD and where he retains an honorary position.

Göran Konstenius is Senior Advisor at the National Library of Sweden, which among other tasks includes research. Relevant for this publication is a research project on legal deposits in a digital media landscape. Göran has extensive experience working in archives and libraries, for example as the Director of the audiovisual department in the National Library and as the Director of Collecting and Documentation in the National Archive of Sound and Moving Images. He has an academic background in cultural and behavioural science.

Danmore Maboreke is a Chief Archivist at the National Archives of Zimbabwe. He is a holder of an MSc in Information Sciences and is currently studying for a PhD. His areas of interest include records management, archives, bibliographic control and access to information.

Jo Ana Morfin is a time-based media conservator who works on projects in the field of digital preservation and digital collections. Morfin, trained as a conservator of traditional artworks, now researches issues of digital heritage and the creative use of documentation and archives, and the crossovers between performance studies and variable media art preservation.

Adrienne Muir was until December 2019 Professor of Information Management at Robert Gordon University Aberdeen. She has researched and taught information policy, law and ethics for over 25 years. Her research has focused on legal and ethical issues relating to digital libraries, including doctoral research on digital legal deposit. She was part of an international study on the impact of copyright law on digital presentation, the results of which were presented at the World Intellectual Property Organization. She was also a member of the NISO License Expression Working Group and an independent member of the UK government's Legal Deposit Advisory Panel.

Bethany Nowviskie is Dean of Libraries and Professor of English at James Madison University. A past president of the Association for Computers and the Humanities, Nowviskie formerly directed the Digital Library Federation at the Council on Library and Information Resources and was founding director of the Scholars' Lab at the University of Virginia Library. She received her PhD in Literature from the University of Virginia in 2004 and has worked on numerous ground-breaking projects in digital libraries and the digital humanities.

Richard Ovenden has been Bodley's Librarian (the senior executive position of the Bodleian Libraries, University of Oxford) since 2014. Prior to that he held positions at Durham University Library, the House of Lords Library, the National Library of Scotland and the University of Edinburgh. He moved to the Bodleian in 2003 as Keeper of Special Collections, becoming Deputy Librarian in 2011. He was educated at the University of Durham and University College London, and holds a Professorial Fellowship at Balliol College, Oxford. He is a Fellow of the Society of Antiquaries, the Royal Society of Arts, and a Member of the American Philosophical Society. He was made OBE in the Queen's Birthday Honours 2019. Richard serves as Treasurer of the Consortium of European Research Libraries, as President of the Digital

Preservation Coalition, and as a member of the Board of the Council on Library and Information Resources (in Washington DC).

Ana Yuri Ramírez-Molina works at the Coordinación de Innovación y Estrategia Digital at the Biblioteca Nacional de México. With a background in information technologies for libraries she now works in the planning and development of digitisation projects and digital legal deposit, both of them from a digital preservation perspective.

Fred Saunderson is Rights and Information Manager at the National Library of Scotland, where he leads on copyright, data protection, and records management. He chairs the UK Libraries and Archives Copyright Alliance (LACA) and is a member of the Europeana Copyright Community Steering Group, the Archives and Records Association Legislation and Standards Working Group, and the Copyright Evidence Wiki editorial board at the University of Glasgow's CREATe copyright research centre. He is co-author of the book *Open Licensing for Cultural Heritage* (2017).

Melissa Terras is the Professor of Digital Cultural Heritage at the University of Edinburgh's College of Arts, Humanities, and Social Sciences, leading digital aspects of CAHSS research as Director of the Edinburgh Centre for Data, Culture and Society, and is Director of Research in the Edinburgh Futures Institute. She is an Honorary Professor of Digital Humanities in UCL Department of Information Studies, where she was employed from 2003 to 2017. She is a Fellow of the Alan Turing Institute and a Trustee of the National Library of Scotland. You can generally find her on Twitter, @melissaterras.

Frankie Wilson is the Head of Assessment at the Bodleian Libraries, University of Oxford. She provides strategic leadership for assessment throughout the Libraries, including training staff in assessment techniques and designing and running assessment activities. She has extensive experience in applying a wide range of assessment methodologies (both qualitative and quantitative) to assess the impact of library provision, effectively communicating the results, and achieving changes in service provision to improve customer satisfaction and productivity. Frankie holds a doctorate in the field of performance measurement, quality and culture change in academic libraries, and continues to be an active researcher as well as practitioner. She is Chair of the Board of the International Conference on Performance Measurement in Libraries, and serves on the Library Assessment Conference board.

Jane Winters is Professor of Digital Humanities at the School of Advanced Study, University of London. Her current and past research projects include CLEOPATRA: Cross-Lingual, Event-Centric Open Analytics Research Academy, Digging into Linked Parliamentary Data, Big UK Domain Data for the Arts and Humanities, Traces through Time: Prosopography in Practice across Big Data, and the Thesaurus of British and Irish History as SKOS (Simple Knowledge Organization System). Her research interests include digital history, born digital archives (particularly the archived web), big data for humanities research and open access publishing.

Foreword

Bethany Nowviskie

On the morning of 9 November 2016 I looked out over a Milwaukee ballroom crowded with librarians, archivists, and specialists in digital preservation. Some were pensive. Many were weeping. Others seemed stricken.

My audience had gathered for the first joint conference of the Digital Library Federation (DLF, the US-based non-profit organisation I then directed) with its new partner, the National Digital Stewardship Alliance (NDSA) – a cross-industry group that had recently come under DLF's wing from its place of genesis at the Library of Congress. We were strangers and friends, largely though not exclusively American, united in a community of practice and the common cause of a dedication to the future of libraries, archives, and their holdings and information services in the digital age. But it suddenly felt as if we didn't know what information *was*, and whether – despite all our efforts, expertise, and the shared infrastructure that our memory institutions represented – its future *could* be made secure.

The unexpected outcome of the US presidential election, announced in the wee hours the night before, had cast a pall over this professional audience that crossed party lines. How could so many confident, data-driven predictions have been so wrong? What shared social understandings – built from the seeming common landscape of ubiquitous digital information that we had met to manage and survey – had never, in fact, *been* shared or were even *commonly* legible at all? And what evidentiary traces of this time would remain, in a political scene of post-truth posturing, the devaluation of expert knowledge, and the willingness of our new authorities – soon to become as evident on federal websites as in press conferences and cable news punditry – to revise and resubmit the historical record?

The weeks and months that followed, for DLF and NDSA members, were filled with action. While the End of Term Web Archive project sprang to its regular work of harvesting US federal domains at moments of presidential transition, reports that Trump administration officials had ordered the removal of information on climate change and animal welfare from the websites of the Environmental Protection Agency and US Department of Agriculture fostered a fear of the widespread deletion of scientific records, and prompted emergency 'Data Rescue' download parties. A new DLF Government Records Transparency and Accountability working group was launched. Its members began watch-dogging preparations for the 2020 US Census and highlighting House and Senate bills meant to curtail scientific and demographic data creation; scrutinising proposed changes to the records retention schedules of federal agencies and seeking ways to make the arcanum of their digital preservation workflows more accessible to the general public; and – amid new threats of the deportation of immigrants and the continued rise of violent nationalism – asking crucial questions about what electronic information *should* be made discoverable and accessible, for the protection of vulnerable persons. The Social Sciences Research Council convened a meeting on challenges to the digital preservation of documents of particular value to historians, economists, cultural anthropologists, and other social scientists, and the PEGI Project – focusing on the Preservation of Electronic Government Information – commissioned a wide-ranging report on at-risk, born-digital information meant to be held by US federal depository libraries and other cultural memory institutions for long-term public access and use.

Over time, reflective, pedagogical, and awareness-raising projects like Endangered Data Week emerged, ties among the NDSA and international organisations like the UK-based Digital Preservation Coalition were strengthened, and conversations on college campuses (fuelled by the Cambridge Analytica scandal and the work of scholars of race, technology, and social media like Safiya Noble and Siva Vaidhyanathan) turned more squarely to data ethics and algorithmic literacy. Frenetic Data Rescue parties gave over to the more measured advocacy and storytelling approach of the Data Refuge movement. And in the UK, an AHRC-funded project, Digital Library Futures, led by Paul Gooding and Melissa Terras (the seed of this edited collection), offered a golden opportunity to reflect – in the light of altered global understandings of the preservation and access challenges surrounding digital information – on the parliamentary Legal Deposit Libraries (Non Print Works) Regulations of 2013, which extended collecting practices dating to the Early Modern Period to new media formats beyond the book.

You hold in your hands (or view on your screens, or listen to through e-readers, or encounter in some other way I can't yet foresee) an important and timely volume. It is well balanced between reflection-and-outlook and practice-and-method in what our editors call the 'contested space' of e-legal deposit-taking on the international and very long-term consequences of our present-day conception, regulation, assembly, positioning, and use of library-held digital collections.

In other words, the essays assembled here cross space and time. The editors take a necessarily global view in bringing together a broad array of national approaches to the legal deposit of materials that already circulate in world-wide networks. And while the authors they've invited to contribute certainly take a long view of digital information, they also frequently address, head-on, the ways that electronic legal deposit forces our attention not just on posterity, but on the here-and-now of what media consumption *means* and how it *works* in the digital age. Rather than asking us to rest our imaginations on a far-future prospect in which reading is conducted *as it ever was* in print (*was* any such act, as Jerome McGann would ask, self-identical?), the authors of these essays, collectively, assert that the kaleidoscopic mediations of e-legal deposit show us we've never *really* known what reading is.

The best thinkers on libraries question the very assumptions that our memory institutions rest upon, while elevating and honouring both their promise and the centuries of labour and careful (if not always disinterested or benign) intent that have made them what they are. Melissa Terras and Paul Gooding are among the best, and the perspectives they have assembled here – from publishers, eminent librarians and archivists, technologists, organisers, and scholars – make this edited collection an essential contribution to the literature on digital preservation. It is a necessary book that grapples with legal, practical, technical, and conceptual problems: with the distinctive visions and values of libraries; with the necessarily concomitant development of policies and platforms; and even with the very nature of our documentary heritage, at a moment when print-era logics break down.

What I most appreciate is that this book – like the notion of e-legal deposit itself – calls for careful consideration of both present-day services and research possibilities not yet dreamt of. In this, it serves the true mission of legal deposit libraries: to be a stable bridge between a past that is perpetually constructed by our acts of preservation and erasure – and the many futures we may mediate but can barely imagine.

Bethany Nowviskie
Dean of Libraries and Professor of English,
James Madison University, Harrisonburg, Virginia

Introduction

Paul Gooding and Melissa Terras

> In the paper world legal deposit and preservation of printed heritage are almost synonymous with libraries. In the digital world it is not a matter of course that libraries are best suited to perform these tasks.
>
> (Larsen, 2005, 86)

Do libraries still belong at the heart of access to our digital heritage? This might seem a strange place to start a volume on electronic legal deposit, but Larsen's provocation remains relevant to our current cultural moment. For centuries, our national and research libraries have been trusted repositories of print production and culture. In terms of comprehensiveness, expertise, and accessibility, their collections were rightly viewed as world-leading. In 2005, the same year that Larsen raised the prospect that libraries could no longer be presumed to occupy that position, the Alexandria Manifesto on Libraries summed up a more aspirational objective for libraries:

> Libraries and information services contribute to the sound operation of the inclusive information society. They enable intellectual freedom by providing access to information, ideas and works of imagination in any medium and regardless of frontiers.
>
> (Australian Library Journal, 2005)

In the past, libraries were undoubted technological innovators, designers of organisational improvements such as card catalogues and complex classification systems. Contemporary libraries are still spaces for innovation, but budget cuts and the growth of networked communications mean that the technological cutting edge has moved elsewhere. Karen Coyle points out that 'if we look … at the timeline of information technology over the 20th Century and into the 21st, we see library technology falling behind the general technology evolution' (Coyle, 2017). Rather than looking towards libraries as their first source for information, individuals now look towards Google or Facebook. Their information-seeking expectations are formed elsewhere, and they increasingly require access for reading on their own devices and in remote locations. Commonly, individuals also want portable data, and the ability to access textual corpora and metadata. And yet the main mode for accessing modern legal deposit materials in a legal deposit library setting is via what Georgi Alexandrov terms 'e-reading' (Alexandrov, 2018, 137): access to a single volume via a terminal within library reading rooms, for the sole purpose of reading. The dynamic process of change surrounding late 20th-century communications technology stands in stark contrast to the print-era logic of e-legal deposit regulations. This disconnect requires us to interrogate the critical and professional library spaces inhabited by the centuries-old regulatory environment of legal deposit in light of the digital turn.

Legal deposit is the regulatory requirement that a person or group submit copies of their publications to a trusted repository. First introduced by France in the 16th century (Larivière, 2000, 6), legal deposit has since been adopted around the world: as of 2016, 62 out of 245 national and state libraries worldwide either benefited from legal deposit regulations or participated in legal deposit activities (De Beer et al., 2016, 88). Many other nations operate legal deposit via government ministries and copyright offices (Staff of the Global Legal Research Directorate, 2017). Regulations permitting legal deposit of printed publications have played a vital role in supporting libraries to build comprehensive national collections for the public good (Brazier, 2016, 42). In the last two decades, the scope of legal deposit has grown to formally incorporate 'electronic' or 'non-print' publication; those published in digital and other non-print formats.

This book was inspired by our AHRC-funded project, Digital Library Futures, which was concerned with exploring the impact of this change in scope from legal deposit to electronic legal deposit. We were specifically interested in analysing the impact of UK Non-Print Legal Deposit (NPLD) upon academic libraries and their users. Throughout the book, electronic legal deposit (e-legal deposit) is used as a broad term to denote legal deposit regulations that apply to digital materials. NPLD is the specific term for the UK's 2013 e-legal deposit regulations, which formalised arrangements for the UK legal deposit libraries to capture digital publications (The Legal Deposit Libraries (Non-Print Works) Regulations 2013).

One of the key interventions of our work to date has been to place users at the heart of debates around legal deposit. In our white paper which summarised the findings of the project, we argued that the literature around legal deposit is built around four key pillars: collection development, including selection, metadata and bibliographic management; questions of long-term digital preservation of e-legal deposit collections; details of technical implementation such as systems, capture, ingest and standards; and regulatory aspects of e-legal deposit (Gooding, Terras and Berube 2019). This volume reflects our belief that users must be understood as the missing fifth pillar of e-legal deposit. The context for the regulations involves a complex interplay between the rights and needs of content creators, cultural heritage organisations, and users, and yet current orthodoxy relegates the third group to the status of an indeterminate group of future users. In the UK, for instance, the government aim for NPLD was to 'mirror the level of access to printed materials' (Hansard, 2013), a largely retrograde failure of imagination in the face of immense change. The presence of a dedicated section that addresses user contexts is thus a vital contribution not only to our understanding of this intellectual space, but to the shape of future debates.

Furthermore, while our own work to date has focused upon the UK regulations, legal deposit is a global phenomenon. The UK is not the only country either to introduce some form of e-legal deposit or to wrestle with the critical and professional challenges posed by such an undertaking. In particular, we are excited to bring together perspectives from across the globe, including Latin America, Africa and Europe. At the heart of our initial provocation lies a simple question: what is it that makes libraries, and legal deposit, distinct from other content providers? This concept of distinctiveness is important to libraries. Caroline Brazier has argued that the digital turn requires libraries to 'see themselves in a completely new way, not just as digital equivalents of traditional collecting organisations' (Brazier, 2016, 54). She argues for the distinctiveness of libraries from other sectors, whereas a global approach to the challenge demonstrates the need to address the local, national and global contexts of e-legal deposit as separate but overlapping challenges. The common ground that emerges assists us to interrogate the extent to which e-legal deposit can, and should, adapt to shifting forms of digital communication.

As both a concept and a regulatory environment, the centuries-long outlook of legal deposit places it in opposition to the fast pace of change that has resulted from digital publishing, and from networked online communication platforms. Libraries, which are already spaces for innovation, collaboration and support for discovering knowledge, have been forced to rethink their services, collections, staff, and users. Publishers have revisited established forms of publication, developed new revenue streams in response to changing online platforms; researchers are adapting to the datafication of knowledge in every domain from medicine and engineering to art history; and user behaviour adapts in response to the differing affordances of digital media platforms. New research methodologies are simultaneously emerging that take advantage of these affordances: text and data mining, natural language processing, digital humanities, and the computational sciences all promise to have a significant impact on how we interrogate and reuse the printed past. Throughout all of these changes, legal deposit continues to speak primarily to posterity, even as the materials that are gathered under its purview change beyond recognition.

E-legal deposit, then, represents a contested space. This space challenges notions of digital materiality, and technological affordances of national library collections. It forces long-established notions of ownership to be reassessed, requiring us to consider whether access protections enshrined in law truly reflect the fragmented rights status of digital publications. It demands that we debate the fundamental questions that surround contemporary libraries: for whom do library collections exist? What is the purpose of a comprehensive national collection? What should various stakeholders be able to do with these collections? And how should libraries respond to shifting information production and consumption patterns in order to remain not just synonymous, but relevant in an era where the likes of Google represent a first port of call for millions of individuals?

By concentrating on various aspects of scholarship, publishing and library practice in light of e-legal deposit regulations, we believe the contributions in this book have an important contribution to make to these ongoing debates. The varied global perspectives represented here help us to consider the broader frames of reference that interact with e-legal deposit. Legal deposit stands as one of the monumental collaborative achievements of governments, libraries, and content creators. It preserves published work that would otherwise be lost, and provides a priceless cultural inheritance for future generations. But like all library roles, its precious status is neither fixed nor universal. It is therefore right and proper to address the challenges faced by the various partners involved in delivering legal deposit, and those who stand to benefit from its existence. This volume aims to provide a space to interrogate e-legal deposit in light of existing library practices, international approaches, theoretical perspectives, and legal and technical contexts. We hope that it will trigger new directions of thinking about the collections of the future that help to define the complex socio-cultural frameworks for legal deposit collections in the digital age.

About this collection

It was important to us, when conceiving the table of contents for this collection, that we framed the systematic retention of published output amid the societal shift from print to digital as an international issue facing libraries around the globe. Despite different local and regional contexts, institutions worldwide are navigating the combination of the changing information environment, expectations that they will remain the trusted custodians of the print outputs of their societies, and legal frameworks that are often playing catch-up with the digital turn. The first section of this book concentrates on institutions, and their implementation of systems and frameworks to tackle electronic legal deposit. Starting from the standpoint of our Digital Library Futures project, which analysed the impact of UK Non-Print Legal Deposit (NPLD) upon academic libraries and their users, the table of contents begins with setting out the UK context, although it then draws parallels with contributions from colleagues and institutions worldwide, showing commonalities, trends and parallel issues. We begin with a chapter from Bodley's Librarian at the University of Oxford, Richard Ovenden, and Linda Arnold-Stratford, who detail the development of legal deposit in the UK, focusing on rapid changes that have taken place during the past 20 years, and reporting on the UK's large-scale shared digital infrastructure project undertaken to allow systematic collection of published output within the digital context. Providing insights into the scale and scope of such an endeavour, the chapter also elucidates unexpected benefits from the transition from print to digital deposit. This is followed by a chapter from colleagues at the National Library of Scotland, by Paul Cunnea, Gill Hamilton, Graeme Hawley and Fred Saunderson , which looks at the implementation of the Legal Deposit Libraries (Non-print Works) Regulations 2013 from the perspective of one UK institution, contextualising both the benefits and challenges presented, and outlining the growing digital expertise that is both necessary and being supported within the UK's legal deposit libraries.

Our third chapter elucidates how the Biblioteca Nacional de México (BNM) is faced with similar issues. Isabel Galina Russell, Jo Ana Morfin and Ana Yuri Ramírez-Molina offer a history of legal deposit in Mexico, and discuss the frameworks being put in place to facilitate e-legal deposit, including legislative context, the creation of a working party, and the development of a digital platform shared between the BNM and UNAM to facilitate e-legal deposit. The fourth chapter in the book, from Collence Chisita, Blessing Chiparausha and Danmore Maboreke shows the importance of maintaining an updated bibliographic record of intellectual input to support legal deposit. Although Zimbabwe has structures and institutions which should enforce legal deposit laws, there is a need to strengthen systems for bibliographic control in order to support learning, teaching, and research in the Zimbabwean context, indicating how electronic legal deposit systems are dependent on numerous facets and parties to be effective, and considering the ramifications of non-compliance, noting in particular the challenges facing African countries with regards to bibliographic control. Finally, in this section, the view from Sweden is presented by Eva Lis-Green and Göran Konstenius, describing the history and implementation of Swedish legal deposit legislation, showing how recent evolutions in media create problems for this current design, calling for revised legislation and corresponding regulations.

The second section of this text foregrounds the user experience, within the emerging technical, legal, and social environment facing the stakeholders of electronic legal deposit. Adrienne Muir highlights the mixed attitude towards legal deposit from UK publishers, assessing the impact of electronic legal deposit on their industry, and their working approach to its implementation. William Kilbride addresses the challenges libraries are tackling via the lens of digital preservation, calling for a renewal and enhancement of the mission of legal deposit libraries, foregrounding their role as solution providers in this emergent digital media space. Jane Winters addresses the nature, scale, and scope of web archiving, both within and beyond the electronic legal deposit framework, suggesting that academic researchers should both become educated about the complex legal issues that surround e-legal deposit and web archives and also contribute their voices to lobby for better, supported, access to our digital cultural heritage, in order to improve the research environment. The two closing chapters directly look at the user community, and what we know of use of e-legal deposit, to date. Linda Berube and Frankie Wilson explore the role that non-print legal deposit collections can play in library discovery and assessment, and the recognition of the unique nature and delivery of these resources, calling on legal deposit libraries to guide users to understand the wider role these collections can play in their research, despite the legal and technical challenges to access, which, in turn, will also allow a greater understanding of potential users of these collections and their needs. Finally, your fearless editors, Paul Gooding and Melissa Terras, demonstrate that the current framing of the UK's Non-Print Legal Deposit Regulations restrict and close off access to researchers and users, advocating for a new understanding of access in relation to the textuality of digital media, showing how these collections could support new, innovative approaches to the study of our digital cultural heritage, if the NPLD Regulations were reframed to support use and users.

Together, these chapters indicate the complexities of a shifting information environment, where highly skilled library and informational professionals navigate technical, professional and legal frameworks, often with relatively limited resources, in order to safeguard our published outputs at a time of social and technological change. We hope that this volume, drawing as it does from a multiplicity of voices around the world, presents a holistic view in which to consider the activities and role of our libraries in the changing information environment. Our foreword, from Bethany Nowviskie, reminds us that all these issues are political: retaining the outputs of the present is crucial to understanding the development and history of our society. At a time when information literacy is tested by wilful manipulation of veracity by broadcast venues, trusted information repositories have a crucial role to play, and the decisions made regarding electronic legal deposit now will cast long shadows for future historians, individuals, and societies. No book comes into physical – or digital – being without concerted effort from a variety of people.

We would like to thank our colleagues at Facet Publishing, particularly Helen Carley, for believing in this volume, and the contributors for drawing together their fascinating professional and scholarly experiences into the first combined overview on this topic. The image on the front cover is a point cloud visualisation of the stacks at the George IV Building of the National Library of Scotland, undertaken by Edinburgh College of Art student Asad Khan (www.theentropyproject.com) in summer 2019. Asad Kahn was assisted by Patricia Wu Wu, and supported by Ryan Gibson, Mark Hemingway, Mark Lamb, Stuart Lewis, Rafiq Jawad and Mike Boyd, in a project directed by Melissa Terras. This image is used with permission from both Asad Kahn, and the National Library of Scotland, and we thank them for allowing us to use it here. We also thank our families for their patience (in particular, Melissa thanks Os for his unfailing support, and Anthony, Edward and Fergusson, for their bemused encouragement. Paul thanks Sian for embracing our own personal Scottish chapter). We hope that these essays, brought together in this way, can show both the progress and the problems, the hard work and the hurdles, in the attempt by our libraries to shape the library collections of the future by retaining and stewarding our digital print present.

References

Alexandrov, G. (2018) Transformation of Digital Legal Deposit in Terms of Legislation and Public Access, *Knygotyra*, **70**, 136–53.

Australian Library Journal (2005) The Alexandria Manifesto on Libraries: The Information Society in Action, *The Australian Library Journal*, **54** (4), 415.

Brazier, C. (2016) Great Libraries? Good Libraries? Digital Collection Development and What It Means for Our Great Research Collections. In Baker, D. and Evans, W. (eds) *Digital Information Strategies: From Applications and Content to Libraries and People*, Chandos Publishing, 41–56.

Coyle, K. (2017) Creating the Catalog, Before and After FRBR, paper presented at the Encuentro di Catalogacion y Metadatos, Universidad Nacional Autonoma de Mexico, 12 September, http://kcoyle.net/mexico.html.

De Beer, M., Van der Merwe, M., Ball, L. and Fourie, I. (2016) Legal Deposit of Electronic Books – A Review of Challenges Faced by National Libraries, *Library Hi Tech*, **34** (1), 87–103.

Gooding, P., Terras, M. and Berube, L. (2019) Towards User-Centric Evaluation of UK Non-Print Legal Deposit: A Digital Library Futures White Paper, University of Glasgow, http://elegaldeposit.org/resources.

Hansard (2013) *HL Deb. 2013*, v. 743, https://hansard.parliament.uk/Lords/2013-03-06/debates/13030683000250/LegalDepositLibraries(Non-PrintWorks)Regulations2013?highlight=%22legal%20deposit%22#contribution-13030683000082.

Larivière, J. (2000) *Guidelines for Legal Deposit Legislation*, United Nations Educational, Scientific and Cultural Organization, http://unesdoc.unesco.org/images/0012/001214/121413eo.pdf.

Larsen, S. (2005) Preserving the Digital Heritage: New Legal Deposit Act in Denmark, *Alexandria: The Journal of National and International Library and Information Issues*, August, http://journals.sagepub.com/doi/abs/10.1177/095574900501700204.

Staff of the Global Legal Research Directorate (2017) *Mandatory Deposit Laws in Selected Jurisdictions (2017 Update)*, The Law Library of Congress, www.loc.gov/law/help/deposit-laws/mandatory-deposit-laws.pdf.

The Legal Deposit Libraries (Non-Print Works) Regulations 2013 (S.I. 2013/777) www.legislation.gov.uk/uksi/2013/777/contents/made.

PART 1

Institutions and implementation

CHAPTER 1

UK non-print legal deposit: from regulations to review

Linda Arnold-Stratford and Richard Ovenden

Legal deposit is the statutory requirement for any publisher to deposit a copy of their publications with designated libraries. It plays a critical role in ensuring preservation of the nation's cultural heritage by allowing systematic collection of the published output. It is the record of human memory, creativity and discovery collected and preserved for future generations. In this chapter, we will detail the development of legal deposit in the UK, focusing on the rapid changes that have taken place during the last 20 years, leading to the implementation of UK Non-Print Legal Deposit (NPLD) in 2013. We explore the difficulties encountered when undertaking a digital infrastructure project of this magnitude, along with the unexpected benefits derived from the transition from print to digital. The chapter concludes with the findings and recommendations of the Post-implementation Review, a mandatory review of whether the UK NPLD regulations are fit for purpose and achieve their intended objective: to preserve our nation's cultural heritage, whether digital or print.

UK legal deposit today

Legal deposit legislation in the UK has evolved over the centuries since it was introduced into the statutes for England and Wales in 1662 (Licensing of the Press Act 1662) and for the whole UK in 1710 (The Copyright Act, 1710). The origin of this privileged status dates back even further than the legislation, to 1610, when Sir Thomas Bodley obtained the agreement of the Stationers' Company to permit the Bodleian Library to claim a copy of everything printed by its members under royal licence (Bodleian Libraries, 2017); in effect making it the first legal deposit library in the British Isles.

The first Copyright Act of 1710 extended this privilege to the Royal Library (later to become the British Library), the library of the University of Cambridge, the Library of Sion College in London and the library of the Faculty of Advocates in Edinburgh (to become the home of the National Library of Scotland), and the ancient universities in Scotland. Over the years other libraries were added or removed. Trinity College Dublin was included in 1801[1], at a time when Ireland was part of the United Kingdom of Great Britain and Ireland and governed by the UK parliament. The inclusion of The National Library of Wales in the 1911 Act[2] means that each nation of the United Kingdom and Ireland was represented in the legal deposit libraries, along with the University Libraries of Oxford and Cambridge due to their historic background and research status (the Scottish universities exchanged the privilege for a one-off cash payment in 1837).

The biggest change in a century came in 2003, when The Legal Deposit Libraries Act 2003 extended existing legal deposit provisions for printed material to cover non-print works. The 2003 Act gave the Department for Culture, Media and Sport (later Digital, Culture, Media and Sport, DCMS) the powers to make secondary legislation bringing new and emerging publishing media under its scope. After an extensive consultation period, the Regulations came in to force on 5 April 2013.

What do the UK regulations allow?

The legal deposit libraries are now able to collect a multitude of published digital material. In addition to being able to collect e-books and e-journals, the legal deposit libraries can now collect websites with a domain name originating in the UK. Complex digital publications such as born-digital sheet music and born-digital maps can also be collected. This has resulted in a very large corpus of material that would have been lost without the regulations.

The regulations recognised the potential size of this collection and allowed for automated web harvesting to limit the burden on publishers and on the legal deposit libraries. The framework allows, wherever possible, for publications to be automatically harvested from a website, with the intention to reduce the burden on both the libraries who ingest and safeguard the collections and the publishers who produce them.

However, the regulations were created in the backdrop of a print world and mimicked that world without recognition of how users interact with digital material as opposed to printed material (Gooding, Terras and Berube, 2019). This is especially apparent when looking at the permitted activities and reader access. The Legal Deposit Libraries Act 2003 restricts use of NPLD materials except where provisions are made by regulation (2003), meaning that a range of activities is restricted. Firstly, all publications received under NPLD are limited to single concurrent access: only one reader in each library can access the content at any one time. This replicates a user taking a printed book from a shelf and it therefore not being available for a second user. However, since most journals are deposited at article level under NPLD the single concurrent access is at article level rather than issue level, which improves availability to users. Secondly, unlike some purchased journals (and the treatment of print legal deposit in some libraries), no digital copies are to be removed from the reading room; which means that users have to print a full article or a part of a monograph if they wish to continue to read away from the reading room. Thirdly, the use of data analytics on this material is prohibited by exclusion of permission, limiting the use of the Web Archive, since it is difficult to meaningfully navigate such a large data set without the use of data analysis tools.

A rapidly changing world

Between the passing of the Act in 2003 and the enforcement of the Regulations in 2013 the world had changed considerably. The financial crash of 2008 had made its impact; the uptake of handheld mobile devices such as iPads, tablets and smart phones had dramatically increased (We Are Social, 2013); and the extent of electronic publishing was greater than expected, especially the uptake of e-books. User expectations have also grown, as their growing familiarity with e-books and e-journals in academic settings comes alongside increased use of iPads, tablets and other mobile platforms for reading articles, newspapers and books on the move.

In fact, 2003 was probably a turning point in digital content creation. In 2010 Eric Schmidt from Google made the claim 'every two days we create as much content as from the dawn of man up to the year 2003' (Siegler, 2013). Whilst the statement is sensational and difficult to prove, the notion that we are creating more and more digital content cannot be doubted. A report funded by the American computing corporation EMC in 2010 put the figure at 1.2 Zettabytes (10^{21} bytes) per year (Gantz and Reinsel, 2010) and figures for 2018 estimate 2.5 quintillion (10^{18}) bytes of data are created per day (Marr, 2018). These numbers are too big to comprehend, but they highlight the speed of growth in data proliferation. The increased amount of digital information makes collecting it all complex and ultimately some information will fall through the gaps. The purpose of the NPLD Regulations was to limit what falls into the 'digital black hole' described by Dame Lynne Brindley in 2009 (Brindley, 2009).

Implementing the largest collaborate digital transformation project

With the regulations in place the first hurdle was overcome, but the libraries and the publishers then faced the reality of implementing these regulations within a complex and rapidly changing environment. Prior to the regulations, during the consultation period, an impact assessment was carried out. During this assessment, it became clear that efficiencies of scale could be achieved if a single infrastructure for all six legal deposit libraries was built instead of six separate systems.

In the 10 years leading up to the passing of the regulations the British Library, the National Library of Scotland and the National Library of Wales had a tripartite agreement working together to build what would eventually be the Digital Library System (DLS). A secure digital store was constructed, with nodes in Scotland, Wales, Yorkshire and London, which was capable of storing the NPLD material once it could be collected. This arrangement satisfied the requirements for each nation to have a copy on their soil, plus the preservation requirements of having the material replicated four times and in different geographical locations. Building the DLS without access to the content was relatively straightforward compared to the challenges that would follow.

Once the regulations were passed, the difficult task of collecting digital material began in earnest. The principles and workflows had been tried and tested under the previous voluntary digital deposit scheme, but extending those to the vast amount of material liable for NPLD proved challenging and in some cases expanded the workflows beyond their capacity. In order to test the systems at scale it was important that the libraries had a large amount of data to work with. They needed to ingest a large amount of material in a short space of time. The best way to do this was to focus on large publishers, producing a large number of journals. This posed a dilemma, as this type of content was at low risk of being lost, since most of it was available in print and digital and therefore was already being collected under print legal deposit. This process became known as transitioning publishers, as the libraries were moving large publishers from print deposit to electronic deposit.

Transitioning publishers is the first step in the process of ingesting the material into the DLS. The process around this that relied on close liaison with the publishers was novel, and had to be newly developed. New relationships had to be forged, and in-depth knowledge about the type of content and metadata that would be eventually received had to be gleaned. In most cases this process took an average of two years: thankfully some of these discussions had started in advance of the regulations being passed, so the libraries were ready to start collecting immediately. However, the diversity of formats and metadata from each individual publisher, even within a content type (i.e. e-journals), created its own problems. Normalising metadata and content is very labour-intensive (British Library, 2015). For this reason, the libraries agreed to use a third party, wherever possible, in order to get a consistent normalised stream of content. An arrangement was made with Portico (British Library, 2013), a US company that many publishers use for storing and preserving content, to provide the British Library with the copies of e-journals from publishers they had an arrangement with. This arrangement provided the opportunity for the British Library to open negotiations with the substantial number of large publishers who were already using Portico's services and were liable for deposit under the UK Act 2003.

Once the content had been ingested into the DLS, the libraries now had digital material to access. Having a single infrastructure certainly had its advantages when it came to the cost and the practicality of storing. In an environment where the market was too immature to support an off-the-shelf product, the cost of developing the DLS was considerable, at approximately £30 million over 10 years. The shared infrastructure meant that this had to be developed once instead of six times. For preservation purposes, a system of replicating to four nodes was adopted. All six libraries can access the content on one of the four nodes. If the infrastructure had not been shared each library would have had to take responsibility for preserving the content individually. If a similar approach had been taken by each library, then 24 copies of the NPLD content would be stored, increasing the cost of implementation considerably.

However, using a single infrastructure made providing access and printing facilities to six diverse libraries more challenging. Integrating the DLS into the diversity of local infrastructures proved a mammoth challenge to which the libraries rose.

A phased approach

By May 2014, it was clear that implementation of the regulations throughout the six legal deposit libraries was not going to be straightforward and a phased implementation was going to be necessary. This was managed by an Implementation Group (LDIG), supported by the Legal Deposit Liaison Manager and her staff, which brought together local legal deposit leads, for co-ordinated planning, decision-making, and implementation.

Although it would have been ideal to have a single technological solution, the different local access arrangements within each library has meant that we have a single infrastructure to which all the libraries' local systems connect. At the local level, each library has implemented the harvest of metadata from the central system, the facility to print and the facility to access content, individually in accordance with their own infrastructure, and reading room arrangements. This does mean that future developments need to interact seamlessly for six different local environments. Wherever possible, similar solutions are applied but it would be unrealistic to think that six diverse libraries could all operate the same library management system and have the same resources to apply to the developments of NPLD. Phase 1 was to provide access and printing of e-journals, e-books and websites in each of the legal deposit libraries' reading rooms (British Library, 2013). It took 2½ years from the passing of the regulations for this first and most important phase to be complete. The legal requirement to have single concurrent access and to prevent digital download of the material presented the libraries with interesting technical challenges. The IT department at the British library, on behalf of all the legal deposit libraries, first had to find a way to control access to the NPLD material. The access solution had to restrict access only to readers who were physically present on the premises of the legal deposit libraries and permit only one reader to access a piece of content at each location at a time. In addition, the access solution had to prevent users from downloading or copying the content, whilst allowing them to print small amounts in line with copyright regulations.

The scale of the challenges faced becomes clearer when you add the technical complexity arising from the fact that the digital content received under legal deposit is in a wide variety of formats. To view an e-journal article in PDF, readers need a PDF viewer application capable of displaying older PDFs and current PDF formats; to view e-books they need an e-reader; and to view the Web Archive they need a browser that can render the captured website. To improve the user experience the IT team wanted to make it possible to access all content streams from one platform and via a direct link from the libraries' existing resource discovery platforms, without the need for multiple readers on each machine that would constantly need updating.

The British Library worked with a company called Ericom to deploy a solution based on their HTML5 client (Ericom, 2013). The resultant AccessNow solution is an HTML5 remote desktop gateway that works from any device with an HTML5 compatible browser. This solution allows end users to gain secure access to content stored centrally in the DLS without the need to download any additional software regardless of the format.

Unfortunately, the remote desktop solution also prevented locally managed print and sign-on services from interacting with the DLS. A simple and necessary requirement to print off NPLD content became a very large infrastructure project. Complexities around printing were exacerbated at the universities, where the printing and IT is not managed by the library but by the university IT services. In the greater scheme of university facilities served by IT services, being able to print NPLD material was a small consideration given the small amount of material available at that point; however, for legal deposit libraries it was a fundamental provision.

Once the basic minimum requirements of Phase 1 were met, it entered a perpetual phase of research and development with iterative developments taking place in order to: improve the user experience; automate more of the process; and improve the handling of exceptions.[3] Exceptions are items which fall out of the automated ingest process and can require technical or manual intervention. When operating at the scale that the legal deposit libraries require for ingest, different problems become apparent and the number of exceptions in the ingest process increase. The manual exceptions are usually minor errors or changes in the metadata accompanying a collection item, which prevents it auto-matching to records already held in the library management system. A manual correction is then carried out to allow for the content to auto-match. The technical exceptions usually require a piece of code to be rewritten or can be as simple as a server failure requiring the server to be rebooted and the process restarted.

To understand the scale of processing it helps to understand that every single issue acquisitioned in print equates to 15 separate acquisitions in digital format. In simple terms, each individual printed issue of a journal now translates into about 15 individual articles to process and each article may have several associated files making up the single article. As described, exceptions usually come about because of problems with metadata. Metadata from a single publisher can vary across publications and blank fields or incorrectly filled-in fields can mean that an article is rejected. Metadata incorrectly describing the format can mean that the item is wrongly ascribed an associated file and cannot be rendered properly. Unfortunately, the different types of errors are numerous and each week the team of staff processing the content will find new errors that will send an item or a group of items into exception. Exception handling, requiring manual intervention, is manageable when ingesting a few thousand articles per week. Once the operation is scaled up to ingesting around 200,000 items per month, a small percentage of exception handling becomes a large amount of manual intervention. Although most of the processes are automated, the work required to ensure that the digital content is ingested correctly into the DLS is a massive undertaking.

Phase 1 focused on collecting the big collections, the material most used, such as e-journals and e-books, and the largest collection, the Web Archive. The second phase of implementation aimed not only at improving current processes but also at increasing the scope of material that could be collected, looking at the more complex material, born-digital mapping and born-digital sheet music. The libraries had been collecting born-digital maps from Ordnance Survey GB since 1998 and in 2013 they partnered with thinkWhere, a company specialising in providing cloud-based GIS platforms and services to find a solution for securely storing and providing access to this digital map data across all six libraries. At this time the data was around 4TB and included large-scale map data. The solution developed was based upon the platform Location Centre. The solution was an online system designed to securely store an access copy of the Ordnance Survey annual snapshot data and provide access via an intuitive full-screen digital map viewer (thinkWhere, 2019).

In 2016 it was necessary to expand this viewer to cope with geospatial data from other publishers. The legal deposit libraries jointly funded a three-year project working with thinkWhere: the first phase, completed in March 2016, was to build a geospatial data application services system based on thinkWhere's theMapCloud platform, which allowed the libraries to provide access to many different digital maps through the one viewer. This allowed comparison across maps of different years as well as across different publishers, opening up the opportunity to collect material never collected before and at high risk of being lost. This content is at higher risk than standard Ordnance Survey maps because born-digital map publishers are diverse in nature and so have not necessarily agreed standards of preservation formats. Most map publications are updated regularly, and the publishers may not keep copies of previous versions of the maps because of the sheer size of the data. We have collected over 40 datasets, amounting to about 12 TB of data, and are continually engaging with more geospatial publishers. As legal deposit libraries, we are mandated to keep the older versions. This separates the legal deposit libraries from libraries that may subscribe to map content and just supply the most recent update to their readers. These snapshots in time allow researchers to see how a landscape changes over time. In the print world one could refer back to paper maps but in a digital world, where the latest update overwrites the previous version, the ability to look back at an older version can be lost.

The second and third phases of this particular project are still under way and involve the ingest and preservation of these massive datasets within the DLS. The complexity and size of geospatial material makes the preservation element of this project difficult, as formats change over time and, unlike with journal and book publishers, there is no agreement within the industry about which format is best for preservation.

Born-digital sheet music is a completely new content stream for the libraries and represents content that would be lost to future generations if not collected. Unlike the large book and journal publishers, most born-digital sheet music publishers are small enterprises producing material in a unique format. Some of the smaller publishers, such as AFS Music,[4] Michael Thomas Andrews[5] and Divine Music[6] are arrangers and composers selling directly to the public. This type of content is at great risk of loss because the scale of the operation makes it more difficult to put in good preservation planning, due to the prohibitive costs to small enterprises. Engaging with a substantial number of this type of publisher is more difficult than with large-scale sheet-music aggregators because they are not generally part of bigger publishing networks like traditional journal and book publishers and they do not always understand or know of their requirement to deposit content under legal deposit. Building a system to cater for a diversity of formats such as Music XML and Sibelius or file formats with associated sound files was not within current capabilities, so the initial collection focus was on born-digital music that was available via an aggregator and published in PDF format. This allowed the collection of born-digital sheet music in a uniform format. Metadata has been the most difficult element of collecting this material to date, as music publishers do not produce metadata in the same way as journal and book publishers. Indeed, from discussions with sheet-music publishers, it is apparent that many do not know what metadata is. It is hoped that in the coming years music publishers will work together to create standard formats and standard metadata formats. We have so far collected 56,000 born-digital music scores from two major aggregators, Faber Music Factory and Music Sales. The collection of born-digital sheet music that is in more complex formats as described above and has associated sound files will fall into a new phase of implementation: Phase 3, Emerging Formats.

Publishers are continually pushing the boundaries of technology to come up with new and innovative ways to present reading matter, such as reading apps, interactive narratives or simple text books with associated video files. They are using technology to their best advantage to turn directories into databases, thereby making the material more accessible to their audiences. Often the publications derived from databases are bespoke, in that a query is entered into a database and a resulting report is produced which the consumer purchases. This poses the question of what is liable for deposit: the database behind the query, or the resultant report?

Whilst advantageous for the user, these new formats present challenges for libraries that have to collect, preserve and provide access to these new formats for decades to come. In time, as new formats become standard, the experience of how to handle them will develop, but the risk of loss comes from those formats which ultimately do not become standard formats but are superseded by something new. This kind of material is a glimpse into the history of the book and forms part of the UK's cultural heritage. Researchers of the future may be interested to know how we transitioned from flat PDFs to EPUB3 through to the latest new format and capturing those emergent formats will provide a useful insight into this progress. However, capturing them may not be possible, as the complexity of the technology may make the cost prohibitive (Smith and Cooke, 2018). A good way of explaining this would be that a narrative-based app purchased for use on an iPad would in theory be eligible for collection under NPLD. Imagine this app is only available for iPads so can be purchased from the Apple store. This app is software- and hardware-dependent. Three weeks after collection the app has an upgrade; does this count as a new version? If we just continue to accept upgrades, how do we keep a record of the previous versions? Five years down the line the original iPad is not supported, and the original app will not work on a modern iPad. In the print world this is the equivalent of loose-leaf publications, but in print we could keep all the previous leaves to show how the publication has evolved. Trying to do this in a digital world is very difficult. You only have to look at how often we need to replace smart phones to start to understand the complexities the libraries will face around emergent formats. The term 'emerging formats' indicates that new formats will continually emerge, as once they have become stable the libraries will have experience to collect them. Therefore, emerging formats represent a constant phase of research and development for the libraries as they figure out how to store, preserve and present to future generations the latest emergent format.

Collaboration is key

The magnitude of this undertaking across six diverse institutions would not be possible without great collaboration and governance. Decisions, which each institution has been used to making for itself, now have to be made collectively. As soon as the 2003 Act was passed in parliament, the legal deposit libraries started working together on a shared infrastructure in preparation for the resultant regulations, not expecting it to be another 10 years before they came into force. In fact, the libraries had been preparing for digital legal deposit as early as 2000, when the British Library started collecting digital material under a voluntary deposit scheme (Boulderstone, 2006).

The main committee formed by the libraries to manage this process, the Legal Deposit Implementation Group (LDIG), consisting of senior management decision makers, was originally formed in 2006. The very first meeting was held on 7 September 2006 and was made up of the following members: Richard Boulderstone, Director of eStrategy at the British Library; Caroline Brazier, Head of Collection Acquisition and Development at the British Library; Peter Burnett, Head of Technical Services at the Bodleian; David Dinham, Chief Information Officer at National Library of Scotland;

Margaret Flood, Keeper (Collections Management) at Trinity College Dublin; Andrew Green, Chief Librarian, National Library of Wales; Avril Jones, Director of Collection Services at National Library of Wales; Patricia Killiard, Head of Electronic Services and Systems at Cambridge University Library; Cate Newton, Director of Collections and Research and Deputy Librarian at National Library of Scotland; Dave Price, Head of Systems and e-Research Service at the Bodleian; Helen Shenton, Head of Collection Care at the British Library; and John Tuck, Head of British Collections at the British Library. The meeting was chaired by Andrew Green.

LDIG, albeit with a different membership, under the chairmanship of Richard Ovenden, has worked together highly collegially to deliver the collective goal of implementing NPLD. LDIG and its many sub-groups have met frequently since 2013, involving a substantial commitment of time and expertise to ensure that the regulations have been implemented according to the agreed plans. In working together to overcome some of the extremely difficult and complex problems arising, the group have developed mutual respect and have created a very supportive network bringing the libraries closer together. Sharing of information and best practice has resulted in successful working relationships and facilitates the delivery of better reader services. The libraries share experiences around library management systems and reader survey responses and learn from each other in order to improve their own offering. When contemplating a change in library management systems, discovery layers or digital preservation and asset management tools the libraries have utilised lessons learned from other libraries to improve their own procurement or process.

Collection management

In the print world every book published is taken by the British Library and at least one other of the legal deposit libraries. Most academic publications are taken by all six libraries but the less academic publications, such as parish magazines, local newspapers, popular fiction or children's literature may be taken selectively and each of the libraries have a responsibility for collecting material for geographical regions or a particular genre. With NPLD the need for that selection is removed as the publisher deposits one digital copy and all of the libraries have access to it. In theory the libraries could decide to harvest metadata only for the publications they choose but in reality the work required to be selective in the harvest is greater than the work required to collect all the records. Therefore in most cases the libraries will have more content via NPLD than they did with print. This does not mean that selection plays no part in NPLD, but the reasons for that selection may be different.

In the early stages of implementation of NPLD, whilst the workflows and processes were being established, the university libraries requested that the academic e-books were not selected for transition to digital deposit. This was primarily to limit the impact on their researchers. The librarians anticipated a negative reaction from some readers who have a preference for printed books. The lack of pagination for citation purposes was their biggest concern, along with the inability to mark a page and go back to it and the difficulty of reading long texts on a screen. Evidence shows that students prefer e-books for searching and finding information, but if they are tasked with reading several chapters they would prefer a printed book (Enis, 2018). The librarians also suggested that the restrictions on downloading, saving and printing are also factors in choosing not to have a digital copy. Readers have an expectation that if something is digital then they can access it from the comfort of their own office or home and that since they can't with NPLD then it would lead to frustration amongst readers. However, recent research among American academic students indicates that there is only a moderate level of frustration around restrictions (Enis, 2018). It would be interesting to see whether the frustration was greater amongst users of NPLD content than other e-book content, given the different restrictions.

As time has gone on, and the workflows and processes have become more robust, the transition to academic e-books was not only inevitable but also desirable amongst all libraries. Most of the libraries have offsite storage for print material, meaning that ordering a book to a reading room can take 24–48 hours. Once these publications were deposited digitally they were available instantly to users within the reading room. The exception to this is if another reader is already viewing that item, in which case they would get a turn-away notification which advises the reader that the item is currently unavailable as it is being accessed by another reader and to try again later. The amount of time a publication is unavailable because another reader has it is considerably less than if it was a print item requested to the reading room, because of the time it takes to re-shelve an item and make it available to another reader. Another advantage is that readers can scan an electronic volume and decide whether they want to read further without having to order it to the reading room.

Other considerations were made when deciding which publications to transition to NPLD, including the type of content. Certain content types really do not transition well to the digital world: e.g. image-heavy material and, for different reasons, some legal publications. Trying to read a book on art history with beautiful images of art works, or books on architecture, is often a poorer-quality experience with e-books. One of the advantages of digital publications is being able to increase the font size to facilitate reading; this itself is an issue with image-based material, as the text increases but the images don't, making annotated images unusable in the digital format. A good example of an e-book where this happens is *Infographica: the World As You've Never Seen It Before* by Martin and Simon Toseland (Toseland and Toseland, 2012).

As described earlier, it was important to work with the large publishers to allow the libraries to test the systems to scale. This meant that collection criteria were based not on what was likely to be lost, but which content could be collected easily using the workflows already created. Partnerships with Portico and Ingrams meant that publications from publishers with existing relationships with these two organisations were prioritised, although transition of other publishers was also carried out in parallel. Most publishers that fell into these categories produce large volumes of books and journals and have found they have benefited from the transition to digital. The larger the publisher, the greater the cost-saving benefits, because once they transition the costs associated with depositing print copies such as printing, shipping and administration are gone (Department for Digital, Culture, Media and Sport, 2019).

Over time other publishers have become interested in transitioning and have approached the libraries asking to transition. When publishers request transition, the libraries have always tried to accommodate them, regardless of whether they are publishers on their prioritisation list. Unfortunately, the libraries aren't always in a position to transition from print to digital. This can be due to lack of workflows to cope with that particular content type at that time; a lack of metadata from the publisher; or a digital format that is not within scope. An example of content not currently in scope is that from publishers wishing to supply a PDF copy of their print publications even though the original publication was not published electronically.

The libraries are not currently able to take digital facsimiles of printed publications. For some publishers where deposit is cost prohibitive this would be an ideal solution but since they are not published in an electronic format they cannot be supplied electronically under legal deposit. In some circumstances it would be beneficial to the libraries as well as the publishers to be able to collect a digital version of a print-only item. An example would be newspapers, where the long-term preservation of the artefact requires them to be digitised from the print. A PDF version exists as part of the printing process, so it feels retrograde to have to scan and digitise a print copy in order to preserve the item for future generations.

The libraries have been very successful in engaging with the large monograph and serials publishers and have transitioned most of the large publishers liable to deposit under UK legislation to NPLD. You can see with which publishers we have a direct relationship in Tables 1.1 and 1.2 on the following pages.

Table 1.1 *Monograph publishers that have transitioned to non-print legal deposit from print* (Source: British Library)

Publisher	Transition Year	Publisher	Transition Year
Accent Press	2014	Troubador/Matador	2016
Cicerone	2014	Ubiquity Press	2016
Critical Publishing	2014	UCL IoE Press	2016
Hachette Group	2014	Xlibris	2016
Kogan Page	2014	Zed Books	2016
Severn House	2014	Andrews UK (AUK)	2017
Canongate	2015	Austin Macauley	2017
Do Sustainability	2015	Berghahn Books	2017
Edinburgh University Press	2015	Burleigh Dodds	2017
Elsevier	2015	Chicago University Press	2017
Institute of Physics	2015	Dorling Kindersely (inc. Rough Guides)	2017
Jessica Kingsley	2015	Emerald	2017
Manchester University Press	2015	Faber & Faber	2017
Oberon	2015	Globe Law & Business	2017
Palgrave Macmillan	2015	Head of Zeus	2017
Pan	2015	John Hunt Publishing	2017
Pluto Books	2015	Karnac Books	2017
Rowman & Littlefield International	2015	Legend Press	2017
Sage	2015	Legend Press	2017
Scion	2015	Panoma Press	2017
Taylor & Francis	2015	Pearson	2017
UCL Press	2015	Pelagic Publishing	2017
University of Exeter Press	2015	Penguin Random House	2017
University of Wales Press	2015	Rowman & Littlefield (US)	2017
Wiley	2015	Wordcatcher	2017
Amberley Publishing	2016	APA	2018
Anthem Press	2016	Arc Humanities Press	2018
AuthorHouse	2016	Catholic Truth Society	2018
Becker	2016	Claret Press	2018
Bloomsbury	2016	Infinite Ideas	2018
Bonnier	2016	Letts Educational	2018
Cambridge Scholars	2016	Lyons Press	2018
Canelo	2016	Nick Hern Books	2018
Edward Elgar	2016	Quarto	2018
European Respiratory Society	2016	Ryland Peters & Small	2018
Future Science/Medicine	2016	Silverwood Books	2018
Harper Collins	2016	SPCK	2018
IB Tauris	2016	Verso	2018
Intellect Books	2016	White Rose Press	2018
Lippincott Williams & Wilkins (LWW) / Wolters Kluwer	2016	Agenda Publishing Ltd	2019
Liverpool University Press	2016	Bookouture	2019
Multilingual Matters / Channel View	2016	CIPFA	2019
Packt Publishing	2016	Goodfellow	2019
Pluto Press	2016	Intech Open	2019
Policy Press	2016	ISTE Editions	2019
Reaktion Books	2016	Lazy Bee Scripts	2019
Rowanvale Books	2016	Paths International	2019
Royal Society of Chemistry (RSC)	2016	Scribe Publications	2019
Springer London	2016	Trigger Publishing	2019
The Stationery Office (TSO)	2016		

Table 1.2 *Serial publishers that have transitioned to non-print legal deposit from print* (Source: British Library)

Publisher	Transition Year	Publisher	Transition Year
Emerald	2013	Future Science Group	2016
Informa Healthcare	2013	Pluto Journals	2016
Maney	2013	Policy Press	2016
Oxford University Press	2013	Springer	2016
Sage	2013	Taylor & Francis	2016
Wiley	2013	The Stationery Office (TSO)	2016
Cambridge University Press	2014	BJBS	2017
Edinburgh University Press	2014	Huddersfield University Press	2017
Manchester University Press	2014	Nature	2017
Elsevier	2015	Palgrave	2017
Equinox	2015	Royal Society	2017
Inderscience	2015	UCL IoE Press	2017
Institute of Physics (IOP Publishing)	2015	Cardiff University Press	2018
LWW / Wolters Kluwer	2015	Veruscript	2018
Liverpool University Press	2015	Berghahn	2019
Royal Society of Chemistry (RSC)	2015	Hindawi	2019
ADIS	2016	ICE (Institute of Civil Engineers)	2019
BioMed	2016	Microbiology Society	2019
Bioscientifica	2016		

In addition, we collect content from small publishers (those who publish less than 50 items per year) via a publisher portal: these publishers register for deposit and can deposit their items one at a time. We currently have over 900 publishers registered to use the portal and have received over 1,100 items for the collection. Now that most of the large publishers have transitioned, the libraries can take a more proactive role in selecting which publishers to focus on for collection. Work over the last two years has been focusing on the material at greatest risk of loss. This is because the publications are only available in electronic format or that the publishers are known not to be good depositors in print.[7] These publishers are more likely to produce a mixture of print-only and digital-only publications, so it is not possible to transition their whole catalogue. These types of publishers are more complex to deal with. It is critical to ensure that the libraries do not miss out on either the print-only or digital-only publications. Dialogue and negotiations are important for making it work with such publishers, as identification of their full catalogue is likely to be more difficult.

Creating new workflows and processes is resource-intensive and the same amount of work will go into creating a workflow for a publisher with 50 titles as for a publisher with 500. Therefore the libraries have now reached the long tail of collecting, where the ability to collect content is determined by the availability of staff and technical resource. This will become apparent as the rate of collection growth slows. Up until 2019 the rate of growth for both e-books and e-journals has increased at a steady rate, as can be seen in Figures 1.1 and 1.2 on the next page. The ingest statistics show the e-journal rate of ingest has increased from approx. 750,000 per year in 2017–18 to 1 million per year in 2018–19 (Source: British Library). The ingest statistics for e-books show that the rate of ingest has increased considerably since 2014, when the libraries ingested nearly 10,000 e-books in the first year, 35,000 in 2015, 57,000 in 2016, 134,000 in 2017, and 144,000 in 2018. The increase in growth over the years is a combination of improving workflows in order to cope with more content and increasing the number of publishers the libraries have an arrangement with.

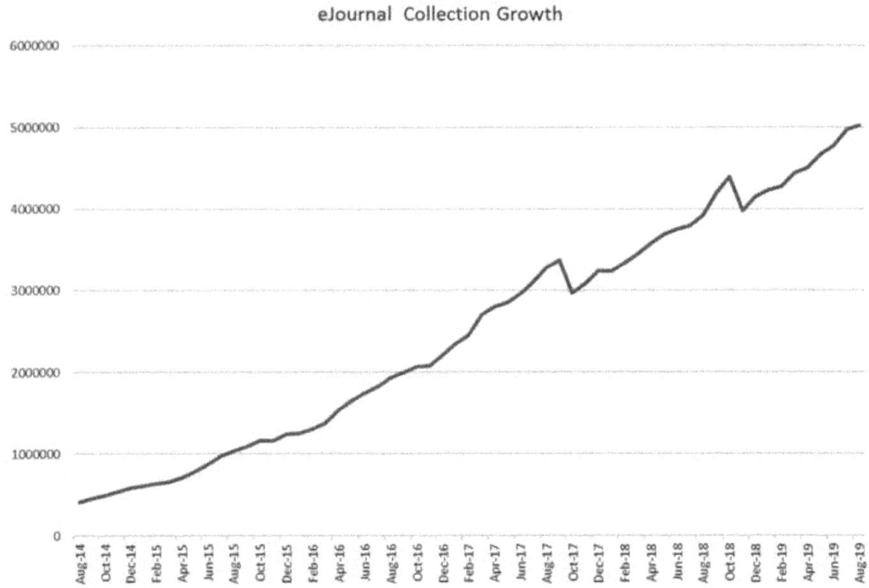

Figure 1.1 *Ingest rates for e-journals* (source: British Library)

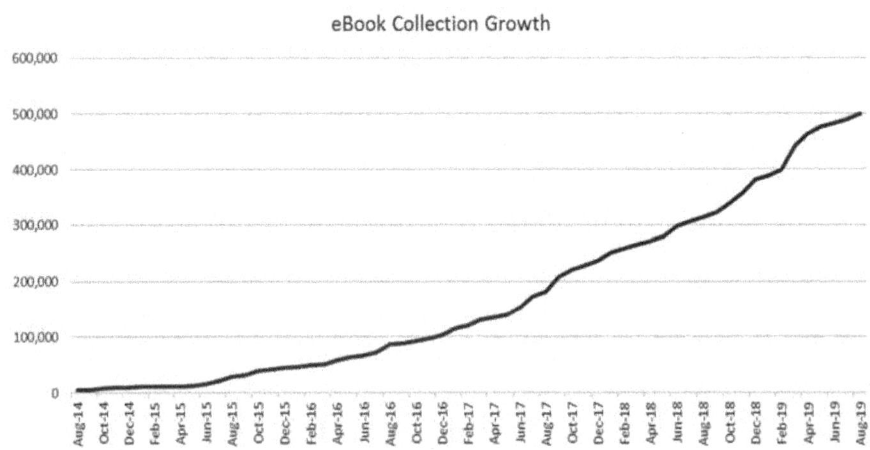

Figure 1.2 *Ingest rates for e-books* (source: British Library)

Six years of collecting

In September 2019 the libraries had more than 5 million journal articles available via NPLD. It is hard to imagine how long it would have taken Sir Thomas Bodley to reach this number of items following his original request to the Stationers' Company; it certainly wouldn't have been in his lifetime, let alone within five years.

In this time the libraries have also collected about 500,000 e-books. Most publishers who have transitioned to e-books have also supplied a digital copy of their back catalogue if they have digitised it. The oldest book received via NPLD was originally published in 1904 and is a digitised copy of *The Sea Wolf* by Jack London (1904). Other titles over 100 years old include the *Brecon Beacons Rifle Range: Bye-laws* (War Department, 1905), and *Morbid Fears and Compulsions: Their Psychology and Psychoanalytic Treatment* by H. W. Frink (Frink, 1918). NPLD is therefore providing access to material which has probably not been out of store for decades, bringing old publications to a new generation of researchers. The age profile of the publications collected to date (see Figure 1.3) predictably shows that the majority have a publication date after 2013, when the regulations were enforced, but the wide range of original publication dates would indicate that the publishers perceive a demand for digitising old publications.

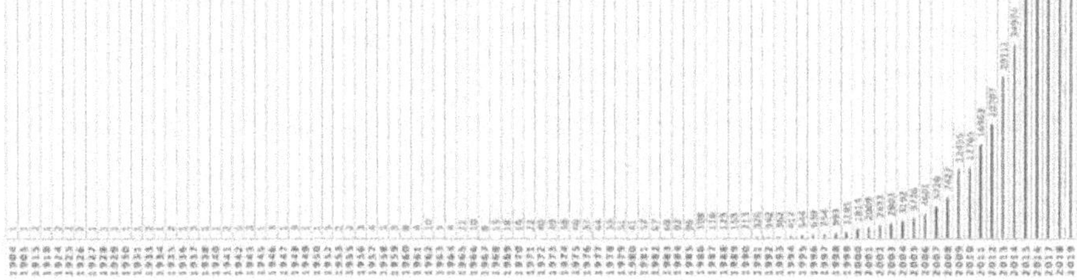

Figure 1.3 *The age distribution of monographs collected under NPLD and stored in the Digital Library Store* (source: British Library)

The largest collection is undoubtedly the UK Web Archive, which is by far the largest digital collection within the libraries, now standing at 500TB of data. It is also the most valuable in terms of achieving the aim of the regulations to limit the loss of our digital heritage. There have already been high-profile examples of its use when websites have been taken down but they have been found in the Web Archive.[8] Research into the disappearance of websites shows that within two years 50% of web pages have been deleted or are not to be found in the original location (Hartmann, 2015); this is information which would have been lost to researchers if it hadn't been collected in the Web Archive. A dataset of this magnitude is very difficult to explore manually. The search engine produces so many results that a user cannot always meaningfully interpret them. Large datasets like this are used to produce innovative research when data analytical tools are applied. Using a different web archive, a major study of the history of UK web space from 1996 to 2013, including language, file formats, the development of multimedia content, shifts in power and access was carried out.[9] The project team could not use the UK Web Archive, due to the legislation preventing investigation using analytical tools. The libraries are working with researchers and policy makers in the hope of making this valuable resource accessible to researchers in a way that can benefit research whilst maintaining the rights of the content providers. Currently a change in the legislation would be required to allow researchers to use the Web Archive to its full potential. However, the fact that all this data is being collected is a fundamental step in preventing the loss of the information which forms a large part of our societal landscape and will allow social historians of the future to understand the tumultuous world we currently inhabit.

What have we learned?

The six years since the regulations were enforced have been a steep learning curve for all those involved with the implementation. There were many technical obstacles to navigate at both a local level and with the central infrastructure as described above. The DLS has now been in use for a decade and some of the components need to be replaced in order for it to work at the ever-increasing scale required of the system. The lessons learned from the original development and the ongoing R&D will be applied to the development and delivery of a new central infrastructure over the coming years. As with many things, the market has moved on since the three national libraries first built the DLS. Other large institutions have the need to collect, store and provide access to a large number of digital objects and the market has responded to this need. The experience and requirements of many institutions has provided the environment for large-scale digital asset management and preservation service providers to exist, negating the need for a bespoke DLS to be built by the British Library. The legal deposit libraries will be working with third parties over the coming years to build a new central infrastructure for the collection, preservation and presentation of the nations' published digital heritage. This will be an enormous project costing the legal deposit libraries millions of pounds over several years. In addition, the increased amount of NPLD material being collected and used means that the libraries are identifying issues that were not necessarily apparent in the early stages.

Issues

Metadata

When working at scale, a consistent metadata format is crucial in order to build automated workflows. As described earlier, metadata is not always uniform across a single publisher, let alone across the thousands of publishers that the legal deposit libraries are collecting from. Working at this scale highlights the need for industry standards in the provision of metadata (British Library, 2015). The regulations themselves do not put any onus on the publishers to produce metadata at all, let alone to a particular standard. Negotiations between the libraries and the publishers who transition help to identify potential problems and aim to get the publisher to provide a certain level of metadata. Not all publishers can provide the metadata required to create suitable records and manual work needs to be done in collecting metadata or creating it from scratch. Unfortunately, this process will limit the libraries' ability to collect at scale, as each library has limited resources to support this activity. It is hoped that in future the publishing industry itself will work with libraries worldwide to create international metadata standards. The librarians are working with publishing colleagues in the Joint Committee on Legal Deposit (JCLD) to progress these discussions.

Citation

As more people use the NPLD content a common issue has been the ability to both cite the electronic version and to translate a print-based citation into a digital-based medium. Researchers are used to citing page numbers to direct readers to source material. Direct quotes, of course, are easier to find in a digital version using search functions. However, if a citation describes a concept that is covered on page 84 of the printed book, it is not straightforward to find where that concept is in the digital version of publications, as the page number is not always fixed. Generally, PDF versions of books mimic the print world and are static. But with the advantages afforded by ePub publishers are moving away from PDF as their format of choice and favouring the versatility of ePub instead. Following an assessment into the best version for long-term preservation[10] the legal deposit libraries agreed that where a publisher produces both PDF and ePub, collecting the ePub version was the best version for preservation. Within the ePub version, pages are dynamic and reflow according to the size of font chosen or the screen it is being read on, and therefore a new way of citing has to be adopted.

Protocols have been adopted by some societies and institutions (Modern Languages Association, 2016; American Psychological Association, 2009) for best practice in citing dynamic content. These protocols include using chapters and paragraphs for citation instead of page numbers. Whilst this approach may work for the digital version where the e-book reader is likely to label and count paragraphs, it is a very cumbersome approach to translating a digital citation into the print world, where counting paragraphs within a chapter is prone to error. Unfortunately, for the legal deposit libraries, this particular issue has caused the greatest concern for researchers[11] and has led to requests for the libraries to purchase printed versions of books collected under NPLD. Again, it is hoped that, since this issue is not unique to NPLD and citation of works is critical to the publication cycle, the publishing industry can work together with researchers and libraries to creatively eliminate this problem.

Changing formats

Publishers by nature want to use the latest technology and technological developments to provide the best reading experience to their audience. Some of these developments may be unnoticeable to the reader but could improve internal processes, whilst others will allow readers to have better functionality from their e-books. Each time a publisher updates its format the workflow created by the libraries has to also change. In the six years since content collection started, some publishers have changed the format in which they send the files to the British Library up to nine times. Format changes are inevitable and when planned for can be seamlessly dealt with. Communication between the publishers and the British Library is key to ensuring that any format changes are handled in a smooth way and that no content is at risk of being lost during the transition from one format to another.

Accessibility software

As described earlier, the legislation requires the libraries to limit concurrent access and prevent digital downloads. The Ericom AccessNow solution used to provide the required security also prevents the content being machine-read. The way the current solution works is that the content is never on the readers' desktop. Instead, a video stream of the content is sent to the desktop. Accessibility software relies on the ability to machine-read in order to make the content available either audibly or in any other non-standard way. The video stream prevents copy and paste functions, which is problematic for users who rely on copy and paste to take notes about an item they are reading. It also prevents the download of metadata directly from the item to bibliographic referencing tools.

Other unintended consequences are to do with the limitations within the legislation. For example, library users who, for whatever reason, cannot access the library can request a photocopy of the printed article, or a proportion of a printed book within copyright limits, to be sent to them without their going to the library. The same cannot be done with NPLD material. Therefore, disabled users are unintentionally unfairly disadvantaged when it comes to accessing NPLD material compared to print legal deposit.

The actual legislation does not include the wider definition of disabled users but agreement amongst the publishers on the JCLD allows the libraries to provide copies of the publication in accessible ways to registered users covered under the wider definition as described in the UK Equality Act of 2010. To date this service is only provided at the Bodleian; however, there are plans to roll this out across all the libraries by the end of 2019 so that disabled users at all of the legal deposit libraries will have equal opportunity to access content in an accessible format.

Unintended consequences

Prior to the regulations a full impact assessment was carried out and the libraries and the publishers identified as many issues as they could foresee at that time, most of which focused on cost and complexity (Department for Culture, Media and Sport, 2013a). Interestingly, it was acknowledged that the legislation would result in a cost to the public purse; however, there was no discussion or agreement that the activities would be funded by the government. With regard to some of the complexity, it was noted that the legal deposit libraries must also ensure that the contents of the archive can still be viewed and used by future generations, perhaps several hundred years from now. Not only must the material be securely stored, but a preservation strategy of active interventions is needed to ensure that the material remains compatible with future technologies and software applications.

However, once NPLD was operating at scale, some unintended consequences came to light. In the university libraries the increased demand for computers within the library space became highly problematic. At a time when licensed content can be accessed from anywhere in the world by university library members the number of people using library computer terminals has dropped, but the increased amount of content being received under NPLD has caused the number of users requiring a computer terminal to increase. The cost of providing the space, the computer, and the support is an extra burden on the libraries at a time when budgets are already restricted.

A more future-focused unintended consequence relates to exhibitions within a legal deposit library. Exhibitions have become more important in attracting users to the libraries in recent years. Many of the exhibitions display material collected under legal deposit over hundreds of years. So how do these libraries exhibit NPLD material? This was a real issue in a recent experience of the National Library of Scotland, which wanted to have a small display of all of Ian Rankin's books. The latest three, however, were collected under NPLD so physical copies were missing from the display.[12]

An unintended consequence for rights holders appears to be to do with the lock-down of content intended to be open. Authors who intend their publications to be open access, either via an author-pays model or another open access licence agreement, find their content being locked down to specific reading rooms in specific libraries to be an infringement of their rights and their original intent. This is both a consequence of the legislation and currently the technology (Gooding, Terras and Berube, 2019).

Some unintended consequences are temporary and result from the technical solution in place to ensure that the libraries are compliant with current legislation. Examples of this would be the accessibility issues relating to the current access software described above or the inability to use bibliographic creation tools. Neither of those examples are explicitly down to the legislation, but are to do with the current technology solutions in place.

Whilst thinking about unintended consequences we must also note that there have also been some positive unintended consequences. The major one is the addition of out-of-print material to the online collection described above and seen in Figure 1.3. Many publishers have digitised back catalogues and have deposited those under NPLD, giving old publications a new lease of life without them having to be retrieved from stores.

In addition, although hoped rather than unintended, the number of serial titles we have collected from the publishers who have transitioned is 43.8%[13] higher than we would have collected in print. There is a combination of reasons, including digitised older material already covered, but the more impressive increases come from publishers who find it easier to send a digital feed for all of their content instead of identifying specific content that is liable. We are also seeing an increased number of publications from the publishers who have been poor depositors in print: this is a testament to how easy it is for the publishers to deposit once they have transitioned and turned on a digital feed.

To calculate the increase in content the British Library and the Agency for Legal Deposit collected information about how many titles had been received under legal deposit in the year preceding transition and compared it with the first year following transition. Some of the largest increases in deposit are from publishers that have large numbers of digital-only titles, such as Springer/Biomed, where we have seen a 1,580% increase, and Ubiquity Press, with a 1,000% increase.

It is not possible to do the same calculations for monographs as the number of monographs a publisher produces fluctuates year by year. However, it is interesting to note how the ratio of print to electronic has changed from 31% electronic monographs in 2015/16 to 72% by 2018/19[14] (Figure 1.4).

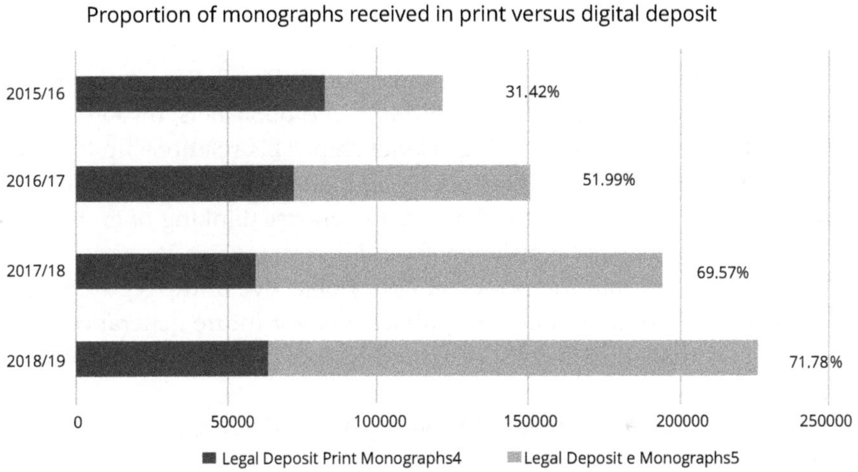

Figure 1.4 *Numbers of monographs received, along with the percentage of legal deposit monographs collected digitally each year since 2015/16* (source: British Library)

Post-implementation review

In 2011 the UK government stated that each piece of legislation passed should be reviewed within five years. Therefore JCLD were asked by DCMS to carry out a post-implementation review (PIR) of the NPLD Regulations by March 2018.

Process of the post-implementation review

The purpose of the PIR was to ensure that the regulations were fit for purpose and that they achieved the stated objectives for NPLD, and to identify any areas for improvement. The main purpose of JCLD is to support co-operation between publishers and deposit libraries for the effective implementation of statutory and voluntary deposit arrangements. A significant amount of work was undertaken by publishers and libraries through JCLD to compile the PIR.

They collated and compiled data from a variety of sources, including publisher questionnaires, management information reports, usage and ingest statistics and financial reports. Independent assessment of the libraries' ability to digitally preserve content supplied under NPLD was also carried out and included in the final report. The final report included areas for improvement which JCLD agreed on, plus views from the libraries and publishers on further areas of improvement that the publishers and libraries could not agree. DCMS published the final PIR in April 2019 (Department for Digital, Culture, Media and Sport, 2019).

Findings of the post-implementation review

What is very clear is that, in the main, the NPLD Regulations have been a success. The DCMS conclude that the libraries and publishers, through JCLD, have developed a positive working relationship. This relationship between the publishers and the libraries is crucial in making the NPLD Regulations work and is an important factor that other countries thinking of embarking on electronic legal deposit legislation should encourage.

The PIR indicates that the principal policy objective of the regulation, to allow the preservation of non-print publications for future generations, has been met and that the majority of the wider policy objectives have been achieved.

The Final Impact Assessment published prior to the Regulations outlined the main policy objectives of the Regulations as:

1. to ensure a national collection of non-print publications
2. to enable an efficient system in which material is archived and preserved in the legal deposit libraries
3. to govern how the deposited copies may be used, balancing the needs of libraries and researchers with the interests of publishers and rights holders
4. to facilitate long-term preservation, so that the material may continue to be used in future
5. to ensure long-term viability by requiring both legal deposit libraries and publishers to share part of the responsibility for archiving without imposing an unreasonable burden on any institution.

The PIR acknowledges that further research and development is required for material which is more complex than standard e-books and e-journals and that the libraries and publishers will continue to work closely to develop workflows. However, it must be noted that whilst there may be a drive to collect even more digital material, such as newspapers, magazines and emerging formats, limited resources in the libraries means that progress on this work is slow and considered by publishers and libraries to be less than ideal.

Two concrete proposals came out of the PIR. The first relates to ensuring accessibility to disabled users in line with the Equality Act 2010, where the definition of disabled is wider than described in the current regulation. As described above, the JCLD currently have an informal arrangement to allow the wider definition to be applied; however, to have this formally ratified will prevent problems in the future. The second agreed proposal is to change the regulations to allow digital facsimiles of publications such as newspapers and magazines where the published output is in print form but a digital deposit would be beneficial to libraries and publishers.

In addition to the agreed recommendations, the libraries suggest that the DCMS should consider aligning the NPLD Regulations with copyright. Currently the two pieces of legislation are separate, and content collected under NPLD is in perpetual copyright and cannot be used under any of the exceptions covered in the amendments of 2014 (Intellectual Property Office, 2014). The publishers on the JCLD did not agree with this recommendation and provided a counter-argument in the PIR.

The libraries also raised the issue of access to the Web Archive being prohibitive for usability and also preservation. They highlighted the anomaly of collecting something from the openly available web and then only allowing access to it from a closed legal deposit reading room. From the perspective of the libraries, limited access along with the inability of researchers to data-mine this dataset makes the Web Archive a redundant archive that cannot be used to its full potential. They argue that this does not represent effective and efficient use of public resources. The DCMS considered the libraries' recommendations and the feedback from the publishers and have agreed that a public consultation should be undertaken to understand how access to the Web Archive can be increased while protecting rights holders, and also how NPLD regulations can better align with UK copyright. Since the agreed improvement would require a change to the primary and secondary legislation these will also be included in the consultation.

At this stage the exact format and timing of the consultation is unknown but what is certain is that any changes to the legislation, however welcome, will not happen quickly. It is therefore important that other countries embarking on electronic legal deposit learn from the experience of others and get it right from the outset.

Concluding remarks

In summary, the implementation of electronic legal deposit in the UK has been the largest collaborative library project of its type in the UK. Six distinct libraries with their unique characters have been working together to create a single digital infrastructure. The six years following the enforcement of the regulations have not been easy and often it is difficult to appreciate the positive things that have been achieved in a relatively short time in the life of these great institutions.

Many lessons have been learned along the way, not least the fact that users need to be at the heart of what the libraries and publishers do. Access, despite not being explicitly explored in the regulations, is the fundamental reason for collecting this material. Much emphasis is placed on preservation but the question has to be asked 'for whom and for what purpose?' If, as mentioned in the final impact assessment and the guidance notes accompanying the Regulations (Department for Culture, Media and Sport, 2013b), it is for future generations, how can we ensure we are preserving this content in a way that is suitable for future generations to use if we cannot properly serve the current generation? Therefore, as described in the Digital Libraries Future white paper, user access and the opinion of the users should be considered at every stage of policy development and implementation (Gooding, Terras and Berube, 2019).

The consultation is an opportunity to improve the regulations and ensure that the UK can be world-leading in the provision and implementation of electronic legal deposit, and shows that the UK's NPLD infrastructure will continue to develop and change, both because of, and within the constraints of, the legislative context.

Notes

1. Trinity College Dublin was included via the Copyright Act 1801, 41 Geo.III, c.107.
2. The National Library of Wales was included in the Copyright Act 1911, Geo.6 5(1911) c.46.
3. LDIG annual updates to JCLD September 2014–September 2019.
4. www.afsmusic.co.uk/brass.html.
5. www.michaelandrewsmusic.co.uk.
6. www.devinemusic.co.uk.
7. Figures from the British Library Legal Deposit Office and from the Agency for Legal Deposit Libraries showing the books deposited compared to the books liable to deposit from publishers.

8. See for example, the controversy caused after the Conservative Party attempted to delete web materials from its website: www.theguardian.com/politics/2013/nov/13/conservative-party-archive-speeches-internet. Additionally, the www.voteleavetakecontrol.org/balance_sheet has been removed but is available in the Web Archive.
9. For further information, see https://buddah.projects.history.ac.uk/about.
10. This information is taken from an internal BL document, Preferred *File Formats for Digital Collection Content,* June 2015. Based on Library of Congress format specifications, www.loc.gov/preservation/resources/rfs/index.html.
11. Gathered from reader survey responses plus feedback channels at all libraries.
12. Personal communication between Graeme Hawley of the National Library of Scotland and Linda Arnold-Stratford, September 2019.
13. Report BL 5a *No of Serial Titles Available in NPLD v Print LD,* Legal Deposit MI Dashboard.
14. Report BL 6 *NPLD Titles Received as a Percentage of LD,* Legal Deposit MI Dashboard.

References

American Psychological Association (2009) *Publication Manual of the American Psychological Association,* 6th edn.

Bodleian Libraries (2017) *History of the Bodleian,* www.bodleian.ox.ac.uk/bodley/about-us/history.

Boulderstone, R. (2006) *The British Library's Archiving Concept and Implementation,* January, www.researchgate.net/publication/28804432_The_British_Library's_archiving_concept_and_implementation.

Brindley, L. (2009) 'We're in Danger of Losing Our Memories', *The Guardian,* 25 January, www.theguardian.com/technology/2009/jan/25/internet-heritage.

British Library (2013) *Path Breaking Partnership Helps National Library Preserve Thousands of E-Journals for Future Generations,* www.bl.uk/press-releases/2013/june/path-breaking-partnership-helps-national-library-preserve-thousands-of-e-journals-for-future-generati.

British Library (2015) *'Unlocking the Value': The British Library's Collection Metadata Strategy 2015–2018,* www.bl.uk/bibliographic/pdfs/british-library-collection-metadata-strategy-2015-2018.pdf.

Department for Culture, Media and Sport (2013a) *Enactment Stage Impact Assessment for the Legal Deposit Libraries (Non-Print Works) Regulations 2013,* www.legislation.gov.uk/ukia/2013/1166/pdfs/ukia_20131166_en.pdf.

Department for Culture, Media and Sport (2013b) *Guidance on the Legal Deposit Libraries (Non-Print Works) Regulations 2013*, https://assets.publishing.service.gov.uk/government/uploads/system/uploads/attachment_data/file/182339/NPLD_Guidance_April_2013.pdf.

Department for Digital, Culture, Media and Sport (2019) *Post-Implementation Review of the Legal Deposit Libraries (Non-Print Works) Regulations 2013*, www.gov.uk/government/publications/post-implementation-review-of-the-legal-deposit-libraries-non-print-works-regulations-2013.

Enis, M. (2018) College Students Prefer Print for Long-Form Reading, E-books for Research | LJ Survey, *Library Journal*, www.libraryjournal.com?detailStory=college-students-prefer-print-long-form-reading-e-books-research-lj-survey.

Ericom (2013) *The British Library Makes the UK's Digital Heritage Accessible with Ericom's AccessNow*, www.ericom.com/successstories/story_britishlibrary.asp.

Frink, H. W. (1918) *Morbid Fears and Compulsions: Their Psychology and Psychoanalytic Treatment*, 1999 digitisation of a 1918 printing, Routledge.

Gantz, J. and Reinsel, D. (2010) *The Digital Universe Decade: Are You Ready?*, IDC Digital Universe Study, www.emc.com/collateral/leadership/digital-universe/2009DU_final.pdf.

Gooding, P., Terras, M. and Berube, L. (2019) *Towards User-Centric Evaluation of Non-Print Legal Deposit: A Digital Library Futures White Paper*, University of Glasgow, http://elegaldeposit.org/resources.

Hartmann, S. (2015) Ten Years of the UK Web Archive: What Have We Saved?, *UK Web Archive Blog*, 18 September, https://blogs.bl.uk/webarchive/2015/09/ten-years-of-the-uk-web-archive-what-have-we-saved.html.

Intellectual Property Office (2014) *Exceptions to Copyright: Research*, www.gov.uk/government/uploads/system/uploads/attachment_data/file/375954/Research.pdf.

Legal Deposit Libraries Act 2003 c.28, www.legislation.gov.uk/ukpga/2003/28/contents.

Licensing of the Press Act 1662.

London, J. (1904) *The Sea Wolf*, digitisation 2014, Adlard Coles.

Marr, B. (2018) How Much Data Do We Create Every Day? The Mind-Blowing Stats Everybody Should Read, *Forbes* (blog), 21 May, www.forbes.com/sites/bernardmarr/2018/05/21/how-much-data-do-we-create-every-day-the-mind-blowing-stats-everyone-should-read.

Modern Languages Association (2016) *MLA Handbook (MLA Handbook for Writers of Research Papers)*, 8th edn.

Siegler, M. G. (2013) Eric Schmidt: Every 2 Days We Create as Much Information As We Did Up to 2003, *TechCrunch* (blog), http://social.techcrunch.com/2010/08/04/schmidt-data.

Smith, C. and Cooke. I. (2018) Emerging Formats: Complex Digital Media and Its Impact on the UK Legal Deposit Libraries, *Alexandria: The Journal of National and International Library and Information Issues*, **27** (3), 175–87.

The Copyright Act, 1710.

The Legal Deposit Libraries (Non-Print Works) Regulations 2013, www.legislation.gov.uk/uksi/2013/777/contents/made.

thinkWhere (2019) *Preserving a Nation's Digital Map Heritage*, https://thinkwhere.com/wp-content/uploads/2018/04/Case-Study-British-Library.pdf.

Toseland, M. and Toseland, S. (2012) *Infographica: The World as You Have Never Seen It Before*, Quercus.

War Department (1905) *Brecon Beacons Rifle Range Byelaws 1905*, https://assets.publishing.service.gov.uk/government/uploads/system/uploads/attachment_data/file/39607/brecon_beacons_rifle_range.pdf

We Are Social (2013) Social, Digital and Mobile Worldwide: Key Statistical Indicators for Each Region Around the World, *Slideshare*, www.slideshare.net/wearesocialsg/we-are-socials-guide-to-social-digital-and-mobile-around-the-world-feb-2013/3-FEB2013_THE_WORLDWIDE_PICTURE_701800000.

CHAPTER 2

The influence of legal deposit legislation on the digital collections of the National Library of Scotland

Paul Cunnea, Gill Hamilton,
Graeme Hawley and Fred Saunderson

The National Library of Scotland, with its centres in Edinburgh and Glasgow, is one of six legal deposit libraries in the United Kingdom and Ireland tasked with responsibility for collecting British published print and non-print resources under the Legal Deposit Libraries Act 2003 and the Legal Deposit Libraries (Non-Print Works) Regulations 2013. In this chapter we give an overview of the history of the National Library of Scotland, and the growing importance and scale of its digital collections, while contextualising the challenges to access and format that come with operating in this space. Pressing issues include considerations of how to widen access to the Library's digital collections and the UK Web Archive, in a legal framework that prioritises access conditions best suited to print. The Library is also grappling with digital preservation issues regarding how best to ingest, safeguard and provide access to structured datasets such as maps, e-books, interactive fiction, and new and evolving media. This chapter outlines the growing digital expertise within the UK's legal deposit libraries, and demonstrates the agile approach that is necessary to ensure that the current, ever-changing UK publishing environment is safeguarded and available for current and future generations to consult.

Context and history

The legal deposit collections of the National Library of Scotland have their foundations in The Advocates Library of the Faculty of Advocates.[1] The Advocates Library was formally inaugurated in 1689, although the Faculty had long been collecting texts and other documents to support legal practice (Solberg, 1938). The Copyright Act of 1710[2] entitled the Keeper of the

Advocates Library to claim a copy of every book published in the British Isles, the first form of legal deposit, thereby broadening the scope of the Faculty's collection beyond legal materials. As a result of the Act, The Advocates Library became Scotland's national library in all but name. By the beginning of the 20th century the ever-growing collection of legal deposit materials was proving challenging for the Faculty, a private members' organisation, to store and maintain. In seeking a solution it approached the UK government for support. In 1925 the National Library of Scotland Act[3] established a new library for Scotland, and the Faculty gifted 750,000 non-legal books, pamphlets, maps and sheet music as the founding collection for the National Library of Scotland. With the Act, responsibility for legal deposit transferred to the new National Library, although the Faculty of Advocates retained the right of legal deposit for legal works.

To store and manage the national collection a new building was erected in Edinburgh's city centre, adjacent to the Faculty, opening in 1956. With the ever-increasing output from UK publishers, the Library soon outgrew these premises, and in 1989 a further building, chiefly for the storage of materials, opened at Causewayside, a mile from the city centre (National Library of Scotland, 2018).

In 2016 a third facility opened at Kelvin Hall[4] in Glasgow, providing access to the Library's non-print legal deposit, digitised,[5] moving image[6, 7] and sound collections.[8] The centre at Kelvin Hall was specifically designed to be a welcoming, comfortable and open space, where anyone may enter and freely view, use and enjoy the digital collections. Unlike the Library's centres in Edinburgh, where membership is compulsory before physical and non-print legal deposit collections may be consulted, Kelvin Hall has no such restrictions. This openness, along with the mix of interactive services for digital and moving image collections, has helped challenge the perception that the Library is an austere, serious research institution, but rather the Library is for anybody and has something for everyone.

The National Library of Scotland and the changing publishing environment

In the 1990s, with the proliferation of low-cost computing and the web as a new, open and democratising platform, publishing underwent a rapid and unforeseen expansion. Works were published in both print and digital formats simultaneously, born-digital works emerged, and a new publishing paradigm arose where potentially anyone could be a publisher. This shift, from print to digital, and the dissemination of digital works outwith traditional publishing routes challenged the Library's ability to comprehensively collect Scotland's published heritage (Lang, 1996). Along with the other legal deposit libraries and interested parties, the Library lobbied government and publishers to extend legal deposit to include digital works (British Library, 1996; Field, 2004). In 1997 the Secretary of State for Culture, Media and Sport (DCMS) set up a working party to advise on how a national archive of non-print content might be achieved. At the end of 1998, following consultation (Department for Culture, Media and Sport, 1998), the government accepted the recommendations of the working party, namely that only statutory deposit could secure a comprehensive national published archive.[9] The Secretary for State recommended that a technical group be set up to look at definitions and investigate impact on business, before drafting legislation, and in the meantime that a voluntary code be developed, agreed between publishers and deposit libraries. This led to the development of the Code of Practice for Voluntary Deposit of Non-print Publications, which was adopted at the end of 1999 (Working Party on Legal Deposit, 1999).

Under the auspices of the voluntary code, and prior to the introduction of the Non-Print Legal Deposit Regulations in 2013, the Library and other legal deposit libraries were able to capture elements of the UK's growing digital publishing outputs. Over this period, the Library negotiated agreements[10] with many Scottish publishers to ensure that their born-digital publications would be deposited with the Library. In a parallel development in 2003, the UK Web Archiving Consortium (UKWAC)[11] was established, with the Library a founding member.[12] This followed a similar voluntary, permission-based approach to collecting digital content, and enabled the Library to harvest Scottish websites and online documents, as well as to test some of the requirements of future legal deposit regulation. Where feasible, agreements also gave permission for these resources to be made available openly. Publishers that entered into these agreements included the Scottish Parliament and other public sector bodies, non-commercial bodies such as the Society of Antiquaries of Scotland,[13] website owners and private individuals. These voluntary deposit and web harvesting approaches led, in 2009, to a memorandum of understanding with the Scottish Government for collecting its digital content.[14] The Scottish Government had by this time switched the majority of its publishing output to digital format, with few publications produced in print, making it essential that the digital copies were retained for posterity in a trusted repository.

With the introduction of the Legal Deposit Libraries Act 2003[15] non-print publications were incorporated within the UK legal deposit framework, but as this was only enabling legislation there was much work still to be done before non-print legal deposit would become a reality. Research was carried over this period to support the development of the regulations (Cunnea, 2005;

Charlesworth, 2003; Day, 2003; Powell, 2006) and an Advisory Panel was set up to manage implementation.[16]

From 2008 the British Library led a collaborative project with the National Library of Scotland and National Library of Wales to build a digital library system to support ingest of non-print works and their metadata.[17] With the passing of the 2013 Regulations, and the resultant legal duty and right to collect non-print works, this technical infrastructure was used by legal deposit libraries to manage and provide access to non-print works. The core facilities of this infrastructure are as follows:

Storage and security

For print materials security is achieved by each legal deposit library receiving a physical copy and storing it in temperature-controlled, secure buildings. For non-print materials the British Library co-ordinates ingest of most digital resources into the shared digital library system. The system then distributes the resources to four digital storage 'nodes' at the British Library at St Pancras, the British Library at Boston Spa, and the national libraries of Scotland and Wales.[18] If a resource on a node becomes damaged, for example through bit-rot, or is lost as a result of a disk failure, the node attempts to resolve the issue from its local disk array. However, if it is unable to do this it will then seek a replacement copy from another node. For digital deposit, a single copy at a single point of deposit – as opposed to six physical copies for each of the six legal deposit libraries – leads to a more efficient deposit method for both publishers and libraries, and ensures that all six legal deposit libraries have access to the same corpus of legal deposit material; this would not necessarily be the case for print deposit, e.g. failure of a publisher to deposit or the libraries to request six print copies.

Access

The Library's access to non-print legal deposit resources is provided via Library Search,[19] a cloud-based resource discovery system that integrates all of the Library's collections, whether physical or digital. For the vast majority of non-print legal deposit works the technology behind Library Search harvests new and updated metadata from the British Library metadata aggregation service. Library Search then processes and indexes this metadata to make it discoverable.

When a user finds a non-print legal deposit work in Library Search there are several layers of control that moderate access and use of the resource, in accordance with the criteria set out in Part 4 of the 2013 Regulations: the user must be on the Library's premises and using a Library provided 'terminal';[20] before using a resource they must accept the terms and conditions of use; and they may not annotate or take copies of the resource, although they may ask Library staff to print limited copies within what is allowed under the regulation.

This is implemented in the Library by providing users with PCs in the reading rooms in Edinburgh and at the Kelvin Hall centre in Glasgow. At the time of writing, users may not use their personal laptops or phones to access non-print legal deposit resources, and this causes them considerable inconvenience as they have to move from the desk where they are consulting physical resources to another location in the Library to consult the non-print legal deposit materials.

In the event of downtime on the Library's node, whether that be planned or unplanned, access to non-print legal deposit resources is maintained by 'failing-over' to another node, usually the node at the British Library at St Pancras in London. That node then provides access to Library users until the downtime has passed and access is restored from the local node. This system has been in place since 2016 and is used on average three to four times a year, most often to support ongoing access during system maintenance.

This infrastructure has enabled the legal deposit libraries to safeguard and provide access to a growing collection of digital material since the non-print regulations came into force, which complement the print holdings. At the time of writing, the National Library of Scotland's collection is in excess of 52 million resources, with approximately 26 million physical items and 27 million digital items. The 27 million digital items are a combination of non-print legal deposit resources, collections digitised by the Library and digital collections purchased, acquired or donated to the Library. The legal deposit collections of the Library are made up of approximately 13 million print titles collected since the Copyright Act, 1710 and more than 16 million non-print legal deposit titles, of which approximately 6.9 million are e-books and articles[21] and 10 million are archived websites, collected since the 2013 non-print regulation.[22, 23]

Receipt and ingest of digital resources is now a core activity for the Library, which brings with it various challenges, opportunities, and issues given the legal frameworks within which the Library operates. The first set of these challenges can be framed as *challenges of access*: how can the National Library of Scotland allow users to access the growing digital collections in ways which respond to their affordances within the legal framework? The second set of challenges can be framed as *challenges of format*: how can the Library effectively deal with ever-changing and developing digital formats, in ways which will allow them to be used, adapted, searched, safeguarded, and preserved for future generations?

Challenges of access

Widening access to the National Library of Scotland's collections

Since 2004, successive National Library of Scotland strategies have made an increasingly strong commitment to widening access to the national collections, and collecting digital content and providing digital copies of its physical collections is a core manifestation of that commitment. The current strategy, *The Way Forward 2015–2020* (National Library of Scotland, 2015), is the most ambitious yet, with a key objective stating that, by the Library's centenary in 2025, it will have further widened access to its collections by having one-third of its holdings in digital format. This ambitious figure (around 15 million on current projections) will include both physical items from the collection that have been digitised and the non-print legal deposit collection. At the time of writing (2019), the Library is over half way towards this target.

Over the years this drive to widen access by providing digital copies has taken different approaches, but always with the same aim. These methods have included:

The digitisation of physical collections

For many years there has been an ongoing programme to digitise physical items, such as books, maps, photographs, posters, and music. Once digitised, these resources are made freely available globally and, where rights and permissions permit, as open access. For example, the Library holds one of the largest and most comprehensive collections of maps in the world[24] and since 2010 a digitisation programme has made available online more than 200,000 maps to a wide global audience via a popular digital mapping service.[25, 26] Other examples include:

- Medical History of British India.[27] This digitised collection, taken from the Library's India Papers Collection, provides access to rare documents and entry into the history of disease and its prevention in 19th- and 20th-century British India, between 1850 and 1950.
- Scottish Post Office Directories.[28] With over 700 digitised directories covering most of Scotland and dating from 1773 to 1911, this collection provides an excellent basis for researching Scotland's family, trade, and town history, enabling users to easily find out where people lived at a certain time and how they earned their living.
- The Word on the Street[29] and the Broadsides from the Crawford Collection.[30] These two collections, amounting to around 4,000 broadsides from 1501 to 1910, provide a fascinating insight into Scotland

over this period, covering crime, politics, religion, romance, emigration, humour, tragedy, royalty and superstitions.
- British Military Lists[31] and the Rolls of Honour.[32] These two collections provide details of officers who served in the British Army, Navy and Air Force in the First and Second World Wars, plus Scottish listings of casualties and those who died on active service in the First World War, provide an invaluable resource for researchers and family historians.

The digitisation programme was expanded in 2018, adding more digitisation stations and staff, with the goal of significantly increasing digitisation throughput.

Digital deposit, harvesting and donation

As noted in the previous section, following on from the earlier voluntary deposit and permissions based access agreements, the Library has continued to seek wider access agreements for digital content and websites collected under legal deposit, where this is feasible and resources allow. Where we have the necessary agreements in place, we make the content openly accessible online.

Purchased and subscription digital resources[33]

When purchasing or subscribing to digital content, the Library negotiates agreements with publishers that determine terms of use and access. To date we have negotiated remote access to over 80% of these collections, which enables Library users who are resident in Scotland to access the content from anywhere. This is a potentially transformative access to knowledge for readers (Gooding, 2017, 167) allowing citizens across Scotland to remotely and freely access resources as diverse as the following:

- 17th and 18th Century Burney Collection Newspapers – full-text digital archive of 17th and 18th century newspapers, broadsides and news pamphlets
- 18th Century Collections Online – full-text digital archive of over 200,000 publications printed between 1701 and 1800
- 19th Century UK Periodicals – 600 full-text titles from the Library's collections
- Access UK and Scotland Newspapers – Full-text current content of local and regional newspapers, from over 860 titles

- Archives of Sexuality and Gender: LGBTQ History and Culture Since 1940 – consisting of 20 individual collections spanning 1940 to 2014 and amounting to around 1.5 million pages
- British Library Newspapers, Parts 1 and 2 – full-text digital archive of 19th-century newspapers, with the complete runs of 70 national, regional and rural daily and weekly publications originating in England, Scotland, Ireland, and Wales
- Making of Modern World – 12 million pages on development of modern business and economics, from 1450 to 1850
- Cold War Intelligence – full-text collection of 2,360 formerly classified US government documents detailing the successes and failures of the US intelligence community in its efforts to spy on the Soviet Union during the Cold War
- Scotsman Digital Archive – every issue of the iconic newspaper from 1817 to 1950
- Perdita Manuscripts – full-text collection of early modern women authors from Britain, 1500–1700
- British and Irish Women's Letters and Diaries – 100,000 pages of published letters and diaries, spanning 1500 to 1950
- D&B Hoovers – a business information database which provides in-depth profiles of companies worldwide, industry profiles, news and market research
- *Scientific American* Archive – full-text digital archive, covering all 4,960 issues from 1845 to 2005, and containing more than 133,700 articles
- SpringerLink – 2000 journal titles and over 65,000 e-books
- Factiva – contents of over 14,000 leading newspaper titles, news sources and company information from around the world
- Electronic Enlightenment – over 70,000 letters and documents from over 8500 correspondents, from 1609 to 1900
- Web of Science – citation database covering over 10,000 high-impact journals in the sciences, social sciences, arts and humanities.

Establishing Kelvin Hall in Glasgow as a 'Digital Access Point'

With the opening of the Kelvin Hall facility in 2016, we not only provided a physical presence for the National Library in the centre of Glasgow, and a suitable, modern facility for consulting the moving image and sound collections, we also provided an additional location for accessing the Library's digital collections, specifically where access is restricted to Library premises. This means we can now provide access from a new geographic location to the 20% of purchased and subscribed digital content that can only be viewed on Library premises due to the licensing conditions noted above. This allows us to deliver these valuable resources to the largest population centre within Scotland, where terms and conditions allow. This also has major implications for increasing access to non-print legal deposit (NPLD) restricted content. Following discussion at the Joint Committee for Legal Deposit (JCLD), and with agreement from the publisher representatives, it was accepted that the regulation provided for access to NPLD content from the Library's new Kelvin Hall premises. This will extend the availability and accessibility of the collections significantly to the people of Scotland, as well as the services provided at the Kelvin Hall facility.

Restrictions on access, use and reuse of NPLD Content

With the advent of non-print legal deposit regulations in 2013, after many years' preparation, the potential for increasing the Library's digital holdings further was enormous. However, the extent to which this would help increase access to the Library's collections for our users was not straightforward, despite some of the developments described above.

The introduction of the 2013 Regulations has greatly advanced the Library's strategic objective of holding a third of its collections digitally. In the first few years of NPLD, many large publishers have 'transitioned' from print to non-print legal deposit and the legal deposit libraries' shared web-harvesting programme has expanded to include annual snapshots of what is now more than 10 million websites from the open UK web domain. However, access and use restrictions in the 2013 Regulations do not align well with the Library's wider access ambitions, and threaten to restrict access to digital content, often despite the interests of many digital publishers, such as bloggers, private individuals and non-commercial organisations and publishers.

The principal objective of the 2013 Regulations, as stated in the final impact assessment (Department for Culture, Media and Sport, 2013), is 'to allow the preservation of non-print publications for future generations'. In the recently published Post-implementation Review of the Regulations (Department for Digital, Culture, Media and Sport, 2019), the JCLD considers three areas in its assessment of the success of this objective so far: collection; preservation; and access and use.

The review recognises that, five years after its introduction, implementation is an ongoing process, but suggests that collection and preservation can be considered to have been largely successful. Indeed, by year 4 (2016/17) 23% more publications had been collected than the highest estimates for year 5, with 58% of all monographs and 35% of all journals identified by the libraries now collected in digital rather than print format. However, the review provides less agreement on the level of success in terms of access and use, with significantly different interpretations between the publisher and library representatives within JCLD. From its inception, a key requirement of the regulations was to achieve a balance between the interests of publishers and rights holders, and the needs of libraries, researchers, and the wider public. As such, conditions controlling terms of access and use are central to the regulations.

In line with this, the use of NPLD content is tightly controlled, with saving, downloading, and taking images of NPLD content prohibited. This is in part technically controlled using a locked-down browser to access NPLD content. Printing is permissible within standard copyright restrictions, and is offered via the Library's networked printers. Data and text mining is also not permitted, restricting the ability of researchers to analyse UK publishing output and the development of the UK web, something which the growing digital corpus is ideally suited to meet, and which would be of value to a wide range of stakeholders, including the publishing industry.

In terms of accessibility, provision is made in the regulations for Libraries to provide accessible copies of relevant material for a visually impaired person. This is achieved by providing access to NPLD content via dedicated terminals with accessibility software installed. However, people with accessibility requirements are unable to use the accessibility tools and software that they are familiar with, which can present a barrier to use. In addition, this provision is limited to people with visual impairments, whereas the current accessibility legislation[34] covers anyone with a disability. This deficit has been recognised by all parties in the Post-implementation Review, which recommends that the regulations are brought in line with current accessibility legislation.

The regulations more fundamentally restrict access to NPLD materials to the premises of a legal deposit library. They also restrict access to only one copy of any one resource within a library at any one time – mirroring the print model. However, these restrictions are notably more restrictive than those that apply to print legal deposit and to other collection formats. As such, although the print environment may have formed the basis for formulating non-print legal deposit access conditions, the regulations can be viewed as enforcing more stringent conditions than apply to print, as highlighted in the Digital Futures White Paper by Gooding, Terras and Berube, (2019).

Compared to print, the digital domain is significantly more diverse and complex. There are a huge and varied number of digital content producers, content owners and publishers, the majority of whom have never produced print works. This diverse group is not represented by traditional publisher bodies, and will have a range of views on digital collecting, preservation and access that are potentially very different from those of both commercial and non-commercial traditional publishers.

For example, many scholarly publications published today are made available under open licences such as Creative Commons[35] to promote open access and reuse. Furthermore, a large amount of public information is made available under Open Government Licensing (National Archives, 2014), to encourage reuse, in accordance with the principles of the Reuse of Public Sector Information Regulations 2015[36] open data strategies.[37] Bloggers and social media content creators are more likely to be more interested in openly sharing their content than restricting access. However, the regulations place the same access conditions across all content collected under non-print legal deposit, irrespective of the interests, wishes or culture of the content and rights owners.

By placing blanket access and use restrictions on this material, legal deposit libraries are in effect limiting access to huge volumes of publicly accessible content. This is not an issue for researchers and the public while this content remains available on the open web, although it does limit the value and utility of the corpus of material, but it does present a problem when this content is no longer available. This disparity in access between the originally published content and the NPLD restricted content is most clearly demonstrated with the UK Web Archive.

Access and the Web Archive

Analysis by Andy Jackson, UK Web Archive Technical Lead at the British Library, found that by 2015, 24 months after UK legal deposit web harvesting began, nearly 40% of the content harvested in 2013 had disappeared from the live web, was missing, or had moved (Jackson, 2015). Indeed, deeper analysis found that link rot and content drift were the norm, and that 50% of web resources were gone or unrecognisable after one year, 60% after two years and 65% after three years.

Looking further back, less than 20% of content archived from 2004 can be confirmed as identical to content currently on the open web. It should be borne in mind that prior to the 2013 legal deposit regulations we were archiving a tiny fraction of the UK domain under permission-based harvesting, so the vast majority of UK web content will be lost unless captured by non-statutory web harvesting bodies, such as the Internet Archive,[38] which has been harvesting the web globally since 1996. This analysis makes clear that a large proportion of even recent web history is no longer extant, or is difficult to find, or has changed out of recognition. Since the NPLD Regulations came into force in 2013 we are able to collect and preserve the

UK web domain at scale. Much of the UK web domain from this period will be available for future generations to view and analyse due to this work, but for the time being much of this originally public content will remain behind closed doors, accessible only on legal deposit library premises.

This demonstrates how the regulations, whilst empowering the libraries to make great strides in collecting and preserving digital content, at the same time limit access to once open, public content that is not readily available by other means. A conundrum is therefore presented: the legal deposit libraries recognise that the interests of the traditional publishing industry require protection, and also that not all free-to-access content is necessarily non-commercial – for example, models for monetising content through click-throughs and advertising. However, the regulations' single approach to access, which gives no provision for granularity in access conditions or publishing models and cultures, is at variance with the intentions of many digital content producers.

This conundrum can be further demonstrated by the options open to the libraries to make archived web content more accessible. The archive consists of an annual snapshot or 'harvest' of the open UK web domain; this excludes any content that lies behind a paywall, or requires membership or a login to access. This annual snapshot is further supplemented by 'selective harvesting'. These selective harvests may focus on a particular event or topic, such as the 2005 G8 Summit in Scotland[39] or the Scottish Independence Referendum in 2014,[40] and harvesting of this content may be carried out more frequently, have higher quality assurance measures, better description, and – of relevance to this section – more resources assigned to pursue open access agreements.

As noted above, since the introduction of the 2013 Regulations the National Library of Scotland has continued to pursue wider access agreements with website owners and non-commercial publishers. Until recently, this has involved collecting a second copy, in addition to the legal deposit copy, and making it globally available, with the rights holder's permission, either on the open UK Web Archive or via the National Library's web services. Over time, and working with the other deposit libraries, this approach has been standardised, and integrated into the non-print legal deposit technical infrastructure, specifically for web and document harvesting. In this context, and where wider access has been agreed, access restrictions may be relaxed to allow the legal deposit copy to be openly and globally available. This approach now applies to content where there is a direct agreement with a website owner or publisher, and through recognised open access agreements, such as the Open Government Licence[41] and the Library's memorandum of understanding with the Scottish Government.[42]

However, adoption of open licences by public bodies is patchy, and despite open access research mandates and campaigns it is still far from being universal in the academic sector. In the meantime, pursuing individual agreements with content producers is resource-intensive, and this, coupled with a low response rate, means that the percentage of the web archive that is openly available using this approach will remain extremely low under the current framework. Taking the UK Web Archive as a whole, less than 1% of the archived content is globally accessible, despite all content being harvested from the open UK web domain.

This impact of restricting access is further highlighted with the merging of the Open UK Web Archive (containing permission-based content harvested since 2004) and the UK Legal Deposit Web Archive through a single search interface.[43] This recent development integrates discovery of the openly accessible archived websites and those that can only be viewed by visiting deposit library premises. The single search interface is a positive development, with restricted-access sites now more visible and sitting alongside open access archived sites. This raises the visibility of the legal deposit corpus, helping to promote the archive to researchers and library users, making it easier to view search results and identify what has and hasn't been archived, even if in most cases it will require travel to a legal deposit library to view the archived websites themselves.

However, levels of use of the content based on access level, whilst not overly surprising, highlight and reinforce the impact restricted access has on this increasingly valuable dataset. As might be expected, the level of use and size of the two archive components – open and restricted – are inversely proportional, with the much smaller open access component (0.15% in 2017) having over 100 times the level of use than the exponentially bigger restricted-access component (Table 2.1). This severely hampers the promotion of the archive to researchers and the public in general, and selling its inherent value to the research community.

Table 2.1 *Comparison of usage and views of legal deposit versus permission-cleared web archives*

	Size		**Uses 2016/17**	**Page views 2016/17**
	Sites	**Data**		
Legal Deposit UK Web Archive (access on LDL premises)	9-10 million	470 TB	2,311	16,036
Permissions-cleared UK Web Archive (access on open web)	15,000	30TB	292,699	1,070,160

In addition to these limitations on access, the restrictions on use noted previously also severely limit the intrinsic value of the dataset for researchers.

What could be an incredibly rich resource using modern text- and data-mining techniques for investigating, for example, social, linguistic, technical, and publishing trends, is instead limited to a search and discovery platform for the UK web over time. Valuable though this is, the research opportunity for mining at scale such an extensive dataset, with its comprehensiveness, span, diversity, cohesion and set boundary, is lost – at least, for the time being.

Future of access and use of NPLD

The JCLD review highlighted the tension between protecting publisher interests and providing public access to NPLD, as well as the diverging views of publisher and library representatives on JCLD in these areas. On the one hand, the libraries assert the value of legal deposit in terms of access and use, advocating in particular a change to regulations to address the issue of access to the web archive in particular. Publisher representatives, on the other hand, question the role of legal deposit beyond collection and preservation for future generations.

Despite the differences in perspective between JCLD members, there appears to be some agreement on how to resolve these differences. While questioning the extent to which access and use is a key objective of legal deposit regulations, JCLD publisher representatives agree that a public consultation on access of the UK Web Archive may be a way forward. However, publisher and library representatives agree that if this is pursued, a framework for protecting the interests of publishers and other rights holders would be required.

For open access advocates this may appear an over-cautious approach. However, there are important considerations to take into account. These include not just commercial interests, but also the moral and legal interests of rights holders in general. Any changes to the regulations need to consider what safeguards would be required, for example to protect future, unforeseen revenue streams. Legal deposit libraries will continue to have a responsibility to ensure that the interests of rights holders are protected, and that legal deposit collections are used responsibly, while also meeting the needs of library users, researchers and the wider public.

UK non-print legal deposit is still in the early stages of implementation. There is an opportunity that a more balanced access framework can be established which not only recognises the interests of publishers and rights holders, and the diverse range of content producers and publishers across the UK digital published and web domain, but also the value that wider access to our digital and web heritage can bring. Such a framework needs to acknowledge that legal deposit libraries are collecting for current as well as future generations, and that within the digital publishing domain there are many more models and interests to consider and adapt to than in the print environment; one size is unlikely to fit all. If an effective balance is struck between the varying interests and needs of publishers, content producers, rights holders, researchers and the public, a non-print legal deposit access framework may emerge for the UK that is the envy of the world. In the meantime, developing access points to digital content – such as our centre at Kelvin Hall – encourages further use of our growing digital collections.

Challenges of format

As well as issues of access, non-print legal deposit highlights issues of changing digital formats, and how libraries can deal with a fluctuating and changing digital environment as well as the inherent tension in trying to make often ephemeral formats available for posterity. The 2013 regulations are based on the print world. As such, the UK's legal deposit legislation focuses on the collection of a comparatively traditional understanding of electronic works. Legal deposit libraries are entitled to collect 'copies' of works that are published in non-print formats, whether on- or off-line. Focus on works distributed by 'copies' is historically and legally logical, but not necessarily best suited to the realities of digital content. To understand why this approach may not be the most appropriate for digital works, it is useful to reflect on the historic logic and legal context of collecting 'copies' under legal deposit.

The historic logic for 'copies' reflects the reality found in monographic and continuous print publications: when a monographic work is prepared for print publication, its content becomes complete, fixed and static at the point of printing. This is true regardless of whether the print run is one copy or many copies; continuous works, such as newspapers, journals and magazines, are somewhat different. Individual issues are of course fixed and static copies at the point of printing, but the work itself continues to change through time as more issues are added. As a result, each time a new issue is printed, an extension or continuation of the work is produced.

The legal logic for 'copies' has its roots in copyright legislation. Under the UK's copyright laws, the right to 'issue copies' of a work to the public is the first of six rights reserved to the copyright owner.[44] Thus, the very notion of what it means to create a work worthy of copyright protection has been rooted in the distribution of copies. Non-print legal deposit regulations continue this historical and legal context of copies and this logic gives the framework tangibility. Works are created, copies made available to the public in accordance with a copyright owner's right, and a copy is duly collectable by legal deposit libraries.

The logic relating to 'copies' is suitable and appropriate for some digital content because, in many instances, digital works like e-books and electronic journal articles and issues mimic print works, in that at point of production they become fixed, complete and static. However, there are many forms of digital content collectable under the 2013 regulations to which this simple 'copies' logic is misaligned. In relation to the legislation, we refer to these as 'challenging formats'.

Challenging formats

The nature of digital works can be, and often is, radically distinct from the world of print. Consider a database or a website that is continually updated. When is the legal deposit 'copy' to be created or collected? Or a politician's social media feed, where comments are added and deleted: when is the legal deposit 'copy' to be created or collected here? And what about a publication that is designed to 'decay' each time it is opened: how is this work preserved by legal deposit?

The nature of the digital domain, and its apparent infinite flexibility and adaptability to create new digital presentations, new formats, and content, will continue to pose fresh legal deposit challenges. Who can imagine what a future digital work will look like or how it will function? To focus our discussion, three specific types of challenging formats are explored: structured datasets, e-books as apps, and interactive fiction.

Structured datasets

Substantial datasets, such as business and cartographic databases such as those from the UK's mapping agency Ordnance Survey, can be considered challenging formats in the non-print legal deposit context because of their scale and their continuously developing nature. Of course, there are certain types of print works that are similar to these datasets, and they have their own collecting challenges; consider 'updating services', which require loose-leaf paper updates to be inserted into a work, replacing outdated leaves of information, which are then removed. However, contemporary non-print equivalents present perhaps even more vexing challenges.

The very value of these works is vested in their size and currency. These are works that are made to be remade, to be continually updated and revised with the most accurate and current information. In the age of print this meant frequent distribution of loose-leaf updates. With non-print works, this means databases, normally obtained through subscription, that are updated at intervals. Some data points may be updated numerous times a day. Others may not be updated for years, or at all. But the publication remains as one single 'live' database of the most current data: immeasurably useful to the immediate user, but immensely challenging to the logic of legal deposit and preservation of 'copies' of knowledge. When is the legal deposit 'copy' of a resource such as this to be obtained? Should a fresh copy of a vast dataset be collected afresh every time a data point is revised? Does the adjustment of a single data point mean that the work in its entirety is a 'new' version? Should the work be collected at fixed times, for example annually?

The challenge in terms of use is obvious when considering the future user. In 10 years' time, how will a legal deposit library provide access to the version of this database as it was on 1 January 2020? Not without some logistical effort, perhaps, that same library may be able to provide access to the database as it was on 1 January 1990, by pulling together the correct sequence of loose sheets. There is no ready solution, bar the creation of an unwieldy multiplicity of copies of each database, to ensuring that the database of 1 January 2020 is as accessible to the future user. Consider computer-assisted legal research services that maintain databases of statutes, court documents and judgments that document the evolution of law and regulation. If a library is unable to take continuous copies, or overwrites an existing copy of such a database with the most current version, then what does this mean for a legal professional or court that is trying to understand the legal guidance or practice at a historical point in time? The evidence trail may be lost or incomplete, perhaps with profound consequences.

E-books as apps

While books and e-books are not generally challenging works, books published digitally as apps do pose unique challenges. By 'e-books as apps' we mean digitally published books that are published along with supporting content, or as part of a richer, content-heavy application, for example, e-book apps that not only contain text but also audio or rich imagery. Unlike the scale and speed-of-change challenges of structured databases, it is the richness and presentation style of 'e-books as apps' that are challenging in the non-print legal deposit context. These works are most often created in exceptional detail, with the traditional book text woven through and around other content, from music to video to imagery that supplements and expands on the direct text.

While these works may be more straightforward to collect as 'copies', ensuring suitable access to and engagement with these works presents real hurdles. E-books as apps are likely to be developed specifically for one particular consumption format. How these works can be properly accessed by current and future users of non-print legal deposit collections remains a challenge, as rarely are such works designed for indoor, seated, desktop terminal access.

Interactive fiction

In many respects, interactive fiction manifests the genius of digital. Works, whether or not based on text, that contain geocoding to localise a narrative to a user's time and place, or narratives through which the user can navigate and develop their own plots or conclusions, are examples of interactive fiction. These works make the very best use of 'digital': unlike 'flat' e-journals and e-books, interactive fiction grabs and runs with the beauty and power of digital, combining methods, formats, and data sources and enabling a shattering of a fourth wall between the creator and the consumer.

Under non-print legal deposit, these works are also some of the most challenging to collect, preserve and provide access to, as well as being at more risk of loss. The challenges of access are most acute and obvious: how, within the limited confines of non-print legal deposit access, is a user wholly and properly to seek to interact with and enjoy these works? By their nature, the user experience may be designed to be wholly different on each occasion, or in any given context, location, or scenario. The challenges of collection are similarly not insignificant. What is to be collected? A device that is pivotal to the experience? Whose version of the narrative?

Digital as artefact

New interactive qualities of digital literature, for example where the text of a work alters as the reader physically engages with it, challenges the perception that digital and print works are basically analogous. This is brought into sharp focus when considering how such works may be exhibited as examples of 'electrified literature'. For the purposes of display and exhibition print works are placed in secure, atmospherically controlled cases protecting them from theft and damage, while simultaneously making them visible to visitors to the library. Would it be strange to put a Kindle or iPad behind glass so as to show particular non-print legal deposit publications? When books are placed in cases, they 'change' from literature to exhibit, and in doing so say something additional to the content of the item itself. Should e-books and e-journals be treated in the same way? And if so, how are electronically powered devices to be physically displayed? Consider an exhibition taking place in 2030: should digital works published in 2020 be displayed on the hardware of the time? What does it actually mean to preserve an e-book over time as a piece of cultural heritage, or has the carrier become meaningless? And if so, what does this imply?

Non-print resources as an agent of change

With the introduction of the regulations in 2013, the expansion of digitisation and the growing investment in purchased digital collections, the Library has, in the past ten years, seen an unparalleled growth in its digital collections. This growth comparatively dwarfs the growth of the physical collections. The need to manage the expansion in digital collections has required a change to the Library's skills portfolio, and has led to investment in digital skills development, retraining of staff and the creation of new positions. This shift has also required the Library to consider new approaches and processes.

Specifically, some 'traditional' skills, techniques and processes have become redundant with the management of non-print legal deposit collections, while others are evolving, and some are new. For example:

- The acquisitions role and function remains, with staff claiming digital publications that have fallen outwith the legal deposit libraries' mainstream non-print legal deposit collecting. With print collections staff would normally unbox and process (for example, by adding the stamp of ownership and moving items to temporary shelving) up to 3,000 new publications a week. These processes are redundant with non-print collections, freeing staff to carry out intellectual rather than physical work.
- The metadata description function remains essential with non-print legal deposit. However, given the volume of this material the Library is unable to provide the quality of description previously feasible with print collections through the Legal Deposit Libraries Shared Cataloguing Programme.[45] The Library does not have the capacity to routinely create new descriptions or upgrade and enhance existing descriptions for non-print legal deposit resources that have been provided by publishers or, in the case of the UK Web Archive, information scraped from the home pages of websites. However, the scale of non-print collections brings considerable opportunity for developing new tools and techniques of description, through the use of 'big data' analysis and machine-learning techniques. There is also untapped potential in using 'the crowd' as an intellectual source for description of non-print collections, whether via analysis of search activity or involvement in tagging, annotating, etc. Collaborating in the design of such tools and services will require metadata staff at the Library and the other legal deposit libraries to develop their knowledge and skills in data processing and in developing networks of expertise and participation.
- The traditional role of the Library's Collection Support staff who place recently received physical items on shelves is redundant in relation to

non-print materials. The digital equivalent of this role is carried out by the Digital Department's technical infrastructure team, which oversees the maintenance and support of the 'node', for example by adding storage as required. Outwith planned upgrades and maintenance support, the 'node' requires few hours of trained technician time per month, compared with many hours of ten Collection Support staff per month in respect of physical materials. However, as the print legal deposit intake declines and Collection Support colleagues spend less time placing books and journals on these shelves, they are able to spend more time on value-added duties, such as managing and optimising the Library's 130 miles of shelving, auditing and checking the collections, and processing requests for the Library's mass digitisation programme.

- The systems librarian role has evolved from overseeing the library management and resource discovery systems to a more data-centric role, with added responsibility for processing and automating non-print legal deposit and other digital collection metadata.
- In 2013, in recognition of the challenges associated with ensuring continued access to its digital collections, the Library created the new specialised role of Digital Preservation Manager, and in 2019 added a further supporting position. These roles co-ordinate and champion digital preservation in the Library and are responsible for safeguarding the Library's digital culture. They provide advice on digital preservation issues and practices including to the UK and Ireland legal deposit libraries to ensure digital legal deposit content is adequately cared for. Working in this field requires the development of new digital skills, expertise and workflows that support the Library and are regularly shared with others who have a growing realisation of the need for digital preservation.

The non-print legal deposit collections, along with other digital collections, have challenged the Library's 300 year-old print-based processes and practices. In just 10 years it has become rapidly necessary to develop the digital skills of those staff working with and managing these resources. Digital collections are compelling the Library, and other libraries, to modernise, embrace the digital, and to look to new techniques and tools for processing these materials.

Conclusion

The nature of 'non-print' collections and non-print legal deposit legislation presents opportunities and challenges in considering access to, engagement with, and display of such works. Overarchingly, this is about the very nature of non-print collections, to expose and celebrate what makes digital works distinct from, and similar to, print legal deposit works. However in many respects the regulations so restrict and limit the access and use of non-print legal deposit collections that they are in fact inferior in these aspects to print collections. These boundaries and constraints need to be explored and pushed. The National Library of Scotland and other UK legal deposit libraries are open to further discussions and public consultation on this, in particular focusing on the access issues relating to the UK Web Archive and its alignment with regulations and UK copyright law, and the challenges in the increasing complexity and sophistication in forms of content.

The development of non-print collecting has been of wider benefit and welcome to the Library and the legal deposit libraries, enabling collection growth in increasingly significant areas of digital publication and communication, and in the development of new and varied digital skills and competencies among staff. It is perhaps unsurprising that the legislative framework remains challenging; unlike its print counterpart, non-print legal deposit remains a new development, which is certain to continue to evolve, refine, and to present new opportunities as well as complexities.

Notes

1. The Faculty of Advocates is a Scottish body of independent lawyers, www.advocates.org.uk.
2. Copyright Act 1710, www.copyrighthistory.com/anne5.html.
3. National Library of Scotland Act 1925 (repealed), www.legislation.gov.uk/ukpga/Geo5/15-16/73/contents.
4. National Library of Scotland at Kelvin Hall, www.nls.uk/kelvin-hall.
5. Digitised collections, National Library of Scotland, https://digital.nls.uk.
6. Moving image collections, National Library of Scotland, www.nls.uk/collections/moving-image-archive.
7. Moving Image Archive at Kelvin Hall, National Library of Scotland, www.nls.uk/collections/moving-image-archive/visit.
8. Sound collections, National Library of Scotland, https://scotlands-sounds.nls.uk.
9. House of Commons (1998) 'Publications.' Hansard written answer, 17 December 1998, pt. 43, col. 682.
10. Recorded within the Library's Legal Deposit Claims & Receipts Database.
11. UK Web Archiving Consortium, https://en.wikipedia.org/wiki/UK_Web_Archiving_Consortium.
12. UK Web Archive Consortium members, https://web.archive.org/web/20100807233342/www.webarchive.org.uk/ukwa/info/about.

13. Society of Antiquaries of Scotland, www.socantscot.org.
14. Memorandum of understanding for the collection and preservation of Scottish Government web content ... between National Library of Scotland and Scottish Government, 1st July 2009 (internal document).
15. Legal Deposit Libraries Act 2003 c.28, www.legislation.gov.uk/ukpga/2003/28/contents.
16. Department of Culture, Media and Sport, Legal Deposit Advisory Panel terms of reference, 2007. Archived copy available at: https://web.archive.org/web/20080727030355/www.culture.gov.uk/images/publications/LDAPToRMarch2007.pdf (Internet Archive, open access).
17. Memorandum of Understanding between the British Library Board, The National Library of Scotland, and the National Library of Wales for Shared Technical Infrastructure for Managing UK Electronic Legal Deposit Materials, 2009 (internal document).
18. Security for NPLD publications, www.bl.uk/legal-deposit/security-for-publications.
19. Library Search, National Library of Scotland, https://search.nls.uk.
20. The Legal Deposit Libraries (Non-Print Works) Regulations 2013, Reader access to relevant material, paragraph 23, www.legislation.gov.uk/ukdsi/2013/9780111533703/part/4.
21. Library Search for non-print legal deposit articles and e-books, https://search.nls.uk/primo-explore/search?query=any,contains,44NLS_NPLD&tab=tab1&search_scope=TAB1_SCOPE1&vid=44NLS_VU1.
22. National Library of Scotland, Annual Review 2019/19, www.nls.uk/about-us/publications/annual-review/2018-2019.
23. Annual Acquisitions and Projected Intake (internal statistics, unpublished).
24. National Library of Scotland map collections, www.nls.uk/collections/maps.
25. National Library of Scotland digital maps service, https://maps.nls.uk.
26. maps.nls.uk Google Analytics Apr 2018–Mar 2019; 1.32 million users, 3.33 million view sessions, 33.3 million page views.
27. Medical History of British India, https://digital.nls.uk/indiapapers.
28. Scottish Post Office Directories, https://digital.nls.uk/directories.
29. The Word on the Street, https://digital.nls.uk/broadsides.
30. Broadsides from the Crawford Collection, https://digital.nls.uk/broadsides-from-the-crawford-collection/archive/144782273.
31. British Military Lists, https://digital.nls.uk/british-military-lists/archive/97343435.
32. Rolls of Honour, https://digital.nls.uk/rolls-of-honour/archive/100261716.
33. National Library of Scotland, eResources, https://auth.nls.uk/eresources.
34. Equality Act 2010, www.legislation.gov.uk/ukpga/2010/15/contents.
35. Creative Commons website, https://creativecommons.org.

36. Reuse of Public Sector Information Regulations 2015, www.legislation.gov.uk/uksi/2015/1415/contents/made.
37. Scottish Government Digital Directorate (2015) Open Data Strategy, www.gov.scot/publications/open-data-strategy.
38. Internet Archive, https://archive.org.
39. G8 Summit 2005 UK web archive collection, www.webarchive.org.uk/en/ukwa/collection/2398.
40. Scottish Independence Referendum UK web archive collection, www.webarchive.org.uk/en/ukwa/collection/65.
41. Open Government Licence for Public Bodies, www.nationalarchives.gov.uk/doc/open-government-licence/version/3.
42. Memorandum of understanding for the collection and preservation of Scottish Government web content ... between National Library of Scotland and Scottish Government, 1st July 2009 (internal document).
43. www.webarchive.org.uk.
44. CDPA s.16 as amended.
45. Legal Deposit Libraries Shared Cataloguing Programme, The British Library, www.bl.uk/bibliographic/clscp.html.

References

British Library (1996) *Proposal for the Deposit of Non-Print Publications to the Department of National Heritage from the British Library.*

Charlesworth, A. (2003) *Legal Issues Relating to the Archiving of Internet Resources in the UK, EU, USA and Australia: A Study Undertaken for the JISC and Wellcome Trust,* Centre for IT and Law, University of Bristol. Originally available at http://library.wellcome.ac.uk/assets/WTW039230.pdf.

Cunnea, P. (2005) Selective Web Archiving in the UK: A Perspective of the National Library of Scotland within UK Web Archiving Consortium (UKWAC), *SCONUL Focus,* **34** (Spring), 44–9.

Day, M. (2003) *Collecting and Preserving the World Wide Web: A Feasibility Study for the JISC and the Wellcome Trust,* UKOLN for Wellcome Trust and JISC, https://web.archive.org/web/20041028035721/http://library.wellcome.ac.uk/assets/WTL039229.pdf.

Department for Culture, Media and Sport (1998) *Legal Deposit of Publications: Summary of Responses to the Consultation Paper Issued by the Department of National Heritage, the Scottish Office, the Welsh Office and the Department of Education Northern Ireland.*

Department for Culture, Media and Sport (2013) *Enactment Stage Impact Assessment for the Legal Deposit Libraries (Non-Print Works) Regulations 2013,* www.legislation.gov.uk/ukia/2013/1166/pdfs/ukia_20131166_en.pdf.

Department for Digital, Culture, Media and Sport (2019) *Post-Implementation Review of the Legal Deposit Libraries (Non-Print Works) Regulations 2013*, www.gov.uk/government/publications/post-implementation-review-of-the-legal-deposit-libraries-non-print-works-regulations-2013.

Field, C. (2004) Securing Digital Legal Deposit in the UK: The Legal Deposit Libraries Act 2003, *Alexandria: The Journal of National and International Library and Information Issues*, http://journals.sagepub.com/doi/abs/10.1177/095574900401600204.

Gooding, P. (2017) *Historic Newspapers in the Digital Age: 'Search All About It'*, Routledge.

Gooding, P., Terras, M. and Berube, L. (2019) *Towards User-Centric Evaluation of Non-Print Legal Deposit: A Digital Library Futures White Paper*, University of Glasgow, elegaldeposit.org/resources.

Jackson, A. (2015) Ten Years of the UK Web Archive: What Have We Saved?, *UK Web Archive Blog*, http://blogs.bl.uk/webarchive/2015/09/ten-years-of-the-uk-web-archive-what-have-we-saved.html.

Lang, B. (1996) The Legal Deposit of Electronic Publications, Conference of Directors of National Libraries, UNESCO, https://unesdoc.unesco.org/ark:/48223/pf0000105504.

Legal Deposit Libraries Act 2003 c.28, www.legislation.gov.uk/ukpga/2003/28/contents.

National Archives (2014) *Open Government Licence for Public Sector Information*, www.nationalarchives.gov.uk/doc/open-government-licence/version/3.

National Library of Scotland (2015) *The Way Forward: Library Strategy 2015–2020*.

National Library of Scotland (2018) *Brief History of the National Library*, www.nls.uk/about-us/what-we-are/history.

Powell, D. (2006) *Refining the Map of the Universe of Electronic Publications Potentially Eligible for the Legal Deposit Advisory Panel*, Electronic Publishing Services, https://web.archive.org/web/20080727024130/http:/www.culture.gov.uk/images/publications/EPS_Report_to_LDAP_Nov_2006.pdf.

Solberg, T. (1938) History of the Legal Deposit of Books Through the British Empire, *The Library Quarterly: Information, Communication, Policy*, **8** (4), 526–38.

The Legal Deposit Libraries (Non-Print Works) Regulations 2013 (S.I. 2013/777) www.legislation.gov.uk/uksi/2013/777/contents/made.

Working Party on Legal Deposit (1999) *Code of Practice for the Voluntary Deposit of Non-Print Publications*.

CHAPTER 3

E-legal deposit at the Biblioteca Nacional de México (National Library of Mexico)

Isabel Galina Russell, Jo Ana Morfin
and Ana Yuri Ramírez-Molina

The Biblioteca Nacional de México, Mexico's National Library, was founded in 1867. Together with the Biblioteca del Congreso de la Unión, Mexico's Library of Congress, the BNM is the institution responsible for receiving legal deposit in Mexico. The chapter offers a general introduction to the National Library of Mexico and the history of legal deposit in the country in order to frame the current discussion on e-legal deposit. We then go on to discuss three projects that are currently under way at the BNM in which we have participated: a new legislation proposal for legal deposit in Mexico; the development of an e-legal deposit platform between the Universidad Nacional Autónoma de México (UNAM) and the BNM; and the creation of a working group on digital preservation in Mexico. It is within this context, and with these ongoing initiatives, that we explore the current implementation of e-legal deposit within Mexico. Finally, we reflect on how these projects can continue to move forward and future challenges for the BNM.

Introduction

Mexico's national library, the Biblioteca Nacional de México (BNM),[1] was founded in 1867 and opened its doors to the public in 1884. This was a time of political turmoil in Mexico and it was with great difficulty and many setbacks that the library was able to assemble and begin work on cataloguing its collection (Brito Ocampo, 2017). Although from colonial times and during the 19th century there were different ordinances, mandates and decrees that pointed in some way or another to creating collections in order to protect the written heritage of the country, it was not until 1936 that a decree made the Biblioteca del Congreso de la Unión (BCU) responsible for receiving two copies of books, journals or magazines published in Mexico and in 1957 the BNM was added (Diario Oficial de la Federación, 1991a). In 1944 the Hemeroteca Nacional de México (HNM),[2] the national newspaper library, was created to handle the periodical collection. Although officially these are two institutions, they are closely linked and so for the purpose of this chapter we shall use BNM to refer to both.

The BNM was originally administered directly by the government but in 1929 the decision was taken to give custody of the library to the Universidad Nacional Autónoma de México (UNAM),[3] Mexico's national university. Only a handful of national libraries in the world are run by universities (Fernández, 2000) making them particularly interesting case studies. For the BNM, belonging to the UNAM implies particular administrative, legal and financial issues for legal deposit that result in important challenges and possibilities for e-legal deposit. Currently the BNM is administered by the Instituto de Investigaciones Bibliográficas (IIB), a research institute of the UNAM dedicated to bibliographic studies. The BNM receives funding through the UNAM, which in turn receives financial resources directly from the federal government. The UNAM's legal position with regard to the BNM is complicated, as the collections are officially considered national heritage but under the custody of the UNAM. This is particularly relevant when attempting to implement e-legal deposit.

The BNM and the BCU[4] are currently the two institutions that are responsible for receiving legal deposit of the material published in Mexico. As elsewhere, the decree has undergone modifications over time (Diario Oficial de la Federacion, 1991a) but it currently refers to books, pamphlets, periodicals, newspapers, maps, sheet music, posters and other printed materials of cultural, scientific and technical content (Diario Oficial de la Federacion, 1991b). One of the biggest problems with attempting to make legal deposit more effective is that there are few reliable indicators of publishing activity in Mexico. The Cámara Nacional de la Industria Editorial Mexicana (CANIEM),[5] Mexico's national association of publishers, produces annual statistical reports but this information is general and lacks detail, in particular with digital publications (CANIEM, 2017). Due to the lack of reliable indicators the BNM currently has no accurate means of correctly identifying legal deposit compliance in the country but estimates calculate a low deposit rate (Mora Pérez-Tejada, 2017). It is even more difficult to identify and measure electronic materials.

Deposit of e-legal deposit materials

Currently the 1991 law includes the deposit of electronic materials. This modification came from a proposal from the Libraries Commission belonging to the LIV [54th] Legislature from the Cámara de Diputados, Mexico's House of Representatives. It was presented on 26 June 1991 and approved on 23 July of the same year. Unfortunately, we were unable to find any documentation regarding this initiative and to our knowledge the BNM was not involved in the process. It is important to note, however, that these modifications were not introduced with a focus on electronic materials but rather they were included with the introduction of a new paragraph which refers to non-printed material in general. It states that a copy of microfilms, slides, disks, diskettes, audio- and video-cassettes and other audiovisual and electronic materials that contain information similar to the printed matter materials (Diario Oficial de la Federación, 1991b) should also be deposited.

Since then the BNM has received in legal deposit a significant amount of non-printed matter, mainly, but not restricted to, diskettes and CD-ROMs. Currently, these materials are being catalogued and they are available to users in an area of the library known as Electronic Resources, which was created in 2000. The librarian in charge, despite not receiving any particular training in preservation, has been able to develop local practices for refreshing and transferring contents from obsolete storage devices into new platforms. However, the area lacks sufficient infrastructure and staff and despite the sole librarian's efforts it has become increasingly difficult to guarantee access to the required hardware and software needed to read these early electronic records. Additionally, there is no reliable instrument that can be used to know what electronic materials are published in Mexico in order to know how much of these types of materials is being collected via legal deposit. We do not know how representative or complete this collection is.

The BNM, like many other libraries in the world, has seen the scope of its work greatly enhanced with the arrival of digital online materials. However, although the Library receives electronic materials as physical objects, there are currently no procedures in place for capturing online digital materials. There is some work on defining these from a research point of view (Galina, 2015) as well as internal discussions within the BNM but there is still much work to be done. Another pressing issue, both with the physical electronic objects and the planned deposit of online materials, is that there is no preservation plan in place for them. Already technological obsolescence and how to ensure long-term access are major issues for the Library. Internal discussions regarding capturing online materials as well as major digitisation projects, such as the 9 million digitised newspapers images for the HNDM,[6] have highlighted the urgent need for creating sustainable digital collections and for defining policies, standards and procedures of digital preservation.

At the BNM one of the greatest obstacles has been procuring the necessary human resources and technological infrastructure to be able to adequately deal with these new types of materials. In 2016 the Coordinación de Innovación y Estrategia Digital (CIED) was created, a digital scholarship department designed to work in collaboration with the research institute and the BNM to better develop digital platforms and collections as well as integrating digital humanities projects from the Institute. Within financial and staff constraints the CIED has managed to work on three projects that aim to contribute towards establishing the desirable administrative, technical and legal infrastructure that will facilitate e-legal deposit:

1 *New legislation proposal* The BNM and the BCU are working together to propose changes to legal deposit in order to ensure that our Mexican documentary heritage, including printed, electronic and born-digital documents, are collected and preserved by the designated legal deposit libraries and institutions. We are also working in partnership with other cultural heritage stakeholders to develop a proposal for a new national policy.
2 *E-legal deposit* As a means to explore the legal, practical, and technical challenges posed by the legal deposit of born-digital materials, the BNM is working in partnership with the UNAM's publishing house, one of the largest and most important publishers in the country, in order to develop an e-deposit prototype. The first phase of this project will focus on the acquisition, collection, preservation and bibliographic control of, and access to, e-books. Through this prototype we aim at developing a model of e-deposit for documents created and disseminated digitally, thus paving the way to the present and future of non-print legal deposit in Mexico.
3 *Digital Preservation Group* Given the lack of policies, strategies and standards within Mexican institutions aimed at guaranteeing long-term access to non-print materials and preservation of our digital cultural heritage, the National Library established a digital preservation group, Grupo de Preservación Digital (GPD). The group brings together leading scholars, researchers, practitioners, and technicians from several cultural institutions. Its objectives are to stimulate collaborative and interdisciplinary research and widen the knowledge and best practices of digital preservation across memory organisations.

New legislation proposal: from print to born-digital materials

Legal deposit in Mexico has included electronic materials since 1991, which was fairly advanced for the time (Diario Oficial de la Federación, 1991b). Mexico connected to the internet two years beforehand, in 1989. However, the 1991 decree does not refer to online materials but rather the term 'electronic materials', placed in a paragraph related to non-printed materials, such as slides, disks, videocassettes, etc., suggesting that legislators were not contemplating online materials but rather focusing on actual objects.

It was not until 2000 that the BNM first began discussing how new technologies, in particular the arrival of online publications, were changing the concept of a national collection and because of this the importance of reviewing the current legal deposit legislation and proposing the necessary adjustments (Fernández, 2000). In 2002 the BNM and the BCU first began work on proposing changes to the legislation which better addressed collecting materials published online. Some of the main issues found were:

1 Electronic books and other types of materials that were available only online were not delivered to the institutions in charge of legal deposit.
2 The INDAUTOR, which is the institution responsible for registering copyright in Mexico, only provided a list of works published with ISBN or ISSN but had little or no information on material published online without this registration number.
3 The current legislation did not adequately consider the budgetary allocation necessary for the BNM and the BCU to handle legal deposit.
4 Legal deposit was governed by a decree and not by a law. In order to be more effective the new instrument should be a law of legal deposit (Sistema de Información Legislativa, 2002).

The proposals suggested by BNM and the BCU in De Ley de Depósito Legal (Sistema de Información Legislativa, 2002) explicitly make a distinction between electronic objects (diskettes, DAT tapes, CDs, magnetic tapes) and those materials which are available through systems such as the internet. They refer in particular to electronic books and databases. It also adds the INDAUTOR as the institution responsible for managing legal deposit (receiving, verifying, etc.), whilst the BNM and the BCU would be in charge of keeping the materials, making them accessible to the public as well as publishing statistical information about the collections. The proposal was passed between different commissions and houses (Congress and Senate) until 2009, when it was rejected (Secretaría General de Servicios Parlamentarios, 2009). The reasons are unclear but they do not seem to be related to the incorporation of digital materials but rather to issues related to the distribution of roles and responsibilities between institutions, specifically the INDAUTOR.

However, the BNM and the BCU continued working together and at the end of 2013 promoted a new proposal in which Mexican publishers would be obliged to deposit their publications both in digital and paper format (Sistema de Información Legislativa, 2013). This proposal considered the following:

1 that all materials produced in the country or published through digital information transmission systems or in any other medium should be deposited
2 that legal deposit should include both the digital and the printed versions of each publication published in Mexico
3 that depository libraries should be granted the legal power to request from publishers legal deposit of publications which the libraries considered particularly relevant (Notilegis, 2014).

This new proposal was met with opposition from the CANIEM, Mexico's national publishing council, with the president issuing a statement considering the initiative illegal, as publishers do not necessarily have the rights in the digital edition. He also expressed concern about editors losing control of their publications if these could be placed online (Jaubert, 2014).

This again caused obstacles to the desired legislative changes as the Senate took up the issue (Talavera, 2014). Both the BNM and the BCU attempted to address them by organising working groups and events with Congress groups, publishers and specialists in documentary heritage in order to discuss the needs and benefits of legal deposit. Changes to the administration of the BNM delayed further work. It was not until 2016, under the current administration, that the BCU and the BNM renewed their collaboration to work once again on a new proposal for legal deposit in Mexico (Mora Pérez-Tejada, 2017).

A great effort was made to incorporate all the elements mentioned in the previous proposals since 2002, as well as new considerations, in particular those regarding digital preservation. An important change to the working group was the inclusion of other national institutions in charge of cultural heritage in the discussion, specifically the Cineteca Nacional,[7] Mexico's national film archive, the Fonoteca Nacional,[8] Mexico's national sound archive and the Filmoteca of the UNAM,[9] the film department of Mexico's national university. The aim was also to work towards better establishing how to distribute the deposit and the responsibility of the different types of cultural heritage materials. Important topics were also addressed, such as budget allocation, sanctions, the structure of the deposit, the discarding of material, the organisation and co-ordination between depository institutions and the differences between the objects deposited in each one and the functions of each receiving institution.

Throughout the sessions for discussing the new legislation proposal the complexity and the media diversity of Mexican documentary heritage became evident. A clear example was the attempt to describe the notion of bibliographic heritage, which has become a field concerned with a variety of types of documents ranging from paper-based materials to electronic, digitised, non-printed, online and born-digital materials. During the meetings, mainly held at the BNM, stakeholders expressed their concerns related to collection development in the digital age, as well as matters such as digital archiving, digital preservation, long-term access, and new competences, skills, workflows and human and technical infrastructure within their organisations. Given the complexity of these issues, it was decided that each depositary institution would develop its own theoretical and practical frameworks to address the challenges of e-legal deposit.

The group has been working for almost three years. Documents from these meetings are not public but a final document is expected. As we have attended the meetings we can broadly state that regarding e-legal deposit the main points are:

1 Electronic legal deposit is explicitly expanded to include online digital publications.
2 The different cultural heritage institutions where e-legal deposit is required are now explicitly named.
3 In appropriate cases e-legal deposit is only required in one institution but it may share with others, thus eliminating the need for dual digital deposit.
4 To allow digital preservation the depository institution must receive not only the digital object but also additional software to access it.

The proposed law will be sent to Congress for review. Over a year ago there was a change of government and unfortunately in Mexico issues are highly sensitive to presidential terms and the political climate, making it difficult to anticipate results. So despite the legislation changes that have been proposed over the past 16 years, the current legal deposit decree has not been updated for 27 years. Considering the important technological changes in publishing platforms during this period, it is urgent that this be addressed in order to adequately consider new digital formats, in particular online materials. Political lobbying will be essential, as well as sensitivity from the legislators to this pending issue. In the meantime, however, regardless of much needed changes to current legislation, the BNM has begun working on implementing the legal deposit of digital materials as described in the following section.

E-legal deposit platform

Leaving the normative and legal changes that are required to better enable the BNM to deal administratively with digital materials, in particular online and born-digital ones, it is still essential that the library begin implementing the necessary internal changes in procedures, human resources and technical infrastructure to address the pending issue of identifying, collecting, storing, preserving and providing access to online digital materials. Within a framework of limited resources and personnel we have managed to design a modest but important project.

One of the advantages of the BNM being so closely linked to the IIB is that library personnel have been able to work closely with researchers on a number of issues related to digital materials. One of the most recent projects has been to develop a prototype for e-legal deposit. Additionally we have sought to take advantage of the fact that the BNM is so closely linked to the UNAM. This project is an example of the type of applied research that the CIED was created to promote.

The UNAM is the largest publisher in the country, with 118 publishing units either as editorial departments or publishing areas (Ayala Ochoa, 2015, 185). Almost every faculty or research institute has its own publishing department and the Dirección General de Publicaciones y Fomento Editorial (DGPyFE)[10] is responsible for promoting, distributing and commercialising all UNAM publications. The DGPyFE produces annual general reports which form part of the general statistical information produced yearly by the UNAM.[11] In 2016 the DGPyFE published general guidelines for all publishing activity in the UNAM (UNAM, 2016). One of the many issues the guidelines address is related to registration and preservation of all university publications and to this end it states that all publishing departments must submit a 'digital copy of all books and pamphlets' to the Centro de Información de Preservación de Publicaciones UNAM, the information and preservation centre of UNAM publications. Previously to this the UNAM published a statement promoting open access at the UNAM (UNAM, 2015) and in recent years has been heavily promoting the publication of born-digital books only.

In 2017 the DGPyFE and the BNM began working together (Mora Pérez-Tejada, 2018). The main issue identified was that despite both having the obligation and responsibility for receiving digital files, neither had the necessary procedures or infrastructure in place, or even the financial support to implement on a large scale. In 2017 both institutions joined forces to work together on a pilot project to build a prototype platform for the deposit of UNAM digital publications (hereafter referred to as e-Legal Deposit Pilot). Given the vast number and variety of digital publications that are currently managed and published by UNAM, it was decided that the pilot would focus only on electronic books, including both born-digital e-books and digital versions of printed books, as these are considered relatively 'easy' compared to other types of publication. A second stage would include journals, as the UNAM is also a major journal publisher, with 140 published online using Open Journal Systems (OJS).[12] From a research point of view, in particular from the digital humanities and open data perspective, we would like to address in the future all types of UNAM academic production, including dynamic content, multimedia material, databases and digital humanities projects, to name a few.

Little research has been done on e-book production in Mexico (Torres Vargas, 2012) and in particular that by the UNAM. There is some previous work on visibility of UNAM online digital resources and repositories (Galina Russell and Héau, 2010; Galina Russell, 2011; Russell, Ainsworth and Díaz-Aguilar, 2012; Peñaloza Báez, 2014). Some studies have been done on UNAM publishing practices, for example Ayala Ochoa's book (2015) on academic editorial practices, but it is mainly print-orientated. The general overview is that the academic digital production at the UNAM is extremely rich and diverse, but the overall management and production is disjointed, with numerous independent initiatives over the past two decades that are only now beginning to come together.

It was therefore critical for the project to set a methodology that would allow us to understand the current panorama with regard to electronic books in the UNAM. As a result, the e-Legal Deposit Pilot was divided into the following four stages:

1 assessment of the current practices followed by the BNM and DGPyFE
2 assessment of the current practices using convenience sampling of five key UNAM publishers
3 research and proposal for developing a pilot platform for e-legal deposit
4 development, implementation and evaluation of the pilot platform for e-legal deposit.

The first two stages are aimed at finding out current approaches to creating, collecting, managing and providing access to e-books. We are also interested in existing practices for collecting and/or depositing e-books under legal deposit mandate and UNAM general guidelines for publishing. Initially we conducted in-depth interviews with personnel working at both the DGPyFe and the BNM. At the DGPyFE we interviewed the three key players who are responsible for electronic book production and management. We followed these interviews with seven interviews at the BNM with library personnel involved in cataloguing, acquisition and special collections and who deal with or are related in some way with electronic materials. We then interviewed five editorial departments from a variety of disciplines: Art History, Law, Bibliographic Studies, Distance Education and Open University and Sciences.[13]

We are still processing the results from these interviews but initial findings from the research indicate that in recent years, digital publishing, and specifically the production of e-books has increased among UNAM editorial departments. Most likely the production will continue to grow due to the current trend of digitising paper-based books; in addition to this, publishers state that they are keeping the digital versions of printed books and creating born-digital books. However, despite this growing trend neither the BNM nor the DGPyFE have been actively collecting e-books.

The assessment reveals that neither BNM nor the DGPyFE have the means to adequately collect, preserve and ensure long-term access to e-books, even if publishers did choose to deposit. The main issues identified are: lack of technical and storage infrastructure, limited human resources, restricted funding and traditional print based procedures for handling of materials, as well as an aversion by some workers to incorporate new practices which would better allow the inclusion of digital materials. Neither the BNM nor the DGPyFE have established tools, schemas, strategies and procedures aimed at guaranteeing the longevity, integrity, preservation and access of materials collected through e-legal deposit mandate.

There is a lack of awareness by UNAM editorial departments of the UNAM general guidelines for publishing activity and the absence of a more robust law specifically aimed at the legal deposit of digital materials, leaving a grey area that does not incentivise e-legal deposit. In addition to this, despite the publication of the general guidelines for all publishing activity in the UNAM by the DGPyFE in 2016 and updated in 2018,[14] each UNAM publishing entity has its own practices and perspectives. For instance, there is not a unique criterion about the formats for publishing e-books; some publishers have decided to use PDF as the *de facto* format while others select a format depending on the contents of the book. In addition to PDF and ePUB formats, editors have also used iBook format. Generally speaking, PDF is selected over an ePUB format when the contents are static, that is to say, where there are not videos, hyperlinks or other types of dynamic media.

In terms of distribution, all surveyed editors obtain and use ISBN identifiers for their publications, most commonly an ISBN identifier for each digital version they created, as established by the INDAUTOR (Cifuentes and Chaverra, 2018). There are differentiated practices around the DOI: some publishing entities use it for the publications that cannot receive an ISBN (such as manuals or guides), whilst others obtain it for all their digital works. In addition to this, most editorial departments have created online platforms as means to make visible, circulate and allow access into their e-book collections. These platforms vary in their accessibility, functionality, usability and extent, however all of them allow the users to have online access and in most cases download entire e-books.

The initial findings also show that each editorial department has taken the responsibility of organising, storing and keeping accessible their electronic books. However, all of them share concerns regarding the preservation, long-term access and storage of digital collections. They all coincide in the need to have a shared and automated platform that would allow them to deposit digital materials but they have concerns regarding the extra workload that this procedure would imply.

We are currently moving towards a proposal for developing a pilot platform for e-legal deposit, as outlined in the following section.

Avoiding digital oblivion: a proposal for building a platform for e-legal deposit

As described in the previous paragraphs, depository institutions face similar challenges in order to meet the essential requirements for collecting digital publications under legal deposit mandate. Initial findings from our research indicate that it is essential that these institutions focus on strategic planning aimed at preserving and providing long-term access to digital publications. We observed that a fundamental challenge is the lack of best practices in these institutions to meet the needs of e-legal deposit, as well as establishing the proper protocols for preserving them. In addition to the lack of regulations, policies, standards and workflows, there is also the absence of proper technical infrastructure within the BNM and DGPyFE. Therefore, the aim of the pilot platform is to provide a tool for these institutions that helps them with the challenges they are currently facing.

The platform is inspired by the Open Archival Information System (OAIS) model[15] and thus considers issues about ingest, administration, archiving and preservation of and access to digital objects (Rodríguez Reséndiz, 2016). Our main object is to provide a user-friendly platform that allows publishers to deposit e-books (PDF and ePUB formats) while submitting controlled and normalised metadata required by BNM and the DGPyFE to adequately fulfil their preservation and long-term access needs. At this moment we are working on defining the core characteristics of the three main packages of information that the OAIS model proposes, specifically on the Submission Information Package (SIP) (Rodríguez Reséndiz, 2016). We are evaluating metadata schemes that would be useful for publishers as well as for depository institutions. So far we have focused on ONIX, Dublin Core and MARC 21. In addition to this, we are evaluating types of repositories, software and tools that enable us to carry on tasks such as content access control, collection management, integrity and authenticity control, and overall, the application of preservation-oriented workflows.

Given the lack of technical expertise, proper funding, and aiming to find a sustainable approach to long-term digital preservation, we want to experiment with small open-source tools that can be integrated into large and scalable systems. Our main objective is to ensure the integrity and authenticity of e-books over time, through transfer processes and migrations; therefore, the proposal for the platform must consider tools that allow us to monitor and manage the integrity of digital files, as well as technical metadata for storage planning, obsolescence monitoring, and so forth (Van Malssen, 2012).

This platform will address some of the most pressing issues regarding digital preservation with regard to e-book published at the UNAM and will hopefully set the basis for future work on a wide variety of materials as well as deposits from other publishing houses. However, there are still many pending issues which the small work group at the BNM and DGPyFE cannot possibly address, as interinstitutional and interdisciplinary expertise is required. It is clear that matters regarding the archive, preservation, long-term access and sustainability of digital bibliographic materials consists of 'technology, people and policies' (Van Malssen, 2012). In order to be able to address 'the bigger picture' we have also formed a digital preservation working group, described in the following section.

Digital preservation group: building communities of expertise

In 2013, the first attempt was made to form a working group within the BNM to deal with issues related to digital preservation as the number of inaccessible electronic publications increased, mainly in the newspaper library. At that time the group had only five members, from technical backgrounds in the computing and microfilm departments. The most important work of this first group was to document and review the work done in other countries, as this led them to create awareness and underline the importance of forming alliances with other organisations to seek common solutions to common problems, particularly on a national scale.

In the following years awareness about digital preservation increased, with many cultural heritage and memory institutions identifying the challenge, although hardly any practical work was being done. From anecdotal evidence it seems that those institutions who claimed to be doing digital preservation were actually focused more on secure backups (Galina, 2018). At the UNAM, researchers at both the IIB and another research institute for library and information science, the IIBi, are doing some work in the area. The IIBi leads the Latin American team for the International Research on Permanent Authentic Records in Electronic Systems (InterPARES),[16] aimed at developing the knowledge essential to the long-term preservation of authentic records created and/or maintained in digital form, from a primarily archive perspective, which has been doing work since 1999. At the end of 2016 the Conacyt,[17] the national council for science and technology, issued a call for the creation of national laboratories. Led by the BNM, a multi-institutional group was put together to write a proposal for creating a national laboratory on digital preservation. Due to an administrative omission the proposal was not sent but the work on the grant proposal established both the urgent need to address the issue as well as identifying many of the key individuals who could work on this together.

In 2016 the Grupo de Preservación Digital (GPD),[18] a working group on digital preservation was formed, as a trans disciplinary and multi- institutional initiative aimed at enhancing research in the preservation and long-term access of digital heritage. It currently has between 20 and 30 members, ranging from scholars and postgraduate students to practitioners working in the fields of digital humanities, digital preservation and digital curation, as well as people from the computing services departments. The GPD is currently divided into four task forces: Technology, Research, Legal Deposit and Management-Outreach. The purpose of the group is to contribute to the development and promotion of models, theories, best practices, principles and platforms for sustainable digital preservation programmes within Mexican memory and academic institutions. In recent times, GPD has established strategic partnerships to further strengthen its mission by translating into Spanish resources, guidelines and core tools for digital preservation.

The legal deposit task force has worked closely with the initiative that will be presented to Congress that was mentioned in the previous section. The group has identified digital preservation as a complete cycle which ideally should begin with the creation of the digital object (Harvey, 2010). It was therefore considered that the e-legal deposit decree should contribute to the long-term preservation of the object by promoting the use of certain standards as well as appropriate metadata. As mentioned previously, the legal deposit reform is a general framework and it is expected that each cultural heritage institution will then provide the necessary specific guidelines for e-legal deposit. Now that work for the proposal to Congress is almost concluded the next step will be to begin work on these guidelines, most likely in conjunction with the UNAM prototype.

As mentioned, one of the main issues identified during the writing of the grant proposal was the urgent need to address digital preservation in Mexico. The research task group is currently working on a proposed national survey of key memory institutions in order to benchmark the situation regarding digital preservation in Mexico as a first step towards further work. For the time being, the DPG is planning to remain involved and present in international initiatives such as the annual World Digital Preservation Day.

In the longer term the DPG is planning to publish technical reports and white papers concerning decision-making models for implementing policies, standards and procedures for digital preservation. The idea is that these documents will be based on research carried out by its members, whose approaches reflect the specificity of the Mexican cultural and academic institutions: that is to say, the limited financial resources, shortage of expertise and the lack of competencies around sustainability, governance, and implementation of digital preservation plans within a culturally rich country with firmly established cultural heritage institutions.

Conclusions

In order to ensure that Mexican documentary heritage, in particular early electronic and born-digital documents, is collected and preserved by BNM, it is of vital importance that the legal deposit regulations be revised and updated. But perhaps even more importantly it is necessary to increase awareness within cultural heritage institutions of the need to co-operate and work collectively to address digital preservation requirements. Most often, this co-operation has been accomplished by assembling small communities of practitioners who share their knowledge and expertise. It is important that the BNM works together with other custodians of documentary heritage to develop strategic policy frameworks, as well as preservation principles, strategies and workflows that meet the needs of new hybrid and complex collections.

The fact that the BNM is part of the national university creates a particular situation with distinctive challenges and advantages. One of the main opportunities is the close working relationship that can be established between researchers at the IIB and other UNAM research institutions. The UNAM also has established research collaboration networks both with other Mexican academic institutions and with international ones, thus allowing the BNM to ground its work on strong theoretical and methodological research on important issues related to e-legal deposit. The fact that the UNAM is one of the biggest publishers in the country offers the possibility to apply this research in real-case scenarios. This strong academic environment also allows us to pursue funding through academic research grants.

One of the main difficulties is that despite the fact that the BNM is the national library of Mexico, the administrative and financial structure is within a university environment. Therefore, the BNM is in many aspects subjected to the staffing and funding restrictions of the university, as well as a focus on academic productivity for evaluating personnel. Additionally, it is not clear who has the administrative or even legal capacity for many of the key decision procedures for e-legal deposit. This is complicated further by the fact that the currently valid legal deposit decree from 1991 does not adequately address e-legal deposit, in particular of that of online digital materials, as has been discussed. Additionally, other cultural heritage institutions are administered directly or indirectly by the government, whilst the BNM is not. The UNAM is an autonomous institution that although funded by the government is not administered by it. This means that the different institutions have different administrative decision makers and procedures, despite all being legally designated custodians of Mexican cultural heritage. Therefore, the route to implementing proposals at a national level is not straightforward and at times even contradictory.

The core values, understanding and scope of documentary heritage are always evolving, transforming and embracing new domains. A clear example is the scope of Mexican bibliographical heritage, which has continued to expand in order to include new forms of documents beyond manuscripts and printed materials. Although the implementation of an e-legal deposit mandate will bring complex technical challenges among depository institutions, we believe that there are other subjects that need to be addressed. A central one is the complexity of implementing new workflows and changing traditional approaches for understanding, providing access to, studying and preserving our documentary heritage. In addition to this, both the role and responsibilities of key cultural heritage institutions must be better established, allowing them to make and implement decisions.

As the definition and breadth of documentary heritage continues to grow, requiring new approaches for the adequate study, protection and preservation of and long-term access to Mexican documentary heritage, legislation, policies and in general Mexican cultural institutions are only just getting started on meeting these new demands and challenges. We consider that the work being done however, will allow us to address these issues and contribute towards understanding e-legal deposit both in Mexico and in other parts of the world.

Acknowledgements

The authors would like to thank Fernando Cruz Quintana, postdoctoral researcher at the IIB, for his help in revising the text, as well as all members of the projects described in this chapter.

Notes

1. Biblioteca Nacional de México, www.bnm.unam.mx.
2. Hemeroteca Nacional de México, www.hnm.unam.mx.
3. UNAM, www.unam.mx.
4. The SEDIA (Dirección General de Servicios de Documentación, Información y Análisis de la Cámara de Diputados) administrates the Library, the historical archive, museum and provides bibliographic research and analysis for Congress, www.diputados.gob.mx/sedia/biblio.htm.
5. CANIEM, http://caniem.com.
6. Hemeroteca Nacional Digital de México, www.hndm.unam.mx.
7. Cineteca Nacional de México, www.cinetecanacional.net.
8. Fonoteca Nacional, www.fonotecanacional.gob.mx.
9. Filmoteca de la UNAM, www.filmoteca.unam.mx.
10. DGPyFE, www.libros.unam.mx.
11. Memoria UNAM, www.planeacion.unam.mx/Memoria.
12. See Portal de Revistas UNAM, www.revistas.unam.mx.
13. The editorial departments belonged to the Instituto de Investigaciones Estéticas, Instituto de Investigaciones Jurídicas, Instituto de Investigaciones Bibliográficas, Coordinación de Universidad Abierta y Educación a Distancia y Facultad de Ciencias.
14. See Disposiciones Generales para la Actividad Editorial y de Distribución de la Universidad Nacional Autónoma de México, www.publicaciones.unam.mx/Normatividad.html#bloque-i.
15. The Open Archival Information System (OAIS) is a conceptual framework developed by NASA´s Consultative Committee for Space Data Systems. It works as a reference model for describing and analysing digital preservation matters; in 2002 it was approved as ISO International Standard 14721; later in 2012 a revised version was published as ISO Standard 14721:2012. See Lavoie (2014) for an overview.
16. InterPARES, www.interpares.org.
17. Consejo Nacional de Ciencia y Tecnología (Conacyt), www.conacyt.mx.
18. GPD, http://preservaciondigital.org.mx.

References

Ayala Ochoa, C. (2015) *La Cultura Editorial Universitaria,* Universidad Nacional Autónoma de México, 282.

Brito Ocampo, S. (2017) *La Biblioteca Nacional de México 1822–1929*, Universidad Nacional Autónoma de México, Instituto de Investigaciones Bibliográficas, XX.

CANIEM (2017) *Indicadores del Sector Editorial Privado en México*, www.caniem.com/es/content/indicadores-del-sector-editorial-privado-en-m%C3%A9xico-2016.

Cifuentes, D. and Chaverra Y. (2018) Panorama de las Agencias del ISBN en Iberoamérica. Centro Regional para el Fomento del Libro y la Lectura en América Latina (CERLALC), http://cerlalc.org/wp-content/uploads/2018/02/CERLALC_PUBLICACIONES_OLB_Panorama_agencias_ISBN_Iberoamerica_010218.pdf.

Diario Oficial de la Federación (1991a) *El Depósito Legal en México. Órdenes y Decretos Expedidos de 1812 a 1991*, 23 July, www.diputados.gob.mx/bibliot/apotec/decretos.htm.

Diario Oficial de la Federación (1991b) *Decreto por el que se Dispone la Obligación de los Editores y Productores de Materiales Bibliográficos y Documentales, de Entregar Ejemplares de sus Obras a la Biblioteca Nacional y a la Biblioteca del Congreso de la Unión*, 23rd July, http://dof.gob.mx/nota_detalle.php?codigo=4733347&fecha=23/07/1991&print=true.

Fernández, R. (2000) La Biblioteca Nacional de México Hacia el Nuevo Siglo, *Métodos de Información (MEI)*, **7** (40), 72–7.

Galina, I. (2015) Las Publicaciones Digitales dentro del Patrimonio Documental, *Textos, Pixeles y Bits*, UNAM, 12–42.

Galina, I. (2018) La Digitalización de Fondos Patrimoniales – el Caso de México, *Relaciones Estudios de Historia y Sociedad*, **39** (155).

Galina Russell, I. (2011) La Visibilidad de los Recursos Académicos: Una Revisión Crítica del Papel de los Repositorios Institucionales y el Acceso Abierto, *Investigación Bibliotecológica*, **25** (53), 159–83.

Galina Russell, I and Héau, O. J. G. (2010) La Visibilidad de los Acervos Electrónicos en la UNAM, *Revista Digital Universitaria*, **11** (7), www.revista.unam.mx/vol.11/num7/art69/art69.pdf.

Harvey, R. (2010) *Digital Curation*, Neal-Schuman Publishers.

Jaubert, P. (2014) El Depósito Legal Electrónico, *Revista Casa del Tiempo*, vol. I, época **V**, (5), June, www.uam.mx/difusion/casadeltiempo/05_i_jun_2014/casa_del_tiempo_eV_num_5_59_61.pdf.

Lavoie, B. (2014) *The Open Archival Information System (OAIS) Reference Model: Introductory Guide*, DPC Technology Watch Report 14-02, October.

Mora Pérez-Tejada, P. (2017) *Primer Informe de Actividades 2016–2017*, Instituto de Investigaciones Bibliográficas, Universidad Nacional Autónoma de México, 115.

Mora Pérez-Tejada, P. (2018) *Segundo Informe de Actividades 2017–2018*, Instituto de Investigaciones Bibliográficas, Universidad Nacional Autónoma de México, 146

Notilegis (2014) *Aprueban Diputados Decreto para que Editores Depositen Sus*

Publicaciones Digitalizadas a la Biblioteca Nacional, la Hemeroteca Nacional y el Congreso de la Unión, Notilegis, Nota N°594925, 25 February 2014, www5.diputados.gob.mx/index.php/esl/Comunicacion/Agencia-de-Noticias/2014/02-Febrero/25/5949-Aprueban-diputados-decreto-para-que-editores-depositen-sus-publicaciones-digitalizadas-a-la-Biblioteca-Nacional-la-Hemeroteca-Nacional-y-el-Congreso-de-la-Union.

Peñaloza Báez, M. (2014) Toda la UNAM en Línea, *Revista Digital Universitaria*, **15** (10), www.revista.unam.mx/ojs/index.php/rdu/article/view/405/0.

Rodríguez Reséndiz, P. (2016) El OAIS en la Preservación Digital de Archivos Sonoros, *Investigación Bibliotecológica*, **30** (70), 197—220, DOI: 10.1016/j.ibbai.2016.10.009.

Russell, J., Ainsworth, S. and Díaz-Aguilar, J. (2012) Web Visibility or Wasted Opportunity? Case Studies from Mexican Research Institutes, *Aslib Proceedings*, **64** (1), 67–82.

Secretaría General de Servicios Parlamentarios (2009) *Minutas Presentadas en la LX Legislatura Turnadas a Comisión*, Secretaría General de Servicios Parlamentarios, Dirección General de Apoyo Parlamentario, 21 April 2009, http://sitl.diputados.gob.mx/minutas_buscador.php?filit=Devuelta%20inciso%20e)%20del%20art%EDculo%2072%20CPEUM&pert=0&edot=D&comt=0.

Sistema de Información Legislativa (2002) *De Ley de Depósito Legal*, Sistema de Información Legislativa, Cámara de Diputados, 24 September, http://sil.gobernacion.gob.mx/Archivos/Documentos/2002/09/asun_61565_20020924_845445.pdf.

Sistema de Información Legislativa (2013) *De Decreto, por el que se Dispone la Obligación de los Editores de Hacer el Depósito Legal Digitalizado de Sus Publicaciones*, Sistema de Información Legislativa, Cámara de Diputados, 7 November http://sil.gobernacion.gob.mx/Archivos/Documentos/2013/11/asun_3040326_20131119_1383840626.pdf.

Talavera, J. C. (2014) Revisarán Cambios al Depósito Legal, *Excelsior*, 28 August, www.excelsior.com.mx/expresiones/2014/04/28/956184.

Torres Vargas, G. (2012) Retos en la Investigación de la Producción Editorial en el Medio Digital. In Ríos Ortega, J. and Ramírez Velázquez, C. (eds), *Oportunidades y Retos en la Formación, Investigación y Aplicación del Conocimiento Bibliotecológico*, UNAM-Instituto de Investigaciones Bibliotecológicas y de la Información, 117–27.

UNAM (2015) Lineamientos Generales para la Política de Acceso Abierto de la Universidad Nacional Autónoma de México, *Gaceta UNAM*, 10 September 2015, 29, www.unamenlinea.unam.mx/files/TUL_AcuerdoLineamientosGeneralesPoliticaAccesoAbierto.pdf.

UNAM (2016) Disposiciones Generales para la Actividad Editorial y de Distribución de la UNAM, *Gaceta UNAM*, 21 April, supplement, www.gaceta.unam.mx/suplemento/Suplemento/Suplemento_disposicioneseditoriales.pdf.

Van Malssen, K. (2012) Tools for Smaller Budgets: Using Open Source and Free Tools for AV Digital Preservation Workflows, *AV Insider*, **2**, September, www.avpreserve.com/wp-content/uploads/2014/04/AVInsider_OpenSourceTools_DigiPres.pdf.

CHAPTER 4

Bibliographic control in Zimbabwe: the conundrum of legal deposit in the age of digital technologies

Collence T. Chisita, Blessing Chiparausha and Danmore Maboreke

Introduction

This chapter describes the functions of current legislation in ensuring compliance with legal deposit laws of Zimbabwe. It seeks to highlight the challenges that the existing legal deposit laws face vis-à-vis the open access regime. It analyses the legislation for bibliographic compilation in the context of the shifts in the global knowledge landscape. The chapter discusses the weaknesses of the current law with reference to current trends in the legal deposit of multimedia formats. It also examines how bibliographic control can underpin national development goals concerning teaching, learning and research. The authors explain how the absence of a print and online version of a national bibliography affects collection development and scholarly research, and explore the challenges of harmonising print and electronic records in the context of digital divide. Recommendations on possible strategies to utilise modern technologies to capture, process and preserve library records as national heritage in Zimbabwe are suggested.

Universal bibliographic control (UBC) as a global system for the control and exchange of bibliographic information acknowledges the resource discovery metadata requirements of modern, global-scale users of information (Dunsire, Hillmann, and Phipps, 2012). The sheer size of global bibliographic control is enormous, as it encompasses the creation and maintenance of a complete record of the sum of human knowledge. Žumer (2009) defines a national bibliography as the accumulation of the authoritative and comprehensive records of the national imprints of a country, which is published regularly and with the least possible delay.

Thapa (2009, 57) views bibliographic control as the activities involved in the process of creating, organising, managing and maintaining the files of bibliographic records, for example the library or archival materials or sources listed in an index, or database, or virtual repository. As such, the locatability, findability, discoverability, accessibility, retrievability and shareability of scientific scholarly content is possible through effective bibliographic control because of scientific description and subject access through uniform catalogue codes, classification schemes and name authorities to enhance precision. Bibliographic tools are published in line with the International Federation of Library Associations and Institutions' (IFLA's) International Standard Bibliographic Description (ISBD) published in 2011. Current developments in digital content have precipitated the development of the Resource Description and Access open standard (RDA) catering for functional requirements for bibliographic records and the functional requirements for authority data (Needleman, 2008). Danskin (2013, 147–58) views RDA and linked data concepts as key standards providing possibilities to make library metadata open, actionable, discoverable and shareable.

Research objectives

The chapter addresses the following research questions:

1. What are the functions of current local legislation in ensuring compliance with the legal deposit laws of Zimbabwe?
2. What are the challenges that the current legal deposit laws face in the context of the open access regime and current trends in the legal deposit of multimedia formats?
3. How can bibliographic control underpin national development goals for teaching, learning and research?

Research methodology

This chapter is based on an analysis of literature on the subject matter, and participant observation. Ahmed (2010) describes documentary methods as the analysis of documents that contain information about the phenomenon studied by investigating and categorising written sources. Mogalakwe (2006) defines documentary methods as the analysis of documents that contain information about the phenomenon being studied. It involves the analysis of primary and secondary sources. Ahmed and Mogalakwe favour the use of this research method because of its cost-effectiveness when compared to social surveys, in-depth interviews and participant observations. The authors note that documentary research is one of the major types of social research that have been most widely used by sociologists. As part of this study, acts of parliament, books and research articles were reviewed for the purpose of data gathering. In participant observation, the researcher 'participates in the ongoing activities or the daily life of a group and records observations' (Mannik and McGarry, 2017, 239). Participant observation was employed in this study because it facilitated access to inside viewpoints and the collection of rich data that could not be easily gathered through other data collection methods. Two library staff and three archivists, one of whom was the participant observer, were involved.

History of legal deposit

Cadavid (2017, 389) highlights how legal deposit emerged as a cultural measure meant to collect and preserve print publications. The author further states that its dispersal took place in line with the developments from print to electronic publishing. The dawn of the digital revolution therefore marks a defining moment for legal deposit theory and practice. Legal deposit reflects the proximal linkage between cultural heritage law and national identity.

History shows that legal deposit has been used as an effective mechanism of collecting and preserving a country's published heritage for over 400 years. The decree of King François I of France known as the Montpellier Ordinance of 28 December 1537 was the first text imposing a legal obligation on printers and booksellers to deposit a copy of each of their publications at the king's library and this enabled the aristocracy to monitor the content of published and widely distributed works (Cadavid, 2017, 380). The king was an advocate of learning and the arts and this was reflected in the aristocratic library that he personally owned. The ruling elite intended to use legal deposit as an instrument that would enable them to gauge the depth and level of intellectual discourse at a time when the 'Gutenberg Galaxy' was threatening to usher in revolutionary ideas that would shape the future of Europe. Fournier (1993, 4) notes that the main idea behind this legislation was to collect and gather current and future publications of editions of books in order to ensure that it would be possible to refer to the original work and not modified editions. Cadavid states that in England the concept of legal deposit was strengthened through a memorandum of understanding between publishers and the Bodleian Library. This development was inspired by the French legal deposit system and eventually it spread to the rest of the British Empire through the promulgation of the Copyright Act in 1842.

Legal deposit is considered important in facilitating access to published materials and providing authors with protection for intellectual property rights through copyright. In addition, legal deposit has been associated with censorship, because lawmakers sometimes use it as a tool to detect and curb treasonous, blasphemous and seditious materials. This has been one reason why some publishers avoid depositing their materials with designated institutions, because of the fear of unknown consequences, for example censorship.

Crews (1988) opines that, the world over, national libraries require legal mandates for delivery of a copy of each new work published in the country in order to create a national bibliographic record. Through enforceable rules of law, national libraries can receive nearly all desired publications, and this serves as a basis for national collection development and library services. Crews traces the development of legal deposit to France in 1537 with the main purpose of buttressing libraries, even though the phenomenon was used for other purposes in subsequent centuries.

Kumar (1998) observes that this new development in France was triggered by the Gutenberg Galaxy in the 15th century, which ushered in a new era of published materials that threatened the status quo: many European countries were forced to introduce similar procedures based on the French model. The Library and Archives of Canada note that initially legal deposit applied to books but in the second half of the 19th century it was extended to include serial publications, sound recordings and multimedia kits, and in the 20th century it embraced microforms, video recordings and currently online publications. In the Soviet Union (1922–91) bibliographic control was exercised by the All-Union Book Chamber commonly known as *Vsesoiuznaia Knizhnaia Palata,* whose responsibility was to produce a complete and current national bibliography, centralised cataloguing, statistical accounting of all printed matter and the establishment of a system of depository libraries (Whitby, Lorkovic and Gracheva, 1979). The agency maintained a comprehensive and well arranged legal deposit system for all Soviet republics with their own publishing output. Canada revised its Library and Archives Act (2004) and the Legal Deposit of Publications Regulations (2007) to incorporate electronic resources. Bell (1997) notes that over the years, in its initial development, legal deposit was used as a tool for surveillance and censorship as well as copyright. Larivière (2000) notes that through time legal deposit evolved from the original aims of the 16th century, which were mainly to preserve books for future generations, to the constitution of a national bibliography reflecting the intellectual output of a country.

As Musiker (2005) notes, South Africa was the first African country to have a national bibliography, followed by Sierra Leone in 1925 and Ghana in 1932. Many African countries have published retrospective bibliographies to capture all of their publications. When the first International Conference on African Bibliography was held in Kenya in 1967, only a few African countries had national bibliographies, but currently almost all have such retrieval tools.

Bibliographic control in the information and communication technologies (ICT) age

The Library of Congress Working Group on the Future of Bibliographic Control (2008) redefined bibliographic control on the basis of a long-term vision of collaboration, decentralisation, internationalism and web-based activities (Mansor and Jarjis, 2008, 1–11). Information and communication technologies (ICT), development of virtual resources and virtual libraries and virtual learning spaces and the proliferation of information in multimedia formats are impacting bibliographic control. In a networked and globalised world of information, the form of national bibliography is undergoing change, but the primary function remains unchanged: providing information about a country's publication landscape and its cultural and intellectual heritage. Mansor and Jarjis (2008) state that bibliographic control is no longer the preserve of an exclusive group of cataloguers alone because ICTs have made collaboration possible between libraries and non-library entities.

Seys (2004) highlights the value of examining content management in order to understand the impact of online publishing on bibliographic control and access to the various forms of text available online. Content management refers to the process of developing, maintaining and organising and deploying web-based content in order to efficiently support the collaborative efforts of content creators, site administrators and users. Bibliographic control is no longer limited to libraries but extends to the broader horizon of information, including the world wide web (WWW). Larivière (2000) states that UNESCO pushed for the amendment of legal deposit laws to suit the digital trajectory in the 21st century. In 2003 UNESCO published a Charter on the Preservation of Digital Heritage, Article 1–8, which called on member states to adopt legal deposit for digital content (Cadavid, 2017, 384). In the ICT landscape, bibliography encompasses a colossal assortment of materials, including published materials, materials that libraries license for user access, digital artefacts on public networks and materials that are unique to an individual library. Users would be better served if access to these materials were provided in the context of a unified philosophy of bibliographic control. Sulistyo-Basuki (2009) states that electronic documents kept on government websites, as well as those produced and stored at private sites, should be of concern to bibliographic control.

The digital revolution has ushered in Virtual International Authority File (VIAF), which reflects how UBC for bibliographic authority data can be achieved from the bottom up, from local to global, through linking identifiers for local data to an aggregator identifier without transforming or discarding the local data. The future for UBC is anchored on the ability of institutions to utilise distributed architecture and 'reasoning' capabilities of the semantic web to link up data (Dunsire, Hillmann and Phipps, 2012). The authors posit that the lessons of the past and the opportunities facing the modern world combine to suggest strongly that continuing to interpret bibliographic control as a static, top-down effort designed to achieve universality – as the library world has traditionally done – will not spur professionals to take advantage of new ubiquitous technologies or new paradigms about and building on metadata. The authors recommend progressive and innovative paradigms to deal with bibliographic control in the digital world, for example semantic mappings – making the essential shift from controlling the data to controlling the semantics that will allow us to move forward, taking our legacy data with us.

The concept of legal deposit

Legal deposit laws are critical tools for the preservation of national life and heritage and a manifestation of human value and identity. They encapsulate the collective artistic, social, economic and intellectual memory of a nation, according to Gilchrist (2005). Larivière (2000) describes legal deposit as a statutory requirement that any organisation, commercial or public, and any other individual producing any type of documentation in multiple copies is obligated to comply with by depositing one or more copies with a recognised national institution. It helps to secure the preservation and transmission of a national cultural heritage for posterity for the benefit of future generations. The author further states that concept of legal deposit covers all types of published materials, namely those published in multiple copies offered to the public regardless of the means of transmission, and unique or archival materials of enduring value. This requirement was initially limited to print resources but with the emergence of ICT amendments were made to align bibliographic control with the new trends of information representation.

Crews (1988) states that legal deposit serves to develop a resource and to facilitate control. The author further notes that Napoleon used legal deposit for control purposes when he gathered and screened new publications as part of his censorship campaign and to monitor tax evaders. The use of ICTs and emerging digital technologies to enable access to information has become the norm in resource-endowed environments of the modern-day world. Electronic publications are formatted and produced in an electronic environment; for example, electronic equivalents of print publications, interactive databases, bulletin boards, discussion lists and others. These resources save time and space and are relatively easier to maintain. Smith (1999) observes that failure to weigh the positive and negative aspects of digital resources impacts heavily and negatively on collection development. The author further notes how electronic resources raise expectations of benefits, costs reductions and efficiencies that are illusory and that if this is not taken into account, electronic resources can put at risk the collections and services that libraries have provided for decades.

Current ICT developments have resulted in serious challenges and splendid opportunities for the future production of national bibliographies. Lor and Letshela (2002) note how the internet and the growth of electronic publishing has created a serious challenge for national libraries as far as their mandate as the national depositories of all published materials. The two authors also note that before the advent of the internet it was easier to follow up on printed publications but now the digital revolution, with subsequent search engines, web crawlers, collaborative tools, electronic indexing, federated searches and other information retrieval tools, provides an opportunity for bibliographic control. The internet provides authors with opportunities to publish in virtual environments with virtual publishers. Oltmans (2003) notes that the internet's web-based resources require the process of web harvesting, which will ensure automatic delivery of qualitative bibliographic descriptions. Elliott (2011) views web-harvesting as marking a paradigm shift from an obligation to deposit to one of copying. Cadavid (2017, 384) states that the obligation to deposit reflects a passive role for the library, while contemporary web harvesting allows the national library to play an active role through harvesting content from the internet. However, in order for libraries to be involved in web harvesting there is a need to enact the appropriate heritage and copyright laws which then provide for the legal right to copy. Developed countries have embraced the concept of electronic bibliographies while developing countries are still grappling with putting together an up-to-date hard-copy bibliography.

Cadavid (2017, 386) states that the other strategy recommended for building digital collections is through domain harvesting, which involves the collection of websites published within specific internet domains, for example '.zw' for Zimbabwe. The other technique is selective harvesting, whereby thematic collections are manually or automatically developed (Chebbi, 2008). Such collections have to do with a particular theme, for example, sports, politics, elections, violence, crime or development issues.

Larivière (2000) notes that in some countries, such as France, Greece, Zimbabwe and Indonesia, the measure requiring legal deposit appears in a legal deposit act, while in other countries like Australia and the USA it is part of another act, such as the copyright act or the National Library Act, as is the case in Canada, Japan and Nigeria. The author further notes that in those countries with a legal deposit system, published materials make up the basis of the national deposit collection while in other countries like Zimbabwe audiovisual materials are also subjected to legal deposit requirements.

Davidson (1988) observes that legal deposit facilitates bibliographic control, which refers to the system of adequate recording of all forms of material, published or unpublished, printed or audiovisual or otherwise, which add to the sum total of human knowledge and experience. Currently many countries have modified their legislation to encompass electronic publications as subject to legal deposit, while some have excluded online electronic publications because of the technical problems relating to acquisition and preservation of such materials.

Conferences on legal deposit and bibliographic control

Wise (1985, 304) states that there have been a number of conferences organised to promote bibliographic control. In 1967 the International Conference on African Bibliography was held in Nairobi; in 1977 the SCOLMA (Standing Conference in Library Materials in Africa) was held at the Commonwealth Institute in London; and in 2001 the Bicentennial Conference on Bibliographic Control for the New Millennium – subtitled 'Confronting the Challenges of Networked Resources and the Web' – was held. These conferences emphasised the importance of bibliographic control and the need to ensure the enactment of effective legal deposit laws. Ng'ang'a (1990) notes that the concept of legal deposit was further popularised through the 1977 Paris International Congress on National Bibliography (ICBN), which produced recommendations aimed at ensuring that member states had formulated, legislated and implemented legal deposit. These international conventions helped to provide the basis for the establishment of local and international institutions responsible for bibliographic control.

UNESCO is at the forefront in promoting bibliographic control and the universal availability of the world's literary heritage. The International Federation of Library Associations (IFLA) has also put the concept of bibliographic control on its agenda, as it has a section/division (VI) that specifically deals with bibliographic issues. It has also been observed that other countries have also set up bibliographic societies, for example the Royal Bibliographic Society of the UK. Fussler and Kocher (1977, 237) noted that there was need for institutions involved in bibliographic control to keep abreast of current trends, because some of the concepts of handling bibliographic data are undergoing change as the format of library resources also undergo change from print to electronic.

Compliance or non-compliance?

Berger and Luckmann (1966) note that according to the social rule theory, most human activity was organised and regulated by socially produced and reproduced systems of rules which are manifested in the form of codes of conduct, norms and laws, such as the Printed Publications Act of Zimbabwe and Broadcasting Act. Laws, norms and codes of conduct are means or mechanisms for social control. Kyobe (2009) notes that compliance is a state in which someone or something is in accordance with established guidelines, specifications or legislation: for example, the need to ensure compliance with the laws of Zimbabwe. Grossman and Zaelke (2005) discuss various models or theories that explain compliance, namely the rationalist and normative models. The former model focuses on deterrence and enforcement as a means to prevent and punish non-compliance, while the latter encourages co-operation and compliance assistance.

As Burns and Flam (1987) observe, compliance with or refusal to comply with particular rules are intricate and normative processes. Factors which encourage compliance are where the benefits of compliance are higher than the loss of individual identity and status, or tensions such as those between authority or sacredness, or the negative or positive threat of sanctions. Kyobe (2009) states that the normative model of compliance relies on behavioural motivation and is premised on the logic of consequence and logic of appropriateness. In the logic of consequences actors are perceived to choose rationally from among alternatives based on their calculations of expected consequences, while with the logic of appropriateness human action is based on identities, obligations and conceptions of appropriateness of action.

Coleman (1993) notes that the rationalist model of domestic compliance follows the logic of consequences and emphasises that regulated individuals act rationally to maximise their economic self-interest. The model is anchored on enforcement and deterrence as measures to transform individuals' economic perceptions, but the model fails to consider social action based on values, beliefs and emotions. Coleman further notes that the model also fails to consider the aspect of conflict that arises because of lack of reciprocity, as only one side gains at the expense of the other. The model does not also consider the problems and costs of deterrence.

Grossman and Zaelke (2005) note that the normative theory of compliance is premised on the notion that people obey the law because it is in their best interest; however, they fail to give explanations for the impact of social factors such as culture and perceived legitimacy. It is assumed that laws that are developed with wider consultation and implanted fairly will be complied with if people believe that they are legitimate and fairly applied. Guoxin (2007) noted that compliance would depend on a number of factors, for example, the capacity of the regulated entity regarding knowledge, financial and technological abilities and commitment. The model has its shortfalls, in that actors need to be conversant with standards and have authority to initiate actions, and also in failing to recognise that within a dynamic environment where change is rapid and complex actors might be overwhelmed and fail to understand their obligations and the need to comply.

Westra (1997) notes that the only non-compliance library case to be documented in South Africa's legal history was the case between the South African Library and Pippa Skotness from 1993 to 1997. This case is viewed as the only legendary legal case with which South Africa has had to grapple with in the history of South African library services. In this case, Skotness refused to comply by arguing that her copies of her expensive book were a work of art rather than a book; however, the Supreme Court ruled in favour of the South African Library. In Zimbabwe, there are no documented cases relating to the flouting of legal deposit, because of the lackadaisical approach in enforcement of the law.

Factors affecting compliance with legislation

Kyobe (2009) notes that there are a number of factors that affect compliance; for example, economic factors are manifested in the economic meltdown that characterised Zimbabwe's economy in 2008, with an inflationary percentage of over 200 million (McGreal, 2008). The other factors are technological, sociological and psychological; for example, some publishers take advantage of the laxity of institutions responsible for enforcing the legal deposit and they fail to comply. Kyobe notes that where actors are psychologically unaware of the legislation there will be non-compliance.

Kigongo-Bukenya (2000) advocates the merger of legal deposit and copyright offices so that publishers secure relative protection of their works from unscrupulous people in breach of copyright, and benefit from marketing promotions through enlistment in national bibliographies. The author further cites the Australian example, whereby the legal deposit act is section 201 of the Copyright Act (1968–73), and argues that such laws will encourage publishers to deposit their works in order to get security from government.

There are various reasons why people comply or fail to comply with a specific piece of legislation; for example, people will comply where the law is legitimate and fair and there are economic benefits to be derived. On the other hand, failure to comply might result from the fact that there is not enough deterrent or the lack of legitimacy or maybe those bound by the act might not see any benefits arising from compliance. Larivière (2000) states that for a law to be effective it needs to be enforceable and that this can be achieved through pressurising the publisher to comply by means of a penalty structure or clause for contravening the law or some other measure that can deter non-compliance. Larivière observes that legislation does not guarantee compliance, because there are problems associated with enforcement. Lor (1995) notes that there is a need to consider a number of factors when dealing with enforcement of legal deposit, for example legal and administrative costs, because it is expensive to follow a case to its conclusion.

Lor (1995, 110) notes the importance of all stakeholders to appreciate and recognise the exceptional value of legal deposit and its undeniable importance and the need for an effective functioning legal deposit system in South Africa. The author stated that ignoring legal deposit would result in the national published cultural heritage being irrevocably lost. Penzhorn, Snyman and Snyman (2008) highlight the main challenges of legal deposit in South Africa as the lack of mechanisms for identifying material subject to legal deposit and for tracing non-compliant publishers, and inadequate structures for supporting the practical implementation of legal deposit by the legal deposit libraries.

Legal deposit in the Zimbabwean context

Made (2009) highlights the legal mandate of the National Archives of Zimbabwe (NAZ) with regards to its role as a legal deposit centre for the country's intellectual and artistic heritage in accordance with the provisions of the Printed Publications Act 12/1975; 37/1977; 22/2001. Under this Act, it is mandatory for publishers to deliver books published in Zimbabwe to the Directors of the National Archives and National Library and Documentation Services (NLDS):

> (1) Subject to this section, the publisher of each book published in Zimbabwe shall, within a period of thirty days from the date of publication of such book, donate and deliver free of charge a copy of such book to–
>
> (a) the Director of National Archives appointed in terms of section 3 of the National Archives of Zimbabwe Act [Chapter 25:06]; and
>
> (b) the Director of the National Library and Documentation Service referred to in section 6 of the National Library and Documentation Service Act [Chapter 25:10]; and
>
> (c) the authority having control of the Public Library, Bulawayo.

The Printed Publications Act 12/1975; 37/1977, 22/2001 defines a book as '... every part or division of a book, pamphlet, and sheet of printing, map, plan, chart, or table separately published...'. The Broadcasting Act (2001) Section 41(b), which states '... provide a copy of each of its programmes free of charge to the National Archives referred to in section 3 of the National Archives of

Zimbabwe Act...'. The National Archives Act of Zimbabwe 22/2001 Section 3 specifies: 'The National Archives established in terms of the repealed Act shall, subject to this Act, continue in existence for the storage and preservation of public archives and public records and shall be known as the National Archives of Zimbabwe'.

The National Archives of Zimbabwe library is a legal depository of all printed material as well as non-print sound and audiovisual material produced in Zimbabwe. It falls under the Ministry of Home Affairs. It also acquires copies of all works published outside the country about Zimbabwe or by Zimbabweans. The National Archives of Zimbabwe also keeps any material on the southern African and sub-Saharan region that explains or depicts the history, development and any other aspect of Zimbabwe. Most of these resources need to be digitised so that they can be made readily accessible through interlending and document supply networks. In practice, the National Archives of Zimbabwe serves as the national bibliographic centre of Zimbabwe, responsible for the publication of the Zimbabwe National Bibliography (ZNB) and the administration of the International Standard Book Number Scheme (ISBN).

The failure by the National Archives to publish a national bibliography and failure to revise and update the penalties for lack of compliance instilled a sense of irresponsibility on part of the actors who could deposit their items. In line with the new technological trends and borrowing a leaf from other regional libraries, the National Archives of Zimbabwe library has adopted the use of ICT, for instance Koha, for managing its collection. This has then 'forced' the library to move from physically publishing the ZNB. Rather, for one to have access to the Zimbabwe National Bibliography for a particular year, they just have to search it on the library's online public access catalogue (OPAC).[1]

The National Archives of Zimbabwe[2] also serves as the National Repository for UNESCO publications with reference to monographs and serial publications. Genge (2008, 3) notes that the Bulawayo Public Library[3] also serves as a legal depository of printed materials considering that it is the oldest, which has helped to sustain the national memory through its historic reference collection dating back as far as the beginning of the 20th century. Haymes and Rushby (2009) noted that Anglophone African countries did not provide the necessary infrastructure to maintain depository libraries and also the fact that the libraries exercised poor bibliographic controls. The two authors also further noted that legal deposit laws were unsatisfactory and difficult to enforce.

The National Archives of Zimbabwe once made efforts to review the Printed Publications Act so as to accommodate changes that are in line with current trends, but those efforts were thwarted by the fact that the Act in itself is administered by different institutions falling under different ministries. The legal department within the parent ministry was unwilling to take up the issue, citing priority being given to aligning acts to the constitution rather than amendments. It was only in 2015 that the submission for the Act to be realigned to the new constitution of Zimbabwe was undertaken (National Archives of Zimbabwe, 2016).

Challenges of enforcing legal deposit

Igbashal and Tsegba (2012) note that the challenges facing African countries with regard to bibliographic control relate to difficulties in defining the scope of legal deposit material, the difficulties in identifying in-house publishing, and limited co-operation from publishers. Originally, legal deposit was limited to formal literature, for example books, pamphlets and serial publications, but now many countries have embraced grey literature, for example conference papers, theses, and dissertations. Many in-house publishers who use ICT for publishing are not concerned with legal deposit because they are not registered publishers. Capuano and Marfouk (2013) note that the brain drain has resulted in mass emigration by Africans to the developed countries, where some end up publishing with international publishers, thus making it an overwhelming assignment for local legal deposit systems to track such publications. The author further notes that where such emigrants acquire citizenship this will result in their literary output assuming their new national identity at the detriment of their mother countries.

Reynolds (2000) notes that the current explosion in electronic publishing has seen new forms (such as web pages) appearing, and many old forms (such as journals) are behaving in new and different ways, thus creating challenges for bibliographic description. In the electronic age, some publications, including abstracting and indexing services, are issued in parts and are treated as serials but when uploaded online they take the form of a database with seamless updating. These publications fail to meet the criterion of a series, thus rendering themselves as monographs and so creating confusion for librarians and users. The author states also that websites, too, create challenges, because they are neither serials nor monographs.

The main challenge NAZ noticed with regard to enforcing the Printed Publications Act 1975 (PPA) was mainly the emergence of self-publishers. It used to be easier previously, when all prospective authors had to go through recognised and well established publishing houses. However, currently, the majority of books being published in Zimbabwe are by individual publishers of no fixed abode. Efforts to track them are usually futile. Some books are even finding their way on to the market without ISBNs, thereby making it impossible for NAZ to know of their existence.

Most books of a political nature are now being published outside the country, mainly because of costs associated with publishing in Zimbabwe, as well as the fear of persecution for publishing anti-government materials. This is then posing a challenge for the National Archives of Zimbabwe to acquire these books. Such publishers and authors are unwilling to deposit, since they just assume the book will be kept under prohibited or limited access the moment it enters the National Archives of Zimbabwe. In addition, like anywhere else, for example in the UK, legal deposits can be confusing for self-publishing authors and many are not aware of legal deposit or do not know how or where to do it (I Am Self-Publishing, 2017).

Currently many countries have been forced to re-examine their legal deposit acts as a way of dealing with the challenges of the digital world. Larivière (2000) notes that the digital world presents a serious challenge to developing countries because of the complexity of addressing legal, ethical, organisational, technical and operational aspects related to the implementation of a legal deposit scheme. The author observed that Namibia in 1996 and South Africa in 1997 did incorporate electronic publications within their legal deposit legislation, even though the legislation deals with offline material. Generally South Africa has had legal deposit legislation since 1842, and in 1997 this was revised to extend the legal deposit to audiovisual broadcast electronic media. This was achieved through avoiding definition and enumeration of various media through the use of generic terms like document and media. Lor and Letshela (2002) note that Namibia had the opportunity after independence to enact a modern legal deposit act which covered all existing and yet to be created media as recommended by UNESCO and this is what is lacking in the current Zimbabwean legislation.

Cadavid (2017) notes that New Zealand's National Library Act of 2003 encompassed the obligation to deposit e-content. It has been observed that legal deposit of online resources presents serious challenges with reference to copyright, authentication, preservation and the legal and technical expertise needed to ensure the ultimate success of the project. Oltmans (2003) notes that handling, and maintaining electronic resources requires new knowledge, skills and different infrastructure from that of printed publications, and currently there are no best practices pertaining to legal deposit of electronic resources. Tenopir (2003) observed that electronic resources also require the prerequisite hardware for reading, for example, e-book readers. They also require a level of digital literacy to manipulate the hardware and software. In the case of Zimbabwe, the National Archives of Zimbabwe has still to adopt a fully-fledged electronic information management system. Some Zimbabwean publishing houses, such as Weaver Press[4] based in Harare, have many books they are releasing as e-books. A few that were deposited are just stored on laptops without any software to use in accessing them online.

With reference to the South African and Namibian experiences, Lor and Letshela (2002) observe that the promulgation of the act does not entail partial or complete implementation of a legal deposit law, because responsible institutions will be overwhelmed to fulfil all the stipulations in one go unless they opt for a gradual approach. This phased approach involved separation of print materials, audiovisual and non-static resources from the dynamic electronic or online resources. Oltmans (2003) notes that the results of scientific research are currently being published electronically because many publishers feel that they now need to license rather than sell their publications. It is interesting to know that other countries within the Southern African Development Community, for example Namibia and South Africa, have already taken the initiative by harmonising the legal deposit laws with ICT legislation.

Fines as a deterrent measure

Larivière (2000) notes that it is quite a challenge to rely on goodwill to ensure the comprehensiveness of deposit collections and this calls for adequate mechanisms to facilitate enforcement; for instance, the use of deterrent fines to deter non-compliance would help to improve the situation. The Printed Publications Act of Zimbabwe states that a publisher that fails to comply with the stipulations of Section 5 will be deemed guilty of an offence and liable to a fine in line with Section 5(4) of the Printed Publications Act 12/1975; 37/1977, 22/2001: 'A publisher who fails to comply with this section shall be guilty of an offence and liable to a fine not exceeding level four or to imprisonment for a period not exceeding three months or to both such fine and such imprisonment'. In South Africa the maximum penalty stands at R2500, while in the USA it goes as far as US$2500. Crews (1988) notes that if penalties are too low, they may not be significant enough to compel publishers to comply.

The use of fines, however, should be viewed as a last resort, because there is a need to encourage mutually beneficial close co-operation between national institutions responsible for legal deposit, publishers, authors and other stakeholders. Larivière (2000) further states that there is a need to educate stakeholders on how the legal deposit act operates and the benefits that accrue from compliance, for example, increased visibility, wider publicity of publications, effective bibliographic control and long-term guarantees of availability of original copies in the event that disaster strikes.

Conclusion and recommendations

This study confirms that Zimbabwean legal deposit laws need to be updated in order to address contemporary issues in information generation, processing, storage and retrieval in a digital environment. Institutions mandated to facilitate legal deposit should take advantage of the proliferation of digital technologies in order to leverage the information science profession and fulfil constitutional rights of access to information. Even though the National Archives of Zimbabwe has in the past entered into partnerships with educational institutions to help clear the backlog in bibliographic compilation, the project has hit a snag as a result of financial constraints.

Investing in modern technology for effective bibliographic control will also assist in inter-lending and document supply projects. Advancements in technology can help libraries and library users to easily identify, locate, discover and access resources from all over the globe. Bell (1997) warned of the dangers of 'memory losses' in national bibliographies of third-world countries and calls for effective strategies to help improve the situation through worldwide co-operation with other institutions such as UNESCO, the African Union, the Association of Southern African Indexers and Bibliographers, the IFLA section for bibliographic control and other key stakeholders. In light of the foregoing discussion, we recommend the following:

1 There should be continuous support to raise key stakeholders' awareness of the value of national bibliographic control. The stakeholders include publishers, libraries, authors, booksellers, print and electronic media, internet service providers, national research and education networks and government. The key stakeholders in bibliographic control and legal deposit should invest in continuous professional development and workplace learning (CPDWL) in order to strengthen skills in critical areas, including indexing and bibliographic compilations, metadata standards and forensic bibliographic reconstruction among other areas.
2 Investment in ICT should be prioritised in order to enable access to scientific publications in a technologically driven information landscape.
3 The National Archives of Zimbabwe should engage in inter-institutional collaboration with colleges and universities and other institutions involved in similar work.
4 The National Archives of Zimbabwe should broaden the scope of legal deposit to incorporate digital content. This can be achieved by viewing legal deposit as a cultural heritage law and ensuring amendments to extend legal deposit into the digital realms through digital harvesting and web harvesting.

5 The right of a national library to harvest electronic content should be combined with the legal obligation for publishers and other content producers to deposit content according to an agreed-upon appraisal criterion.
6 Key stakeholders involved in bibliographic control, for example publishers, e-content providers, publishers, authors, producers, librarians, scholars and researchers, should work together to ensure successful bibliographic control in line with the transition towards RDA.
7 Forensic bibliographic reconstruction (FBR) should be considered and incorporated into continuous professional development and workplace learning (CPDWL) programmes in order to build capacity for effective bibliographic control and legal deposit. Forensic bibliographic reconstruction is 'the use of Google Scholar (or other tools, usually in multiples and/or in creative ways) to track down missing or incorrect pieces of a bibliographic reference, due to printing errors or human errors in compiling Works Cited lists' (Tara Patterson, cited in Mathews, B., 2015).
8 Bibliographic records should be easily accessible and reusable for posterity through the development of interoperable data sets characterised by optimum interconnectivity.
9 Internet service providers (ISPs) and National Research and Education Networks (NRENs) should assist in developing bibliographic control and legal deposit as a key component of national research infrastructure.
10 Pre-digital content should be digitised to widen access to Zimbabwe's national heritage.
11 There is a need to harmonise bibliographic control of serials with regards to seriality, extent of the record, title changes, descriptions, ISSN issues, multiple manifestations and versions (Reynolds 2000).

An effective legal deposit system will help Zimbabwe contribute to the national development through a collaborative knowledge society that will be instrumental in universal bibliographic control and the provision of wider availability and access to published material in multimedia formats in support of learning, teaching and research. Penzhorn, Snyman and Snyman (2008, 113) are of the view that the implementation and management of legal deposit in African countries is dependent upon the positive and full commitment of key stakeholders, including publishers, legal deposit institutions, authors, internet service providers and others. Even though the above-mentioned studies were mainly focused on South Africa, the findings can be generalised to the rest of the African continent. Zimbabwe stands to gain greatly by revisiting the legal deposit law so that revisions can be made, and new laws that will take into cognisance electronic and other non-print resources should be put in place. The country cannot afford memory loss by ignoring the need of bibliographic control, since the knowledge dispensation is driven by access to all forms of knowledge. Having a regularly and punctually updated physical and digital record will move the country on a progressive and digitally compliant path.

Notes

1. www.moha.gov.zw/index.php?link=naz_library.
2. www.archives.gov.zw.
3. http://byopubliclibrary.org.
4. http://weaverpresszimbabwe.com.

References

Ahmed, J. U. (2010) Documentary Research Method: New Dimensions, *Indus Journal of Management and Social Sciences*, **4** (1), 1-14.

Bell, R. (1997) Legal Deposit (Part 1), *Law Librarian*, **8** (1), 5.

Berger, P. L. and Luckmann, T. (1966) *The Social Construction of Reality: A Treatise in the Sociology of Knowledge*, Garden City.

Burns, T. and Flam, H. (1987) *The Shaping Of Social Organisation: Social Rule System Theory with Applications*, Sage Publications.

Cadavid, J. A. P. (2017) Evolution of Legal Deposit in New Zealand: From Print to Digital Heritage, *IFLA Journal*, **43** (4), 379–90.

Capuano, S. and Marfouk, A. (2013) African Brain Drain and its Impact on Source Countries: What Do We Know and What Do We Need to Know? *Journal of Comparative Policy Analysis: Research and Practice*, **15** (4), 297–314.

Chebbi, A. (2008) Archivage du Web: Quelques Leçons à Retenir, *Archives*, **39** (2), 19–46.

Coleman, J. S. (1993) The Rational Reconstruction of Society, *American Sociological Review*, **58** (6), 898–912.

Crews, K. D. (1988) Legal Deposit in Four Countries: Laws and Library Services, *Law Library Journal*, **80**, 551.

Danskin, A. (2013) Linked and Open Data: RDA and Bibliographic Control, *JLIS.it*, **4** (1).

Davidson, D. (1988) *Bibliographic Control*, Clive Bingley.

Dunsire, G., Hillmann, D. and Phipps, J. (2012) Reconsidering Universal Bibliographic Control in Light of the Semantic Web, *Journal of Library Metadata*, **12** (2–3), 164–76.

Elliott, A. (2011). Electronic Legal Deposit: the New Zealand experience. Paper given at the conference of the International Federation of Library Associations and Institutions (IFLA), San Juan, Puerto Rico, http://www.ifla.org/past-wlic/2011/193-elliotten.pdf.

Fournier, C. (1993) Documentation Bibliotheca, *Le Depot Legal*, **39** (2), 95–9.

Fussler, H. H. and Kocher, K. (1977) Contemporary Issues in Bibliographic Control, *Library Quarterly*, **47** (3), 237–52.

Genge, P. (2008) Historic Reference Collection, Bulawayo Public Library Zimbabwe, *IFLA Round-table on Newspapers*, **8**, May.

Gilchrist, J. (2005) Copyright Deposit, Legal Deposit or Library Deposit: The Government's Role as Preserver of Copyright Material, *Queensland U. Tech. L. & Just. J.*, **5**, 177.

Grossman, D. and Zaelke, D. (2005) An Introduction to Theories of Why States and Firms Do (and Do Not) Comply With Law, *Seventh International Conference on Environmental Compliance and Enforcement*, **9**, 15.

Guoxin, L. (2007) On Reform of Publication Legal Deposit System, [J], *Journal of Library Science In China*, **2**.

Haymes, M. and Rushby, L. (2009) Anglophone Africa Seminar on Government Information and Official Publications, www.innovation.ukzn.ac.za/innovation/Innovation/pdf.

I Am Self-Publishing (2017) *What is a Legal Deposit?*, www.iamselfpublishing.com/legal-deposit.

Igbashal, A. A. and Tsegba, J. F. (2012) Bibliographic Control of Publications: the Impact on African Countries, *Library Philosophy and Practice*, https://link.galegroup.com/apps/doc/A285340823/AONE?u=googlescholar&sid=AONE&xid=0903ac2c.

Kigongo-Bukenya, I. M.N. (2000) The State of Ugandan Bibliographic Control and Strategies into the Twenty-first Century, *Library Review*, **49** (2), 64–76.

Kumar, G. (1998) *Sociology of Information Management*, Har-Anand Publications.

Kyobe, M. (2009) Factors Influencing SME Compliance with Government Regulations on Use of IT: the Case of South Africa, *Journal of Global Information Management*, **17** (2), 30–59.

Larivière, J. (2000) *Guidelines for Legal Deposit Legislation: a Revised, Enlarged and Updated Edition of the 1981 Publication by Dr Jean Lunn*, UNESCO.

Lor, P. J. (1995) Legal Deposit: Some Issues in the International Scene, *Musaion*, **13** (1/2), 94–111.

Lor, P. J. and Letshela, P. Z. (2002) *Implementing Legal Deposit of Electronic Publications in Africa: Progress Report from South Africa and Namibia*, paper presented at the 68th IFLA Council and General conference, 18–24 August 2002.

McGreal, C. (2008) Zimbabwe's Inflation Rate Surges to 231,000,000%, *The Guardian*, 9 October, www.theguardian.com/world/2008/oct/09/zimbabwe.

Made, S. H. (2009) *Project in Resource Sharing in Southern and Central Africa (Botswana, Malawi, Zambia and Zimbabwe). Feasibility Study Part 1*, www.unesdoc.unesco.org/images/0008/000851/0081541/eb.pdf.

Mannik, L. and McGarry, K. (eds) (2017) *Practicing Ethnography: A Student Guide to Method and Methodology*, University of Toronto Press.

Mansor, Y. and Jarjis, J. (2008) *Taming the Bibliographic Universe: Proposed Bibliographic Centre for the Muslim World*, paper presented at the World Congress of Muslim Librarian and Information Scientists, Puntra, http://ddms.usim.edu.my/bitstream/123456789/1967/1/Taming%20the%20 Bibliographic%20Universe-%20Proposed%20Bibliographic%20Ce.pdf.

Mathews, B. (2015) Forensic Bibliographic Reconstruction: Tracking Down Troublesome Citations and the Problem of Lost Knowledge, *The Chronicle*, 4 May, http://chronicle.com/blognetwork/theubiquitouslibrarian/2015/05/04/ forensic-bibliographic-reconstruction-tracking-down-troublesome-citations-and-the-problem-of-lost-knowledge.

Mogalakwe, M. (2006) The Use of Documentary Research Methods in Social Research, *African Sociological Review*, **10** (1), 221–30.

Musiker, R. (2005) History of Indexing in South Africa: a Brief Overview. In *Indexing for Southern Africa: a Manual Compiled in Celebration of ASAIB's first decade: 1994–2004*, http://uir.unisa.ac.za/handle/10500/19459.

National Archives of Zimbabwe (2016) *Directors' Annual Report for the Year 2016*, www.archives.gov.zw/phocadownload/Director%27s%20Annual%20Report%20 2016.pdf.

Needleman, M. (2008) The Resource Description and Access Standard, *Serials Review*, **34** (3), 233–4.

Ng'ang'a, J. M. (1990) *The concept of UAP and its relevance in Kenya*, paper presented at the KLA Annual Seminar, Nairobi, 27 February–2 March, 1990.

Oltmans, E. (2003) Legal Deposit of Digital Materials, *Liber Quarterly*, **13** (3–4), http://doi.org/10.18352/lq.7741.

Penzhorn, C., Snyman, R. and Snyman, M. (2008) Implementing and Managing Legal Deposit in South Africa: Challenges and Recommendations, *The International Information & Library Review*, **40** (2), 112–20.

Reynolds, R. R. (2000) Harmonizing Bibliographic Control of Serials in the Digital Age, *Cataloging & Classification Quarterly*, **28** (1), 3–19.

Seys, D. (2004) *Bibliographic Control and Content Management on the Web*, www.hpl.hp.com/techreports/2004/HPL-2004-2.pdf.

Smith, A. (1999) *Why Digitise?*, Council on Library and Information Resources.

Sulistyo-Basuki, L. (2005) A Rethinking of the National Library Role in Bibliographic Control in the ICT Age, With Special Reference to the Region of South East Asia, https://core.ac.uk/download/pdf/11879244.pdf.

Tenopir, C. (2003) Use and Users of Electronic Library Resources: an Overview and Analysis of Recent Research Studies., Council on Library and Information Resources, http://citeseerx.ist.psu.edu/viewdoc/download?doi=10.1.1.120.3442&rep=rep1&type=pdf.

Thapa, A. (2009) Bibliographic Control: Its Importance, *Infolib* **2** (2).

Westra, P. (1997) Preserving Our Published Heritage: An Exemplary Case, *Alexandria*, **9** (3), 239–41.

Whitby, T. J., Lorkovic, T. and Gracheva, I. B. (1979) *Introduction to Soviet National Bibliography*, Libraries Unlimited.

Wise, M. (1985) *Aspects of African Librarianship: a Collection of Writings*, Mansell Publishing.

Zimbabwe, Ministry of Home Affairs (1975) Printed Publications Act 1975, www.moha.gov.zw/index.php?link=naz_library.

Žumer, M. (ed.) (2009) *National Bibliographies in the Digital Age: Guidance and New Directions*, vol. 39, Walter de Gruyter.

CHAPTER 5

Electronic legal deposit in Sweden: the evolution of digital publications and legislative systems

Eva Lis-Green and Göran Konstenius

Introduction

Recent years have seen much progress and change in both legal and procedural approaches to safeguarding Sweden's digital published output, at a time when Sweden's publishing environment is rapidly changing and evolving. This chapter gives a summary account of the design of Swedish legal deposit legislation and proposes areas that need to be changed in order to achieve its stated purposes. The chapter begins with a description of the history and implementation of Swedish legal deposit legislation. It then describes the design of Swedish legal deposit legislation and its relevance to the digitisation of media outputs. We identify problems linked to the recent evolution of media in relation to the design of current legal deposit legislation, including media that falls outside the current legislation, difficulties in determining the requirement to deposit, and the limits of collecting. In spite of the National Library's extensive and largely automated collection under the E-Legal Deposit Act, these issues mean there are still significant parts of electronically published material produced in Sweden that are not being collected. The chapter concludes with a Nordic outlook that summarises the issues that libraries in our close neighbouring countries also face in the preservation of digital publications and media and highlighting the issues that Sweden will face should the legislation not be adapted. We call for revised legislation and its corresponding regulations, harmonising the Library Act and E-Legal Deposit Act to ensure the preservation of Sweden's digital publications for posterity.

The history and context of Swedish legal deposit legislation

In 2015 the National Library of Sweden[1] (the National Library) was commissioned by the Swedish government to draft a proposal for a national library strategy for all publicly financed libraries. In 2017 the National Library was also commissioned to carry out a study on the role, design and relevance of Swedish legal deposit legislation in relation to the evolution of digital and print media. The study was submitted to the Swedish government in October 2017 and emphasised the importance of adapting the Swedish legal deposit legislation to today's media landscape. It was therefore natural that these findings would contribute to the evolving National Library strategy. The National Library strategy, which was submitted to the Swedish government in 2019, highlights among other things the importance of updating the legal deposit legislation and adapting it to present-day circumstances. As a result of these two studies the government has recently decided to review the current legal deposits laws, and we set out the landscape, scope and need for this in this chapter.

Legal deposit of printed matter has deep historical roots. The first Swedish provision can be found in an act from the year 1661, stipulating that all printing houses in Sweden were required to deliver two copies of all printed matter to the equivalent of today's government offices before they could be disseminated (Larsson, 2011, 29). At that time, collection was not undertaken in order to preserve the printed matter for the sake of cultural heritage, but as an instrument of censorship used by the king for monitoring purposes (Svensson, 2018, 57). Modern legal deposit legislation in Sweden has a broad purpose, encompassing the interests of both the research community and society as a whole. In addition to the significance of legal deposit materials for research purposes, it emphasises the citizen's right to information and knowledge, which is a prerequisite for a functioning democracy. Current collection of legal deposit materials in Sweden is dependent on two pieces of legislation: The Legal Deposit Act for Documents (SFS 1993:1392), and The Legal Deposit Act for Electronic Materials/Documents (SFS 2012:492). The E-Legal Deposit Act of 2012 extends the remit of collection to internet publications.

Well into the 20th century, the obligation to submit legal deposit materials to libraries in Sweden applied only to printed matter. Although Swedish legal deposit legislation dates back to 1662, it was only in 1979 that legal deposit was extended to include recordings of sound and moving images such as music, film, video, radio and television (Larsson, 2011, 33). In 1979 the Swedish National Archive of Recorded Sound and Moving Images (SLBA)[2] was established in order to collect and preserve audiovisual material and to make it accessible. Through the design of the Legal Deposit Act (1993), which includes a deep as well as broad collection of different types of media, society gains access to material that would otherwise have been difficult to collect. The obligation to deliver was also extended to computer games and other interactive multimedia in 1995 (Prop. 1995/96:71). On 1 January 2009 the SLBA ceased to be an independent authority and its operations were subsumed into those of the National Library (Konstenius, 2017, 29). The inquiries on which the current legal deposit acts are based also emphasise the importance of making cultural heritage available and accessible (SOU 1992:92, 87). The purpose of the legal deposit framework is consistent with the opening section of the Swedish Library Act (SFS 2013:801), which states that the public library system shall promote the development of democratic society by contributing to the dissemination of knowledge and free opinion formation.

The Swedish legal deposit libraries currently consist of the National Library as well as the university libraries at Lund,[3] Stockholm,[4] Uppsala,[5] Linköping,[6] Gothenburg[7] and Umeå.[8] The university libraries in Uppsala, Lund and Gothenburg have been a part of legal deposit legislation since 1707, Umeå since 1950, Stockholm and Linköping since 1978. The National Library became an independent authority in 1877, built on the royal library collections. The fact that the legal deposit libraries are spread all over the country is seen as a strength, as it reinforces the regional perspective in the collection of legal deposit copies. With the exception of Stockholm University Library,[9] the legal deposit libraries welcome the legal deposit mandate (Konstenius, 2017, 37). The legal deposit deliveries give a good overview of printed publication activity, provide the higher education institutions with smooth access to publications, and give the legal deposit libraries an opportunity to build up collections that include non-commercial material that would otherwise have been difficult to obtain.

The National Library and Lund University Library are responsible for preserving legal deposit materials for the future. The National Library holds the national copy and Lund University Library is responsible for what is referred to as the national reserve copy. The reserve copy in Lund may not be weeded out, but content may be lent out within the institution and may be borrowed by external libraries and institutions on an interlibrary basis. Other legal deposit libraries are under no obligation to preserve legal deposit materials and may weed their collections based on the needs of the university. The weeding performed at the university libraries at Uppsala, Linköping, Gothenburg and Umeå is generally of a lesser extent than that of Stockholm, yet is quite extensive within certain categories. Several legal deposit libraries say that advertising is one type of material that is subject to extensive weeding, as demand for it is very low. The demand for advertising and commercial printed matter remains significant at the National Library.

The National Library's mandate differs from that of the other Swedish legal deposit libraries, as it is the only institution that collects and preserves all the media forms prescribed by the legal deposit legislation. While printed legal deposit materials are submitted to all the legal deposit libraries, newspapers are only submitted to both the National Library and to Lund University Library. Audiovisual and E-Legal Deposit Act materials are submitted to the National Library only. It is therefore the place of the National Library to comment on and inform others in Sweden of the changing nature of non-print legal deposit materials, and to highlight issues which are arising in this developing landscape.

The Legal Deposit Act for Documents (1993)

The general principle for the Swedish Legal Deposit Act for Documents (1993) is that all publications made available to the public in Sweden are to be collected via legal deposit. A document is deemed to have been made available to the public when it is offered for sale, rent or loan, or otherwise disseminated to the public. Moreover, the information in the document must be written in Swedish in whole or in part, or the document must contain works by a Swedish author in whole or in part, or be performed by a Swedish artist. If none of these conditions are met, the document must nonetheless be submitted via legal deposit if it is primarily intended for dissemination within Sweden. For example, the latter requirement means that foreign film and video, as well as games and other multimedia that have been imported and made available in Sweden, are subject to the legal deposit legislation if the work is subtitled in Swedish, or has otherwise been adapted to accord with Swedish conditions.

In the Legal Deposit Act for Documents (1993), the term 'document' is defined as an object that stores information for reading, listening or viewing. Legal deposit deliveries always refer to the document in the version in which it is made available to the public, with the exception of cinema-screened film, radio and television. Packaging, such as book covers, record and video game covers, is also subject to the obligation to deliver, as is extra material such as liner notes and illustrations.

The Legal Deposit Act for Documents (1993) always refers to physical objects, even in the case of radio and television broadcasts. With regard to radio and television material, the legal deposit legislation pertains to the reference recordings that Swedish broadcasters are required by law (SFS 1994:728) to record and retain for six months. The reference recordings contain everything that the broadcasters have broadcast, and may, for example, be relied upon in litigation when programming content is considered to have violated the rules of a broadcasting licence. When the Legal Deposit Act for Documents was last updated in 1993, the broadcasters' reference recordings consisted of audiotapes and videotapes, indicating how now dated the legislation is. With regard to the routines related to legal deposit deliveries of cinema-screened film, the film distributor is required to submit a copy of the film[10] to the National Library, which is then entitled to produce a video copy of the film. Subsequently, the National Library is required to return the film to the distributor.

In the case of printed material, documents produced at both Swedish and foreign printing houses may be subject to an obligation to deliver these to the National Library for ingest. Printing houses in Sweden are responsible for delivering material printed, while the publisher, or the person who otherwise publishes the document in Sweden, is responsible for legal deposit deliveries if a foreign printing house is engaged. For audiovisual material, the person who makes the document available to the public in Sweden is responsible for the delivery of this material to the legal deposit library. For some imported audiovisual documents, such as music videos, computer games and other multimedia, the Swedish distributor has the obligation to deliver these to the National Library.

The Legal Deposit Act for Documents (1993) proceeds on a principle of completeness, meaning that all editions made available to the public in Sweden and which constitute documents for purposes of the Act are subject to an obligation to deliver. The purpose of the principle of completeness is carefully defined in the legislation to ensure that the selection of material is not left to the discretion of the delivering parties and government agencies. For example, everything printed by Swedish printing houses is collected, including simpler publications such as flyers, restaurant menus, etc. No weeding out takes place at the printing houses or at the National Library. However, an exception is granted from the principle of completeness for community radio and local advertising-financed radio, in which case recordings amounting to no more than four weeks per year are required to be submitted as legal deposits. The legal deposit legislation therefore regulates in detail the criteria that have to be met in order for an obligation to deliver to arise.

The E-Legal Deposit Act

In 2009 the Swedish Government decided to investigate the matter of how to design a constitutionally regulated obligation to deliver published network-transmitted electronic material to a government agency (the National Library). There was a growing volume of electronic media content, especially on the internet, that was not subject to the Legal Deposit Act for Documents (1993), despite the fact that network-published electronic material appeared to be important to preserve, in accordance with the purposes set out in the legal deposit legislation. The legal deposit libraries also emphasised the research community's need for the E-Legal Deposit Act, like the National Library's other digital collection activities, to be in line with the evolution of the media and with other changes in the media landscape. However, the inquiry's mandate did not extend to issues related to how the delivered material could be used and made available. In the mandate for the inquiry that preceded the E-Legal Deposit Act (2012), it was stated that the obligation in the new legislation should not, in principle, extend to material that the National Library is technically able to collect on its own, or to material that substantively corresponds to that already subject to the obligations pursuant to the Legal Deposit Act for Documents (Öman, 2009, 131). Accordingly, the inquiry chair proposed that the E-Legal Deposit Act should be subsidiary to the earlier legislation. The E-Legal Deposit Act (2012), then, was designed as standalone legislation, with the existing 1993 legislation being left largely intact. This means that electronic material that essentially corresponds to that which is covered by the Legal Deposit Act for Documents is to be made exempt from the E-Legal Deposit Act. At the time of the introduction of the E-Legal Deposit Act the government declared that the longer-term objective was to review the legal deposit legislation as a whole in order to unify it into a single act (Prop. 2011/12:121, 16); however, this is something that has not yet been undertaken.

In contrast to the Legal Deposit Act for Documents, the E-Legal Deposit Act does not proceed on the basis of a principle of completeness, but was limited to what was deemed both relevant as well as economically, legally and practically possible to collect by means of an obligation to deliver at the time of the E-Legal Deposit Act commission's inquiry. The Act is limited in its application to what is referred to in the legislation as 'electronic material'. The Act defines 'electronic material' as a specific unit of an electronic recording of text, audio or video having predetermined content that is intended to be presented each time it is used. In practice, the definition means that what is collected must be of a completed, delimited and static character. The E-Legal Deposit Act additionally only applies to what is termed 'distance-transmitted material', which requires that it must be possible for the material to be accessible from a location or device other than that where the creator stores the material. For example, a publication on the internet constitutes distance-transmitted material, but not a film played from a hard disk in a digital cinema. In practice, the subsidiarity principle means that if an e-book has content that is essentially identical to that of a printed book, only the printed book is subject to the obligation to deliver. However, the subsidiarity principle does not apply to municipal authorities and state agencies under the government. For them, both the printed version of a government publication and the version that is distributed online are subject to an obligation to deliver.

The E-Legal Deposit Act's definition of what is to be collected does not include, for example, dynamic databases such as websites, interactive web-based teaching aids, map databases and online games or other interactive media. What is shown in these databases constitutes only a certain portion of the content and depends on the user's interaction. In the assessment by the government, at the time of the introduction of the E-Legal Deposit Act there was no uniform way of saving different representations of, for example, a dynamic web page, website or networked database, or the operation that controls the display. However, electronic material included in a database may be subject to the E-Legal Deposit Act, provided that it is a recording having a predetermined content that is intended to be presented each time it is used, for example a completed news article on the website of a newspaper publisher. Nor is electronic material in the form of pure software subject to the Act. The government indicated that it would be highly unusual to collect software that controlled the display of content to the public, but which has never been made available to the public *per se*. It was also deemed that the National Library would have difficulty preserving many different kinds of software over a long period of time, and that it may require different types of machines in order to re-create the operation.

The inquiry that preceded the E-Legal Deposit Act considered it unreasonable to impose an obligation to deliver which extended to everyone in Sweden who publishes electronic material via the internet (Öman, 2009, 76). According to the inquiry, such legislation would hardly be accepted or complied with by everyone who publish online. As an example, it mentioned private individuals who keep a blog or a website about their families or a hobby. The inquiry chair believed that such a law would risk undermining respect for legislation and for the legislator. The fact that the National Library would have difficulties handling the sheer volume of deliveries that would result from an obligation for private individuals to deliver their electronic material was also cited as a reason to restrict the scope of collection. The resulting design of the E-Legal Deposit Act means that material is exempt from the obligation to deliver if it falls outside editorial responsibility and constitutional protection. Such materials include privately published e-books, images, music, films, blogs and comments on social media, as well as those of non-profit organisations and others who do not automatically qualify for constitutional protection for their publication activity or who produce opinions on a professional basis. The inquiry that preceded the E-Legal

Deposit Act noted that this material is naturally of great importance in terms of understanding our times and for future research. For this reason, the inquiry chair considered the National Library's web harvesting[11] of online material to be an important complement to the E-Legal Deposit Act (see the next section).

The obligation to deliver e-material is therefore directed at publishers who are subject to automatic constitutional protection according to the Fundamental Law on Freedom of Expression,[12] mass-media companies, other professional publishers, and municipal authorities and state agencies under the government. Any party that has electronic material produced, provided that such party is established in Sweden, is also the party that is obliged to deliver the legal deposit. In other cases, the legal deposit must be submitted by the party that made the material available to the public in Sweden, provided that such party is established in Sweden.

The National Library's web collection – a combination of several collection methods

The National Library's web-collecting methods currently consist of a combination of the E-Legal Deposit Act, web harvesting and targeted and event-driven harvesting. A brief description will be given of what is collected by each method, and of how the various methods interact in the building up of the National Library's web archive.

Web harvesting as a precursor and complement to the E-Legal Deposit Act

The National Library has been using web harvesting to collect Swedish web pages since 1997. Web harvesting makes it possible to use a relatively simple set of technical rules to collect large amounts of data. The National Library's web harvesting is not subject to the legal deposit legislation. Because the appearance and structure of websites are captured by web harvesting, such collection provides a context for the publications collected on the basis of the E-Legal Deposit Act.

The web-harvesting process uses very general criteria to target the Swedish internet. For example, harvesting is directed toward all websites having the top-level domain '.se'. With the technical capacity that the National Library's web-harvesting system has today, it is possible to perform one to two scans per year.

It is not possible to predict exactly what will be collected when web harvesting. It is also difficult to adjust the web-harvesting scans in order to satisfactorily capture certain categories of material that are not pure web pages. For example, these categories may include content that is behind paywalls or which require login, such as music, film, television, dissertations, books, reports, etc. However, the result of the National Library's web harvesting does provide an overall view of how the Swedish internet and individual websites are evolving over time. Yet the ability to search web-harvested material with precision and at publication level is limited, as there is no structured description of the content. Unique and permanent identifiers or descriptive metadata are usually missing for individual publications as well.

The development of automated scripts and other tools for web harvesting is occurring in parallel with the development of the web itself. Harvesting technology is becoming increasingly sophisticated, even as the web is growing exponentially and becoming increasingly complex. This means that the challenges posed by web harvesting today are at least as large as those encountered when the E-Legal Deposit Act was introduced.

E-Legal Deposit Act – digital deliveries

As explained previously, the e-legal deposit deliveries only include completed and static publications. Those publishers subject to the E-Legal Deposit Act are obliged to submit e-publications to the National Library. In other words, responsibility for the delivery lies with the publisher, and legal deposit materials are usually submitted to the National Library by transmitting digital files over networks. Because the collection has a statutory basis, the procedures have been designed to achieve the greatest possible completeness, based on the design of the legislation. In addition to close collaboration between the National Library and those subject to a legal deposit obligation, this also requires a technology that is capable of handling large data inflows. In accordance with the E-Legal Deposit Act, for example, each published version of a news article is collected. This is done in order to make it possible to retroactively reconstruct how a news article can be changed over time.

The e-legal deposit deliveries are highly standardised in terms of technical formats and metadata, in order to be able to adapt the deliveries archive standards like METS,[13] MODS[14] and PREMIS[15]. This is the case in order to enable long-term digital preservation, and to make material searchable. The National Library's collection of E-Legal Deposit Act material is therefore quite similar to its physical collection of legal deposits. The collection consists of well defined publications that have been collected, described and stored on the basis of a statutory framework, standardised processes and on the basis of accepted standards.

Thematic and event-based collections

According to the National Library's new formal agency instructions (SFS 2008:1421) from 2018, the National Library is required, in addition to collecting legal deposits, to collect, describe, preserve and provide other physical and digital material that is needed for the discharge of the authority's duties. The opening section of the instructions states that the National Library is required to promote the quality of Swedish research as well as democratic social development by providing source material and an effective research infrastructure. The new agency instructions allow, among other things, for the thematic and event-based collection of e-media that are not subject to the E-Legal Deposit Act. It goes without saying, however, that thematic and event-based collection must not violate other legislation, such as copyright and GDPR.[16]

However, because the agency instructions are new, the National Library still has little experience with thematic and event-based collection. At present, it collects a selection of Swedish newspaper websites using thematic collection. In 2018, it also carried out event-based collection of social media in connection with the Swedish election campaign, among other things.

The National Library believes that thematic and event-based collection will become increasingly important as a complement to the E-Legal Deposit Act and to web harvesting. Because technical tools for thematic and event-based collection – in comparison with the possibilities afforded by web harvesting – can be adapted for specific purposes, it is possible to capture and reproduce the original presentation of specific material in a more accurate way. Tools for thematic collection also make it possible to collect dynamic material such as web pages, interactive media such as online games, and social media.

Regulations define availability

Printed legal deposit collections are made available in the premises of the libraries and through interlibrary loans. However, legal deposit materials in the National Library are only available at the premises of the Library. E-Legal Deposit Act material is collected only by the National Library, and its provision is not yet regulated, but in summer of 2019 the National Library decided to open up the access in its premises. The government intends to revisit the issue, but at time of writing in 2019 this has not yet happened. Access to web content collected by means of web harvesting is limited to specific terminals at the National Library due to provisions related to personal data protection. A priority issue for the legal deposit libraries at the higher education institutions is to gain access to E-Legal Deposit Act material and to other digital collections at the National Library. At present, only the

National Library's digitised newspapers can be accessed via networks. This is done via subscription to a special contract license.[17] The National Library is also negotiating a possible licence agreement for the audiovisual content for remote access for research purposes.

The evolution of media and the current legal deposit legislation

The evolution of media

The evolution of media is spurred on by the digitisation of media and society as a whole. Old conceptual structures, created in a time of clearly delineated types of media and well defined players, are a poor fit in the digital domain. Traditional concepts such as that of the book, newspaper, television, radio and film gain new meanings on the web, where text, sound and images are combined in a way that is impossible in physical publishing (SOU 2016:80). Because technological developments have made it possible for more players to self-publish, the role of traditional publishers and other media companies has also changed. Part of this change includes increased interactivity between publisher and consumer. The web is made up of an interlinked, ever-changing structure of publications, comments and onward links. New forms of media lacking any equivalent in the world of physical publishing are also being developed on the web, for example social media. Here we identify problems linked to the evolution of media in relation to the design of the current legal deposit legislation, including media that falls outside the current legislation, difficulties in determining the requirement to deposit, and the limits of collecting (Konstenius, 2017, 8–13). In spite of the National Library's extensive and largely automated collection under the E-Legal Deposit Act, these issues mean there are still significant parts of electronically published material that are not being collected.

The current legal deposit legislation leads to the growth of collections that lack a clear remit: differing design of the various legal deposit acts creates a media-dependent and illogical collection mechanism entailing, among other things, that certain categories of material collected in physical form are exempt from collection in electronic form. For example, this is the case for material from political parties, associations, self-publishers and companies whose business is in a sector other than media. It is also the case for computer games, interactive educational programs and other multimedia that must only be submitted as legal deposits if they are published in physical form.

The current legislation also means that certain media formats do not need to be preserved: radio, television, and cinema-screened film are currently outside the remit of legal deposit legislation. At present, the broadcasters store their programming recordings as digital files and not on audiotapes and videotapes, as in the past. The reference recordings of radio and television that are to be submitted as legal deposit materials to the National Library are therefore no longer subject to the Legal Deposit Act for Documents.[18] In Sweden, virtually all cinemas are digital, meaning that the screenings are based on files and not physical documents. For this reason, digitally screened film is also not subject to the Legal Deposit Act for Documents. Like digitally screened film, traditional radio and television broadcasts do not satisfy the criteria for the E-Legal Deposit Act, as they do not fall under the legislation's definition of the term 'distance-transmitted material' (see p. 104). The National Library collects radio and television, but this is done on the basis of voluntary agreements at present. This is the case because as used in the Act (and as described above), a 'document' must always have an object as a counterpart.

It can be difficult to determine whether and when the obligation to deliver arises. The Legal Deposit Act for Documents covers physically published media. The Act is designed in the context of an analogue media landscape with well defined forms of media, clear players and a clear division of roles. Digitisation has led to changes in the conditions of production and distribution alike, which in turn has led to a situation where certain formulations in the Legal Deposit Act for Documents are difficult or impossible to apply to the media situation of today. The digitisation of printing technology has led to lower printing costs, which has led, among other things, to increased self-publishing, and to an increase in the number of small print runs. The average cost of producing a book is currently between €10 and €20 per title. For the purchaser, this involves an extra cost of €70–140 per title for the production of seven legal deposits (Fichtelius, Persson and Enarson, 2019, Appendix, 51). The printing houses also incur significant costs related to the packaging and distribution of the books to the seven libraries that currently receive legal deposits. Moreover, in many cases it is unreasonable that publishers should be required to submit seven legal deposits of publications that may then be weeded out by all of the legal deposit libraries except for the National Library and Lund University Library.

Finally, collecting under the E-Legal Deposit Act can be limited at several stages. The overriding problem when it comes to the E-Legal Deposit Act is that it only covers a limited part of the material that is published electronically. The E-Legal Deposit Act is based on an act of selection in which collection is limited at several stages. The legislation encompasses a limited number of publishers, and also only encompasses a limited part of their publishing activities. The E-Legal Deposit Act is also subsidiary in relation to earlier legislation, which limits collection to that which is substantively unique.

Nordic outlook

How does the Swedish provision for non-print legal deposit fare in comparison to that of Sweden's close neighbours? The legal deposit legislation in Norway, Denmark and Finland is quite similar to the Swedish legislation in terms of what is to be collected (Konstenius, 2017, 22–3). Their legal deposit acts cover both printed and audiovisual publications, as well as material that is distributed online. An element that is unique to the Swedish e-legal deposit legislation is that it is designed in the form of an obligation to deliver, i.e. a positive duty on the part of the publisher to be responsible for the delivery of electronic material to the National Library. The e-legal deposit legislation in the other Nordic countries is instead based on a right on the part of their national libraries to collect and requisition material published online. The national libraries have the legal right to collect online publications that are openly published, and have the right to requisition any codes, passwords, etc. that may be needed to access material that cannot otherwise be reached. Examples include material that can only be reached via a subscription or by registered users. Because the web harvesting of the Swedish web domain is not included as part of the E-Legal Deposit Act, the National Library does not have this opportunity.

In Sweden, electronic material that content-wise corresponds to material published in physical form is exempt from the E-Legal Deposit Act. The legal deposit legislation in the other Nordic countries does not incorporate such a restriction. In Norway, the obligation also extends to the digital originals on which printed legal deposits are based, in the form of print files. The reason for this is that the National Library of Norway is required to offer digital access to legal deposits at all university and college libraries in Norway. The legal deposit legislation in Norway, unlike its Swedish counterpart, also extends to Norwegian publications that are published on foreign social media platforms.

Discussion

In the Swedish context, it is clear that there is a need for revised legal deposit legislation and its corresponding regulations. In modern times, the collection of legal deposit copies in Sweden has been characterised by a broad purpose that addresses the interests of both the research community and society as a whole. This includes the citizen's right to information and knowledge, which is a prerequisite for a functioning democracy. The purpose is also consistent with the Swedish Library Act's opening section, stating that the public library system shall promote the development of democratic society by contributing to the dissemination of knowledge and free opinion formation (SFS 2013:801).

However, in the letter of regulation for 2017, The National Library was commissioned to carry out a study on the design and relevance of the legal deposit legislation in relation to the evolution of the media landscape. The National Library's study shows that the current legal deposit legislation has major shortcomings and therefore needs to be revised. In connection with such an overhaul, it is necessary to bring together the two Acts currently in effect and harmonise them into a single Act, with regulation on legal deposits governing the provision of the same. In this section we detail various recommendations, including: expanding digital harvesting to encompass social media; updating the legislation to cover radio, television and cinema broadcasts; expanding legal deposit beyond physical publications; allowing remote access to e-legal deposit and audiovisual materials; and addressing the different weeding-out policies of the legal deposit libraries to maintain consistency in the national legal deposit collection.

As noted in the National Library's study, it is also a particularly serious matter that many electronic publications currently fall outside the scope of the legal deposit legislation in whole or in part, in spite of the passage of the E-Legal Deposit Act. For example, this is the case for social media, games that are distributed online and other interactive publications. In order to be able to collect these media and make them available, the National Library needs a legal basis to engage in supplementary digital collections. Nor is there at present any clear regulation of the conditions for the provision of E-Legal Deposit Act material. It is therefore very important for the legal prerequisites for expanded digital harvesting, and for the appropriate provision of the E-Legal Deposit Act material, to be determined as soon as possible.

In particular, the National Library needs legal support and resources for supplementary harvesting of social media. One example that illustrates the importance of revising the legal deposit legislation is the high-profile #metoo movement. Several of the central arenas in which that debate was held are not subject to the legal deposit legislation currently in effect. The fact that these types of phenomena are not collected creates gaps in the National Library's collections that are difficult to repair, and thus limits the right of researchers and the citizenry to information and knowledge. As part of the effort to counteract information loss following from the current legal deposit legislation, in connection with the 2018 election campaign the National Library carried out a supplementary collection project focusing on the political debate conducted in social media. The project showed that there are techniques for capturing this type of media, but it was also clear that the National Library lacks the technical platform and the other resources needed to establish that kind of expanded supplementary collection capacity. In order for the National Library to be able to perform this type of supplementary collection on a large scale and on a long-term basis in the future, we therefore require changes to the legal deposit legislation or another adjustment enabling such efforts. Increased resources are also needed in order to upgrade the National Library's technical platform. In practice, the National Library needs to be given the resources and the legal prerequisites required to combine the collection of E-Legal Deposit Act material with web harvesting and thematic collection. The National Library believes that thematic collection will become increasingly important as a complement to the E-Legal Deposit Act and to web harvesting.

The National Library's study also shows that the existing legal deposit legislation needs to be updated with regard to traditional radio and television broadcasts, and for digitally screened movies. As a result of digitisation, these media have fallen outside the scope of the legal deposit legislation. The collection of radio and television broadcasts currently only takes place under the auspices of voluntary agreements, an arrangement that is subject to vulnerabilities and that risks leading to deliveries not being received. It is particularly serious that legal deposit deliveries of cinema-screened film have ceased completely as a result of the digitisation of the cinemas. This creates a growing gap in the National Library's film collection. In addition to television programming, subtitles and teletext also need to be included in legal deposit deliveries of television material. As a support for people with hearing impairment, subtitles are currently available for nearly everything broadcast on Swedish television. This information is to be regarded as published. In addition to being used to document this publication form, it could also constitute a qualified access point for collected television programming. Teletext must also be made subject to the obligation to deliver, as it constitutes published news that is not collected in any other way.

A major shortcoming in the current design of the E-Legal Deposit Act is that it is subsidiary in relation to the legal deposit legislation relating to physical publications, which is a missed opportunity for using deliveries of digital originals to form the basis of a national digital library. What this means in practice is that if an electronic publication is published with essentially the same content as a physical document, only the physical document must be submitted as a legal deposit. This design does not take advantage of the possibilities of expanded provision afforded by the digital format. This therefore presents an obstacle on the way to being able to offer society equivalent access to legal deposit materials throughout the country. The subsidiarity principle also ultimately imposes significant costs on the National Library, and thus also on society as a whole. One clear example of this is that the National Library currently engages in ongoing digitisation of legal deposit deliveries of physical newspapers. The digitisation of the physical newspapers is performed as a conservation measure, but also in order to be able, by means of a separate contractual licence, to offer the newspaper content outside the National Library's facilities. The annual cost for the digitisation of daily newspapers currently runs to approximately €600,000. If the digital print file on which the physical edition is based were instead to be delivered as a legal deposit in parallel with the newspapers, over time this could result in significant savings for society. In order for the National Library to be able to abandon this type of digitisation, while at the same time laying the foundation for a national digital library, the legal deposit legislation needs to be extended to digital versions of books, newspapers, music, video and other media as well. The digital versions could either be digital originals of the printed version, or digital versions published in parallel with the analogue edition. Legal deposit legislation extending to digital originals is already in place in Norway.

In addition to these suggestions, there is a need for wider national access to the E-legal Deposit Act and audiovisual legal deposit materials, to encourage use and uptake across Sweden. An underlying concern behind the current system is to lay the groundwork for the regional dissemination of the legal deposit materials. Sweden currently has seven legal deposit libraries. However, only printed material – with the exception of newspapers – is collected by all of the legal deposit libraries. Newspapers are submitted to the National Library and to Lund University Library. Legal deposit versions of electronic publications (E-Legal Deposit Act material), and of audiovisual material, are submitted only to the National Library. The electronic and audiovisual legal deposit material is only made available at the National Library's facilities. This is the case for copyright reasons and/or due to legal restrictions based on the EU General Data Protection Regulation (GDPR). The regional dissemination of this material has thus not come to pass. In order for the entire country to be able to access legal deposits of electronic publications and audiovisual material, the legal obstacles that stand in the way of making these collections available need to be eliminated.

There are also concerns that the weeding of legal deposit materials may erode confidence in today's legal deposit legislation. At present, only the National Library and Lund University Library have been mandated to preserve legal deposit materials, whereas other legal deposit libraries have the ability to weed their collections. Stockholm University Library weeds out nearly all the material that is submitted under the legal deposit requirement, and has also stated that it wishes to be exempted from the legal deposit mandate (Konstenius, 2017, 37). The weeding out performed at the university libraries at Uppsala, Linköping, Gothenburg and Umeå is generally of a lesser extent, yet is quite extensive within certain categories. The digitisation of print production has made it considerably more affordable to produce small print runs, which in turn has led to an increase in self-publishing. Requiring publishers to submit seven legal deposits even for very small print runs in the knowledge that they may be weeded out immediately upon receipt risks undermining confidence in the current legal deposit legislation in the long term. For these reasons, it is an apposite moment to deal with the issues related to legal deposit deliveries and the number of legal deposit libraries, the weeding of items and the need for a national depository library, as well as interlibrary loans.

Conclusion

Swedish legal deposit legislation needs to be revised, as it is out of step with the digital turn in the media and of society as a whole. For example, there is currently no legal basis for the collection of interactive publications on the internet or of the public debate taking place on blogs and in social media. The digitisation of radio, television and cinema-screened film has also led to a situation where these media are no longer subject to legal deposit legislation. The National Library of Sweden has had the opportunity to collect some types of this media in accordance with the intention of the law, but in other cases this has not been possible. For example, radio and television material is collected on the basis of voluntary agreements, but we have not been able to collect films that are cinema-screened digitally. The overall consequence of the shortcomings in the present legal deposit legislation is that important parts of Sweden's cultural heritage are at risk of being lost for purposes of future research and study.

Under the present-day legal framework, legal deposit material is only accessible at the National Library's facilities in Stockholm. For example, this is the case for both web-harvested material and for audiovisual legal deposits. In order to achieve the purposes of the legal deposit legislation, it is important for society to offer equivalent access to the legal deposits, thus contributing to equal conditions for the pursuit of academic studies, research and higher education throughout the country. What is needed in practice is to exploit the potential of digital technology in a better way than we do today, and to bring together and update the provisions governing how the legal deposits can be made available. The legal deposit library system also needs to be reviewed in the context of an overhaul of the legal deposit legislation. At issue are questions related to legal deposit deliveries and the number of legal deposit libraries, the weeding out of items, and the need for a national depository library, as well as interlibrary loan issues. Unless the legal deposit library system is redesigned and adapted to the digitalisation of media and society as a whole, there is a risk that the legitimacy of the current legal deposit legislation will be eroded.

This chapter has set out the development and implementation of Sweden's e-legal deposit framework, pointing to various areas where the current legislation and practice are not ensuring the preservation of Sweden's digital publications for posterity. There are consequences if the recommendations set out in the review, and in this chapter, are ignored: the relevance of the National Library and of the other legal deposit libraries to the research community and academic studies is determined by the quality of the material that the library is able to offer its users. The gulf between the rapid developments in the media landscape and legal deposit legislation that has lagged behind these developments is now causing gaps to arise that may be difficult to remedy. Already outdated legal deposit legislation that is not updated to accord with changes in the media landscape will eventually create collections that represent the past, rather than the present and the future. There is a risk that such a statutory lag in the ability for the legal deposit libraries to fulfil their mission will result in serious consequences, not least for the research community, and thus also for Sweden as a leading research nation. On the other hand, legal deposit legislation that is modernised, coherent and as media-independent as possible will create good opportunities for the Swedish research community to remain at the forefront of research practice in the future.

Notes

1. www.kb.se/kb-in-english.html.
2. https://en.wikipedia.org/wiki/Swedish_National_Archive_of_Recorded_Sound_and_Moving_Images.
3. www.ub.lu.se.
4. www.su.se/biblioteket.
5. www.ub.uu.se.
6. https://liu.se/biblioteket.
7. www.ub.gu.se/sv.
8. www.ub.umu.se/.
9. Stockholm University Library views the current legal deposit delivery system as out-of-date. It is perceived as being sluggish and costly to administer, as being a poor source of acquisition for the university libraries, and as being expensive for the publishers. Stockholm University Library also weeds out nearly all legal deposit material. Instead, their acquisition is based primarily on demand, which is considered to be more cost-effective. Stockholm University Library therefore wishes to be exempted from the legal deposit mandate (Konstenius, 2017, 37).
10. The legal deposit legislation defines a 'film' as a document consisting of images that are intended to be projected in rapid succession (SFS 1993:1392).

11. Web harvesting is an automated process used to collect content and metadata that is available without access restriction on the open web.
12. Fundamental law on freedom of expression (one part of Sweden's constitution, enacted in 1991); (abbreviated YGL).
13. The Metadata Encoding and Transmission Standard (METS) schema is a standard for encoding descriptive, administrative, and structural metadata regarding objects within a digital library. The standard is maintained in the Network Development and MARC Standards Office of the Library of Congress.
14. Metadata Object Description Schema (MODS) is a schema for a bibliographic element set that may be used for a variety of purposes, and particularly for library applications. The standard is maintained by the Network Development and MARC Standards Office of the Library of Congress.
15. The PREMIS Data Dictionary for Preservation Metadata is the international standard for metadata to support the preservation of digital objects and ensure their long-term usability.
16. GDPR (The General Data Protection Regulation) applies throughout the EU and aims to create a uniform and equivalent level of protection for personal data so as not to hinder the free flow of data within Europe.
17. The contract licence gives the National Library the opportunity to make digitised newspapers available at public libraries, universities and colleges, and at the Swedish National Archives.
18. The Legal Deposit Act for Documents always refers to physical objects.

References

Fichtelius, E., Persson, C. and Enarson, E. (2019) *Demokratins Skattkammare: Förslag till en Nationell Biblioteksstrategi,* Appendix, 'Sex strategiska reformer för stärkta bibliotek', Kungliga biblioteket.

Larsson, B. (2011) Från Censurinstrument till Stöd för Forskningen och den Svenska Kulturens Bevarande, *Biblis*, **55**, 29–44.

Konstenius, G. (2017) *Plikten under Lupp! En Studie av Pliktlagstiftningens Roll, Utformning och Relevans i Förhållande till Medielandskapets Utveckling*, Kungliga biblioteket.

Svensson, I. (2018) *Kungliga Biblioteket i Ord och Bild,* Kungliga biblioteket.

Government bills and official reports of the Swedish government

Prop. 1995/96:71. Ändringar i pliktexemplarslagen. Utbildningsdepartementet

Prop. 2011/12:121. Leveransplikt för elektroniskt material. Utbildningsdepartementet

SOU 1992:92. Pliktleverans: Utbildningsdepartementet

SOU 2016:80. En gränsöverskridande mediepolitik – För upplysning, engagemang och ansvar: Kulturdepartementet

Öman, S. (2009) *Leveransplikt för Elektroniska Dokument*, Utbildningsdepartementet (Ds 2009:61)

Legislation

SFS 1993:1392. Lag om pliktexemplar av dokument: Utbildningsdepartementet

SFS 1994:728. Instruktion för Granskningsnämnden för radio och TV: Kulturdepartementet

SFS 1994:728. Instruktion för Granskningsnämnden för radio och TV: Kulturdepartementet

SFS 2008:1421. Förordning med instruktion för Kungl. Biblioteket. Utbildningsdepartementet

SFS 2012:492. Lag om pliktexemplar av elektroniskt material: Utbildningsdepartementet

SFS 2013:801. Bibliotekslag: Kulturdepartementet

PART 2

Users and contexts

CHAPTER 6

Publishers, legal deposit and the changing publishing environment

Adrienne Muir

Introduction

UK publishers have always had mixed attitudes to legal deposit. This chapter focuses on electronic legal deposit in the UK from the perspective of publishers, providing some assessment of what the impact on publishers has been in the relatively short time electronic legal deposit has been in existence, and the role of legal deposit in a dynamic digital environment.

The long opposition to legal deposit requirements from the publishing industry is well documented. Feather's historical account (Feather, 1994, 97–121) brings into sharp focus the often vehement opposition of the publishing trade to the principle of legal deposit, and the trade's history of reluctant or non-compliance with the law. At the beginning of the 19th century, the amount of material being deposited was unsatisfactory for the deposit libraries. Anthony Panizzi, the principal librarian of the British Museum, through his energetic enforcement of legislation, established what may be regarded as 'proper' legal deposit in the UK (Altick 1957, 215; Harris, 1991) with more comprehensive compliance with the law.

The mid-20th century saw the advent of electronic publishing. This was initially limited to textual and numeric data, but increasingly it has incorporated recorded sound and still and moving images. The development of the world wide web and browser software in the 1990s and other developments has profoundly affected publishing practices (Brown and Boulderstone 2008; Deegan and Sutherland, 2009; Martin and Tian, 2010; Ramrattan and Szenberg, 2016). It became clear that restricting legal deposit to print publications would result in an increasingly large gap in the national legal deposit archive. The British Library (BL) commissioned several studies on potential issues arising from the extension of legal deposit to non-print publications (Electronic Publishing Services Ltd, 1996; Hendley ,1996; Martin, 1996). The BL, supported by the other legal deposit libraries and the British Film Institute, then submitted a proposal to the UK government to extend legal deposit to non-print publications (British Library, 1996).

Publishing is an important contributor to the UK economy. The Publishers Association (2019) reported that book and academic journal publishing income was £6 billion in 2018 and that there was 'a 3% increase in digital sales income (to £2.6bn) and a 5% drop in physical sales (to £3.4bn)'. The publishers' report to the five-year post-implementation review of deposit of non-print publications states that the publishing industry creates £7.8 billion gross value added (GVA), supports more than 70,000 jobs and that 57% of total publishing turnover (£29 billion) comes from exports. The industry has an annual trade surplus of £1.1 billion (Joint Committee on Legal Deposit, 2018, 57). The publishing voice is, therefore, a strong one, and tensions between increased digital outputs and electronic deposit requirements have emerged, with the proposed extension of the scope of the law reviving publisher concerns about legal deposit. For example, Whitaker (2001a) described legal deposit as a tax on knowledge and questioned why the industry is penalised in this way. In a later article, Whitaker (2001b) accepted that an archive of published output is a national good, but he did not agree that publishers should be providing the books for free, and repeated that legal deposit is an anomalous tax in kind on the publishing industry. However, the financial burden is not borne solely by the publishers; the State funds the accessioning, cataloguing, storage and preservation of publications by legal deposit libraries and the creation of national bibliographies. Dellar (2001) also pointed out that deposit obligations are factored into business planning, as review copies are.

However, despite the concerns voiced by the publishing industry, the UK government acknowledged the need to expand the scope of legal deposit and new legislation was proposed. UK legal deposit libraries and publishers collaboratively undertook preparatory work leading to the new legislation and publisher concerns were taken into account throughout the process. This was a long process, involving negotiation between the interested parties, as well as exploration of how deposit of electronic publications could work in practice. This chapter provides an overview of the relationship of e-legal deposit frameworks to the publishing industry, including preparation for legislation and the history of negotiations, the working approach taken to electronic legal deposit, the impact upon publishers, and the place of electronic legal deposit in a developing publishing landscape, which includes the intersection of open access, open science, commercial publishing, and user expectations.

Preparing for legislation

In January 1998, the UK Government announced the establishment of a working party (Working Party on Legal Deposit, 1998, s. 1.8), including the legal deposit libraries and publishers Reuters, Thomson Science[1] and Chadwyck-Healy. Its remit was to:

- advise on how to achieve a comprehensive national archive of non-print material, taking into account the concerns of publishers and exploring the potential for the use of secure networking for access
- draw up and agree a voluntary code of practice for digital and microform material, to be used until government introduced legislation
- ensure compatibility between the provisions of this code of practice and existing voluntary arrangements for film and sound material.

The main UK trade associations, the Publishers Association (PA), the Association of Learned and Professional Society Publishers (ALPSP) and the Periodical Publishers Association (now known as the Professional Publishers Association), endorsed the voluntary code of practice developed by the Working Party on Legal Deposit (1999).[2] These associations between them represented commercial and non-profit and independent consumer, educational, scholarly and media magazine publishers. The voluntary code came into effect on 4 January 2000. Publisher representatives and the legal deposit libraries continued to work together in a Joint Committee on Voluntary Deposit set up to monitor the voluntary deposit scheme and work on issues arising in its operation.

The Legal Deposit Libraries Act 2003 was enabling legislation for the subsequent extension of legal deposit from print to other forms of publication through secondary legislation. A range of concerns about the potential impact of extending the scope of legal deposit was raised during the draft legislation's passage through Parliament (Muir, 2005, 32–42). The Act (s. 11) stated that secondary legislation made to extend the scope of legal deposit to non-print publications should not introduce a disproportionate interference with the economic interest of publishers. The BL press release announcing the new primary legislation indicated that the publishers were reassured by the government's responses to their concerns during the passage of the legislation through Parliament (British Library, 2003).

A Joint Committee on Legal Deposit (JCLD) superseded the Joint Committee on Voluntary Deposit. The membership now also included publisher associations reflecting the wider publishing industry: the International Association of Scientific, Technical & Medical Publishers; the Newspaper Publishers Association and the Newspaper Society[3] (two organisations now merged into News Media Association), and the Association of Online Publishers (British Library, 2019a). The Association of Online Publishers (2019) represents publishers across the press, broadcasting and 'pure online media'. The JCLD discusses all aspects of legal deposit, but a major role at the beginning of its existence was to advise the government's Advisory Panel for 'ongoing legislation on legal deposit' (Fell, 2004).

The Legal Deposit Advisory Panel

The Legal Deposit Advisory Panel (LDAP) began its work in 2005 and submitted its final recommendation for secondary legislation in 2010. LDAP comprised 15 members: legal deposit library representatives; publisher representatives and five independent members.[4] LDAP had to identify, understand and work through some complex issues and this process was not without its challenges. Progress was reported through annual reports (Legal Deposit Advisory Panel, 2006; 2007; 2008). Challenges arose because the print publishing paradigm did not transfer well to a rapidly changing digital environment. Difficulties included what 'published in the United Kingdom' means in an online networked environment (Green, 2012, 107). The fluid nature of digital publishing also made it difficult to consider traditional publication categories in isolation from each other (p. 107).

One of LDAP's core tasks in its first year was to address the 'territoriality' issue. This was done in consultation with other parties, including the JCLD and the Federation of European Publishers/Conference of European National Libraries Committee (FEP/CENL).[5] LDAP also commissioned a report on the 'universe' of digital publications eligible for legal deposit (Powell, 2006). This report proposed a typology which split publications into two categories: granular and enquiry-driven. These categories acknowledged that digital publications may consist of several discrete components or may be constructed through interrogation of databases (Powell, 2006, 7–8). Further considerations included whether publications are made available offline or online and whether they are made freely available or protected in some way. This approach facilitated progress by highlighting issues including commercial concerns, how different types of content could be acquired and what additional material, such as software or manuals, would need to be deposited along with content.

LDAP's work initially focused on offline publications, such as microforms and optical discs, freely available (web) publications, and electronic journals. The existing voluntary scheme for offline non-print publications was simplified to ease the burden on participating publishers (Legal Deposit Advisory Panel, 2006). The aim was to invigorate participation and to gather evidence to inform whether deposit of offline material should continue to be on a voluntary or statutory basis. LDAP also initiated a voluntary deposit scheme for electronic journals, building on the existing JCLD pilot scheme (Legal Deposit Advisory Panel, 2008). LDAP developed a definition for electronic journals and commissioned a scoping study to identify the number and nature of UK electronic journal publications (Legal Deposit Advisory Panel, 2008). Work on archiving the public web included developing cost models for the legal deposit libraries, as they would be required to 'pull' web publications rather than have publishers deposit them (Legal Deposit Advisory Panel, 2007). LDAP also considered the implications for publishers of web archiving.

LDAP initially recommended that deposit of offline publications should be on a self-regulated voluntary basis with libraries requesting deposits (Department for Culture, Media and Sport, 2009, 8). Given that this category of publications was considered to be in decline, it was felt that it was unnecessary to introduce statutory deposit (Gibby and Green, 2008, 61). The government reserved the right to regulate at a later stage if the scheme was not achieving comprehensiveness. The government consulted on LDAP's recommendation that harvesting and archiving of freely available online material should be regulated to ensure a more comprehensive national archive. A UK Web Archiving Consortium (UKWAC) pilot had shown that a voluntary scheme involving proactive harvesting by libraries would be hampered by copyright clearance issues (Department for Culture, Media and Sport, 2009, 10). Regulation was supported as the least onerous option by responses to an LDAP survey of both commercial and non-commercial publishers that had participated in the UKWAC harvesting pilot (p. 15). LDAP's work on electronic journals was expanded to examine technical, commercial and other issues of deposit for protected online publications more generally (Legal Deposit Advisory Panel, 2008). LDAP delivered its recommendation to government for deposit of this category of publications in March 2010 (Department for Culture, Media and Sport, 2010a, 4) and was wound up in July 2010.

The legislative process

The government then drafted and consulted on proposed regulations (Department for Culture, Media and Sport, 2010a). The draft Legal Deposit Libraries (Non-print Publications) Regulations 2011 stated that where a publication was available in print and non-print versions, the print publication should be deposited. Where non-print publications were available in more than one medium, the libraries and publishers should agree on the medium to be deposited. If this could not be agreed, it was up to the publisher to decide. The draft Regulations included offline publications. The accompanying impact assessment (Department for Culture, Media and Sport, 2010b) stated that the reason for this was to protect both publishers and libraries from legal liabilities, including breach of contract, copyright infringement and defamation actions that might arise from legal deposit activities. The provisions for online publications (ss. 14, 17, 20) referred to 'delivery' of material, suggesting publishers should deposit material made freely available on the web, although this was not clear, as requests for deposit could be made by a web harvester (ss. 16 & 19). The Regulations set out a range of activities that could be performed on deposited publications by legal deposit libraries. These proposals included provisions to ease the economic impact on publishers. For example, only one person at a time in each deposit library could view a publication (s. 23) and publishers could request embargoes of up to three years on access to deposited publications (s. 25).[6]

During 2011, the government revised the draft Regulations in response to the results of its 2010 consultation (Department for Culture, Media and Sport, 2010a). It seemed that not enough evidence had been provided to show that the Regulations would not impose a disproportionate cost burden on publishers (Department for Culture, Media and Sport, 2011). Publishers had concerns over various issues, including technological implications, security, the need for multiple deposits and access and use of deposited publications (Department for Culture, Media and Sport, 2011). The new draft Legal Deposit Libraries (Non-Print Works) Regulations 2013 (Department for Culture, Media and Sport, 2012a) addressed some, if not all, of the concerns raised by publishers. A key revision was to remove any obligations on publishers to deliver online publications directly to legal deposit libraries. Publishers would, however, have to provide libraries with the ability to harvest protected publications, for example by providing login information. The revised Regulations provided exemptions from depositing offline publications or providing login details for micro businesses (10 employees or fewer) to relieve a disproportionate cost burden on them (Legal Deposit Libraries (Non-Print Works) Regulations 2013, ss. 19–20). However, these provisions would expire in March 2014 (Department for Culture, Media and Sport, 2012a, 8). The draft Regulations introduced flexibility for deposit of protected online publications by agreement between the publishers and libraries. They included provision for secure upload of protected publications by publishers on a voluntary basis and to revert back to the default of library harvesting if desired (p. 14). The consultation document on the revised Regulations included guidance to publishers on how the law would apply to them and to address concerns on security.

The government noted that there was general support for legal deposit in the response to its consultation (Department for Culture, Media and Sport, 2012b, 2). However, it also highlighted remaining concerns of libraries and publishers and proposed the introduction of some further minor revisions and guidance to address the concerns that it accepted (p. 2). The government proposed to explicitly exclude audiovisual material in the Regulations (p. 3). It also indicated that other concerns should be dealt with mainly through the development of policies and procedures and through JCLD deliberations (p. 33). The legal deposit libraries would develop a co-ordinated collections policy to address concerns over the potential impact of multiple web harvester requests (p. 3). The libraries would also have to provide a longer notice period for publishers to respond to requests for login details or to provide content via another delivery method (p. 4). The Regulations would make it clear that the libraries could only use legal deposit material for non-commercial purposes (p. 5). The government deferred taking any action in response to libraries' and researchers' concerns (Department for Culture, Media and Sport, 2013) that access restrictions would apply to material even after it is out of copyright on the basis that this is not an immediate problem (Department for Culture, Media and Sport, 2012b, 8). The final version of the regulations came into force on 6 April 2013 (The Legal Deposit Libraries (Non-Print Works) Regulations 2013, S.I. 2013/777).

Developing a workable approach to electronic deposit

The guidance given to publishers on the libraries' web sites (for example British Library, 2019a) indicates that electronic legal deposit will be gradual, transitioning from print to digital publications over time. The guidance also describes the dispute resolution process that has been put in place in case of disagreements between libraries and publishers (British Library, 2019b).

The legal deposit libraries developed an initial collecting plan for 2013–14 (Agency for the Legal Deposit Libraries, 2019a), and then another for 2015–20 (Legal Deposit Librarians Committee, 2015). The initial plan acknowledged that offline publications were already collected under the voluntary deposit scheme and that the legislation meant no significant change to the collection of these publication categories (Agency for the Legal Deposit Libraries, 2019b). It also set out how and when web crawls are carried out and several alternative approaches to deposit of electronic journals. This included the BL working with third-party service providers, such as Portico[7] for journals and Ingram[8] for e-books. Ingram offers e-book distribution services to publishers and supply services to libraries. Portico provides preservation services for both publishers and libraries. Publishers deposit their content with Portico, which acts as a dark archive until a trigger event, such as the closure of a publisher, occurs and the triggered publications are made accessible. This arrangement means that publishers depositing their journals can authorise Portico to supply publications in preservation formats with associated metadata.

For publishers of journals in other formats, the plan was for the BL, National Library of Scotland (NLS) and National Library of Wales (NLW) to approach publishers to arrange deposit, either through acquiring login details or through publishers using a secure deposit portal set up by the libraries (British Library, 2019a). In the 2013–14 period, the priority for e-books was to collect publications in the ePub format, with other formats being accepted (Agency for the Legal Deposit Libraries, 2019a). For news and magazines published online, the plan was for a higher frequency of crawls to ensure that frequently updated content is collected and also to explore other means of collecting content with publishers. Other types of publication likely to present more challenges were a lower collection priority but with the possibility of proceeding on an experimental basis with publishers.

The 2015–20 framework is a more detailed collection development plan, acknowledging the size and complexity of the task and the resource constraints. The top priority is publications that only exist in digital form at risk of outright loss (Legal Deposit Librarians Committee, 2015, 1). An interesting point at the end of this document is that voluntary deposit of sound recordings is decreasing and that there may be renewed efforts to extend legal deposit to digital sound recordings (p. 5). A similar point is made about exploring with stakeholders whether 'non-traditional' publications such as apps and games could be collected in a selective way and preserved, although not necessarily by legal deposit libraries (p. 5).

Publishers' concerns over security (Department for Culture, Media and Sport, 2011) have been addressed through a joint security undertaking by the legal deposit libraries (Gibby, 2013). This document provides details of the technical and security arrangements for the legal deposit library technical infrastructure. It also explains how the libraries will ensure that access and use of legal deposit copies will comply with the provisions of the Regulations.

While implementation of digital deposit is developing gradually, progress has been made in developing policy, procedures and the infrastructure required. The legislation has now been in force for five years and so it is worth examining how the system is working in practice and what the impact of digital deposit has been on publishers so far.

The impact of electronic legal deposit on publishers

The impact of electronic legal deposit on publishers has been addressed in a post-implementation review of legal deposit of non-print publications submitted by the JCLD to the UK government in 2018. The review drew on data gathered from both the legal deposit libraries and publishers depositing non-print publications (Joint Committee on Legal Deposit, 2018, 17). One aim was to evaluate how successfully the Regulations have met the policy objectives they were meant to address. The review report points out that the implementation is taking place in stages and therefore the conclusions are based on progress so far. There is agreement between libraries and participating publishers that the implementation of the Regulations has been successful in terms of collection and preservation of non-print publications (p. 44). Fifty-eight per cent of deposits are now in digital form and the infrastructure in place has increased the efficiency of the deposit process (p. 9). There have been some issues: for example, libraries are still collecting printed newspapers, as it has not hitherto been possible under the law to collect digital facsimiles and news web sites do not fully replicate the print publications (p. 23). The review recommends that the collection of digital facsimiles should be pursued. The conclusion on effective preservation is supported by an external validation by the Digital Preservation Coalition (p. 26).

The paucity of data makes it difficult to compare actual set-up costs for the publishers, with between £1.9 and £4 million projected for the first ten years of electronic legal deposit (Department for Culture, Media and Sport, 2012a, 14). A questionnaire survey sent to just over 500 traditional publishers resulted in a response rate of 25% (Joint Committee on Legal Deposit, 2018, 28), so the results may not be representative. The majority of respondents reported no set up costs and the review report assumes that any costs were modest enough to be absorbed into general business costs (p. 28). Seven of the ten respondents that did provide figures for set-up costs were micro-companies which reported costs between less than £49 and £1000 (p. 28). These respondents did not indicate whether they felt that these costs were onerous. There were no set-up costs for web publishers, as the libraries harvest web publications (p. 29). If the review's estimate that the overall set-up costs for publishers will be between £30,000 and £2 million in the first 10 years of legal deposit are correct (p. 29), this will be significantly lower than the original projected figures and a tiny fraction of the profits generated by the publishing industry. The report states that none of the potential administrative costs identified by publishers, such as the provision of logins, effect of harvesting on performance, or the need to present access to personal or confidential data, have materialised (p. 29).

The publisher questionnaire did not directly ask publishers to quantify the costs of depositing publications (p. 59). Therefore, it is not possible at this stage to confirm quantitatively whether projected cost savings of electronic deposit have been realised (Department for Culture, Media and Sport, 2012a, 14). The review does address potential benefits to publishers from the transition from print to electronic deposit. Sixty-two percent of questionnaire respondents indicated that they had made cost savings. Twenty-nine percent of respondents were not able to say whether they had realised any cost savings (Joint Committee on Legal Deposit, 2018, 34). The remaining 9% of respondents were either still depositing some or all of their publication in print form or were digital-only publishers (p. 34). Cost benefits were achieved by both large and smaller publishers. Large publishers reported annual savings in excess of the initial start-up costs (p. 34). These savings included staff time, printing, shipping and administrative costs.

Publishers have expressed willingness to engage with deposit of a wider range of materials (p. 60). Collection of more complex digital materials is likely to present challenges because of the technological complexities involved and the need to keep up with a high rate of innovation (p. 40). As noted in the legal deposit libraries' joint collecting framework, these challenges will need exploration (Legal Deposit Libraries Committee, 2015) and adequate funding to support this (Joint Committee on Legal Deposit, 2018, 40).

The post-implementation review paints a reasonably positive picture of a preference for electronic deposit and some indication of efficiency and cost savings. In contrast with the period during which new legislation was introduced, there is a lack of public discussion on how publishers feel about the impact of electronic legal deposit in the trade press or by trade associations. The publishers' report to the review, however, does temper the success of the implementation to an extent. It notes the limited nature of the data available regarding the impact of electronic legal deposit (p. 59). A more realistic assessment will only emerge over time as the legal deposit libraries extend the scope of electronic deposit to a wider range of publications.

There have been no complaints from publishers depositing electronic publications, so it is assumed that the costs have not been prohibitive so far (p. 59). The dispute resolution procedure has not been used (p. 19). The systems in place to enforce the statutory access restrictions to legal deposit material are reported to be working well (p. 33). The independent arbitrator appointed to the JCLD has stated that her role has been conciliator within the JCLD rather than between legal deposit libraries and depositing publishers (Appendix B).

Despite all this, there remain significant differences in perspectives on the matters of access and use between libraries and publishers. The publishers' submission to the review states that 'the use of materials for purposes other than preservation is seen by the Publishers as falling outside the scope of the legal deposit legislation' as the purpose of legal deposit is 'not to provide an alternative route of general non-prescribed access for users or a commercial opportunity for the libraries' (p. 58). Publishers believe that legal deposit provides an archive of last resort when publications are no longer available by other means (pp. 61, 67).

The publishers' report does not make it clear why publishers are concerned about libraries commercially exploiting legal deposit, but the potential for libraries to act as competitors by providing access to publications has also been raised about interlibrary loans (Electronic Publishing Services, 2002, 42). The libraries' report to the post-implementation review refers to the possibility of libraries commercially exploiting material in their collections when copyright expires (Joint Committee on Legal Deposit, 2018, 53). While anyone would be able to do the same with any out-of-copyright publication, the libraries will have large collections easily to hand.

There was some discussion on access restrictions before the new Regulations were implemented. Green (2012, 10) pointed out that the concerns raised about legal deposit of non-print publications reflect the interests of commercial publishers. Gibby and Brazier (2012, 367, 373) note that the aim of access restrictions for material harvested from the open web was to protect advertising income. The publishers' report to the post-implementation review reiterates the point made by Gibby and Brazier (Joint Committee on Legal Deposit, 2018, 61). There are signs that non-commercial online publishers will have a voice in ongoing library and publisher co-operation on legal deposit. The BL's web page for the JCLD suggests that there is an intention to expand its membership or at least consult with non-traditional publishers, such as bloggers, as well as trade bodies and 'official' publishers (British Library, 2019b).

Publishers believe that questions of access should be subject to consultation separately from the post-implementation review process (Joint Committee on Legal Deposit, 2018, 59). This suggestion is consistent with the view articulated throughout the publishers' report to the post-implementation review that preservation and access should be considered separately, and that the purpose of legal deposit collections is preservation and not an alternative access route to currently available material (p. 58).

The place of electronic legal deposit in a developing publishing landscape

In their report to the post-implementation review, the publishers challenge the legal deposit library proposals on access and use of openly available online publications (Joint Committee on Legal Deposit, 2018, 60–8). The library concerns reflect changes in scholarly communication, the publishing environment, how researchers carry out research, and user expectations. The publishers do not accept that such expectations 'should necessarily be the driver for use of another party's digital content' (p. 58).

The publishers' concerns over access extend to material harvested from the open web (pp. 74–5), but analysis of the content of social media sites and of multimedia sources, such as YouTube, is increasingly important in research. The recent scandal that associated political use of data harvested from social media sites such as Facebook (Cadwalladr and Graham-Harrison, 2018) highlights what a rich source of information these sites provide for research as well as the legal and ethical issues this practice raises. The publishers object to the legal deposit libraries' proposal to make the legal deposit open web archive available online (Joint Committee on Legal Deposit, 2018, 74–5). Despite its limited geographical scope, the UK Web Archive could be a useful research resource, particularly over the long term as online content disappears from the open web.

While much content available on the open web is subject to copyright and monetised, the open access movement is changing how publications are being made available (Davis and Walters, 2011; Laakso and Björk 2012; Solomon, 2013; Alahar, 2017) and it may be more difficult to justify restricting access to open access publications in legal deposit collections. These publications are typically made available under a Creative Commons licence,[9] which allows the copyright holder to specify what can be done with the output. The UK's current legal deposit provisions mean that access to such outputs will be restricted, which is contrary to the licence provisions and the purpose of open access. In the UK, UK Research and Innovation (UKRI, formerly Research Councils UK), the public body supporting research across the country, initiated an open access policy in 2005 (UK Research and Innovation, 2013). This policy acknowledges that free and open access to publicly funded research is a societal good (UK Research and Innovation, 2013, 1). The policy has been supported by funding to some institutions to pay for research publications to be immediately openly available under the Gold Open Access route.[10] The policy is also being partially enforced by the requirement for open access for some categories of research outputs to be submitted to the UK's next Research Excellence Framework exercise (REF, 2021).[11, 12] Future discussions over access and use of content in legal deposit libraries should consider what to do about open access publications as well as those that are out of copyright.[13]

Open access is an element of the broader concept of open science. While there does not yet seem to be a single accepted definition of open science,[14] it also encompasses open data, note-books and educational resources as part of a new approach to scientific methods, collaboration and access to knowledge.

Open science implies that source materials are published alongside working records and traditional research outputs. Indeed, some UK research funders require applications for research grants to include data management plans setting out how digital outputs will be managed and made available.[15] If such materials are considered to be published, what role, if any, legal deposit has in preserving access to these sources will need to be addressed.

Researchers are applying analysis tools to draw new insights from large corpuses of scientific, medical, social, financial, statistical data and texts. In 2014, the UK introduced a new copyright exception for text and data analysis for non-commercial research (Copyright, Designs and Patents Act 1988, s. 29A). This exception allows researchers with lawful access to works (for example if they, or their institution, already have a subscription) to make a copy for analysis for non-commercial research as long as they provide an acknowledgement where possible. No further unauthorised copying or sharing of content is allowed. Responses to the UK government's consultation on the proposal to introduce this exception indicated that it was unpopular with publishers, which would prefer to only allow this activity under licence (Department for Culture, Media and Sport, 2012b, 17). The legal deposit libraries argue that legal deposit and copyright laws should be aligned so that changes to copyright law also apply to legal deposit publications (Joint Committee on Legal Deposit, 2018, 53–4). The publishers stated that researchers do not need to use legal deposit collections for this purpose (p. 61) and that this should be done through individual purchase or subscription, library provision and text and data analysis agreements.

Conclusion

It seems that publishers acknowledge the benefit of legal deposit as a means of preserving the UK's published output for posterity. There is also encouraging, if limited, evidence that deposit of electronic publications is not imposing an onerous burden, at least on larger publishers. Indeed, there is evidence to suggest that publishers find electronic deposit to be more efficient. There have been no formal complaints from publishers to the JCLD about the implementation of electronic legal deposit and no need for dispute resolution between publishers and legal deposit libraries, so far. There does not seem to be any evidence of public discussion about the impact of electronic legal deposit on publishers (although this may be happening privately) since implementation. The publishers' formal report to the post implementation review indicates willingness to continue to work to expand the scope of electronic deposit to more complex digital materials. For now, electronic legal deposit seems to be a positive thing for the publishers involved.

However, publishers are concerned that legal deposit collections could be used in ways that interfere with their commercial interests. While the current UK legal deposit legislation aims to balance the interests of different stakeholders, the provisions relating to access and use of legal material are meant to protect these interests. It is understandable that publishers wish to be free to develop products and services based on the content they publish. What is not clear at the moment is whether access restrictions must be applied across the board and in perpetuity, or whether arrangements can be put in place to reflect the diversity in digital publishing so that, for example, material that is openly licensed can be made freely available by legal deposit libraries. It does not make sense that access restrictions should continue after publications enter the public domain, despite publisher concerns about unfair competition.

The tension around access and use, always inherent in legal deposit, but impressively handled so far, thanks to good working relationships between the libraries and publishers, could become far more acute over time because of the rise of open access and the user expectations that the deposit libraries wish to meet. There seems to be a willingness on the part of publishers to open up areas of disagreement to wider consultation, which may lead to compromises and more nuanced access and use permissions in practice. Developments in scholarly communication and open science may also result in a more accessible and usable national published archive, at least for scholarly outputs. Whether this archive is part of a national legal deposit collection or not remains to be seen.

Notes

1. Two separate companies at the time, since merged to form Thomson Reuters.
2. This version of the code is no longer available online; the 2000 version is available at www.bl.uk/aboutus/stratpolprog/legaldep/voluntarydeposit.
3. Now merged into News Media Association.
4. The author was an independent member of LDAP from 2005 to 2008.
5. This Joint Committee's mandate includes monitoring legislation and practice and providing advice in the context of voluntary and statutory deposit schemes. The Committee's most recent joint statement includes reference to publication formats and territoriality issues: see https://fep-fee.eu/FEP-and-CENL-adopt-joint-statement.
6. By 2017, 11 publishers had requested an embargo (Joint Committee on Legal Deposit, 2018, 40). It is not clear how many publications were involved.
7. www.portico.org.
8. www.ingramcontent.com.
9. https://creativecommons.org/licenses.

10. www.ukri.org/funding/information-for-award-holders/open-access/open-access-policy/open-access-block-grants.
11. www.hefce.ac.uk/rsrch/oa.
12. www.hefce.ac.uk/rsrch/oa/Policy.
13. For a broader discussion on the future of scholarly communication and preservation and the preservation of scholarly outputs, see Fitzpatrick, K. (2011) *Planned Obsolescence: Publishing, Technology, and the Future of the Academy*, NYU Press.
14. The OECD describes the concept at www.oecd.org/sti/inno/open-science.htm
15. For example, see www.dcc.ac.uk/resources/data-management-plans/funders-requirements for examples of funder requirements.

References

Agency for the Legal Deposit Libraries (2019a) *Electronic Legal Deposit: Legal Deposit Libraries' Collecting Plans for 2013–2014*, www.legaldeposit.org.uk/electronic/2013-2014-collecting-plans.html.

Agency for the Legal Deposit Libraries (2019b) *Electronic Legal Deposit*, www.legaldeposit.org.uk/electronic/index.html.

Alahar, H. (2017) Academic Publishing, Internet Technology, and Disruptive Innovation, *Technology Innovation Management Review*, 7 (11), 47-56.

Altick, R. D. (1957) *The English Common Reader: A Social History of the Mass Reading Public 1800—1900*, University Of Chicago Press.

Association of Online Publishers (2019) *About Us*, www.ukaop.org/about.

British Library (1996) *Proposal for the Legal Deposit of Non-Print Publications to the Department of National Heritage from the British Library.*

British Library (2003) *Historic Change in Legal Deposit Law Saves Electronic Publications for Future Generations – Bill to Extend Legal Deposit to UK Non-Print Materials Receives Royal Assent*, press release 31 October, http://www.bl.uk/cgi-bin/press.cgi?story=1382.

British Library (2019a) *How to Deposit Your Digital Publications*, www.bl.uk/help/how-to-deposit-your-digital-publications.

British Library (2019b) *Joint Committee on Legal Deposit*, www.bl.uk/legal-deposit/joint-committee.

Brown, D. J. and Boulderstone, R. (2008) *The Impact of Electronic Publishing: The Future for Publishers and Librarians*, rev. edn, K. G. Saur.

Cadwalladr, C. and Graham-Harrison, E. (2018) Revealed: 50 Million Facebook Profiles Harvested for Cambridge Analytica in Major Data Breach, *The Guardian*, 17 March, www.theguardian.com/news/2018/mar/17/cambridge-analytica-facebook-influence-US-election.

Copyright, Designs and Patents Act 1988, Ch. 48.

Davis, P. M. and Walters W. H. (2011) The Impact of Free Access to the Scientific Literature: A Review of Recent Research, *Journal of the Medical Library Association*, **99** (3), 208–17.

Deegan, M. and Sutherland, K. (2009) *Transferred Illusions: Digital Technology and the Forms of Print*, Ashgate.

Dellar, G. (2001) Legal Deposit Accounted For, letter to the editor, *Library Association Record*, **103** (9), 542.

Department for Culture, Media and Sport (2009) *Proposal on the Collection and Preservation of UK Offline and Microform Publications and UK Online Publications: (Available Free of Charge and Without Access Restrictions)*, https://webarchive.nationalarchives.gov.uk/+/http://www.culture.gov.uk/images/consultations/Digital_legal_deposit.pdf.

Department for Culture, Media and Sport (2010a) *Consultation on the Legal Deposit of Non-print Works*, http://webarchive.nationalarchives.gov.uk/20110505103427/http://www.cep.culture.gov.uk/consultations/7449.aspx.

Department for Culture, Media and Sport (2010b) *Digital Legal Deposit - Non-print Off Line Publications*, Impact Assessment DCMS 004, http://webarchive.nationalarchives.gov.uk/20110505103427/http://www.cep.culture.gov.uk/consultations/7449.aspx.

Department for Culture, Media and Sport (2011) *Government Response to the Public Consultation on the Draft Regulations and Guidance for Non-Print Legal Deposit*, http://webarchive.nationalarchives.gov.uk/20110505102314/http://www.cep.culture.gov.uk/publications/8029.aspx.

Department for Culture, Media and Sport (2012a) *Impact Assessment for the Legal Deposit Libraries (Non-Print Works) Regulations 2013*, www.legislation.gov.uk/ukia/2013/1017/pdfs/ukia_20131017_en.pdf.

Department for Culture, Media and Sport (2012b) *Consultation on Copyright: Summary of Responses June 2012*, www.gov.uk/government/uploads/system/uploads/attachment_data/file/320223/copyright-consultation-summary-of-responses.pdf.

Department for Culture, Media and Sport (2013) *Guidance on the Legal Deposit Libraries (Non-Print Works) Regulations 2013*, https://assets.publishing.service.gov.uk/government/uploads/system/uploads/attachment_data/file/182339/NPLD_Guidance_April_2013.pdf.

Electronic Publishing Services Ltd (1996) *The Legal Deposit of Online Databases (British Library R&D Report no. 6244)*, British Library.

Electronic Publishing Services Ltd (2002) *The Impact of the Extension of Legal Deposit to Non-Print Publications: Assessment of Cost and Other Quantifiable Impacts*: study report prepared for the Joint Committee on Voluntary Deposit, EPS Ltd.

Feather, J. (1994) *Publishing, Piracy and Politics: An Historical Study of Copyright in Britain*, Mansell.

Fell, C. (2004) *Legal Deposit Libraries Bill – Update*, http://www.alpsp.org/legdep.htm.

Gibby, R. (2013) *Undertaking to the Joint Committee on Legal Deposit on the Security of Deposited Non-Print Publications*, www.bl.uk/aboutus/legaldeposit/websites/security/joint_security_undertaking.pdf.

Gibby, R. and Brazier, C. (2012) Observations on the Development of Non-Print Legal Deposit in the UK, *Library Review*, **61** (5), 362–77.

Gibby, R. and Green, A. (2008) Electronic Legal Deposit In the United Kingdom, *New Review of Academic Librarianship*, **14** (1–2), 55–70.

Green, A. (2012) Introducing Electronic Legal Deposit In the UK: A Homeric Tale, *Alexandria*, **23** (3), 103–9.

Harris, P. R. (1991) *The Library of the British Museum: Retrospective Essays on the Department of Printed Books*, British Library.

Hendley, T. (1996) *The Preservation of Digital Material*, British Library R&D Report 6242, British Library Research and Innovation Centre.

Joint Committee on Legal Deposit (2018) *Post Implementation Review of the Legal Deposit Libraries (Non-Print Works) Regulations 2013*, www.gov.uk/government/publications/post-implementation-review-of-the-legal-deposit-libraries-non-print-works-regulations-2013.

Laakso, M. and Björk, B.-C. (2012) Anatomy of Open Access Publishing: A Study of Longitudinal Development and Internal Structure, *BMC Medicine*, **10** (124), https://bmcmedicine.biomedcentral.com/track/pdf/10.1186/1741-7015-10-124.

Legal Deposit Advisory Panel (2006) *Legal Deposit Advisory Panel Annual Report September 2005–August 2006*, http://webarchive.nationalarchives.gov.uk/20071207231619/www.culture.gov.uk/reference_library/publications/archive_2007/ldap_annualreport07.htm.

Legal Deposit Advisory Panel (2007) *Legal Deposit Advisory Panel Annual Report September 2006–August 2007*, http://webarchive.nationalarchives.gov.uk/20090902213611/www.cep.culture.gov.uk/what_we_do/libraries/3409.aspx.

Legal Deposit Advisory Panel (2008) *Legal Deposit Advisory Panel Annual Report September 2007–August 2008*, http://webarchive.nationalarchives.gov.uk/20090902220855/www.cep.culture.gov.uk/reference_library/publications/6167.aspx.

Legal Deposit Libraries Committee (2015) *Joint Collecting Framework for UK Legal Deposit (2015–2020)*, http://vll-minos.bl.uk/aboutus/legaldeposit/websites/elecpubs/joint-collecting-framework-for-uk-legal-deposit.pdf.

Legal Deposit Libraries Act 2003 c.28, www.legislation.gov.uk/ukpga/2003/28/contents.

Legal Deposit Libraries (Non-Print Publications) Regulations 2011, http://webarchive.nationalarchives.gov.uk/20110505103427/www.cep.culture.gov.uk/consultations/7449.aspx.

(Draft) Legal Deposit Libraries (Non-Print Works) Regulations 2013, http://webarchive.nationalarchives.gov.uk/20121204120059/www.culture.gov.uk/consultations/8878.aspx.

Martin, D. (1996) *Definitions of Publications and Associated Terms in Electronic Publications*, British Library R&D Report 6243, British Library Research & Development Department.

Martin, W. J. and Tian, X. (2010) *Books, Bytes, and Business: The Promise of Digital Publishing*, Ashgate.

Muir, A. (2005) *Legal Deposit of Digital Publications*, PhD thesis, Loughborough University, https://dspace.lboro.ac.uk/dspace-jspui/bitstream/2134/8469/2/thesis_adrienne_muir.pdf.

Powell, D. (2006) *Refining the Map of the Universe of Electronic Publications Potentially Eligible for Legal Deposit* (unpublished report), Electronic Publishing Services Ltd.

Publishers Association (2019) *Digital Growth Drives Value of UK Publishing Industry to £6bn*, www.publishers.org.uk/news/releases/2019/pa-publishing-yearbook-2018.

Ramrattan, L. and Szenberg, M. (2016) *Revolutions in Book Publishing: The Effects of Digital Innovation on the Industry*, Palgrave.

Solomon, D. J. (2013) Digital Distribution of Academic Journals and its Impact on Scholarly Communication: Looking Back After 20 Years, *Journal of Academic Librarianship*, **39** (1), 23–8.

The Legal Deposit Libraries (Non-Print Works) Regulations 2013 (S.I. 2013/777), www.legislation.gov.uk/uksi/2013/777/contents/made.

UK Research and Innovation (2013) *RCUK Policy on Open Access and Supporting Guidance*, www.ukri.org/files/legacy/documents/rcukopenaccesspolicy-pdf.

Whitaker, D. (2001a) Time to Move on – Free Legal Deposit Has Had Its Day, *The Bookseller*, 18 May, 24–5.

Whitaker, D. (2001b) Nobody Expects the Spanish Inquisition, *Library Association Record*, **103** (8), 492–3.

Working Party on Legal Deposit (1998) *Report of the Working Party on Legal Deposit*, https://web.archive.org/web/20110314061539/www.bl.uk/aboutus/stratpolprog/legaldep/report.

Working Party on Legal Deposit (1999) *Code of Practice for the Voluntary Deposit of Non-Print Publications*, rev. version, September.

CHAPTER 7

Making history: digital preservation and electronic legal deposit in the second quarter of the 21st century

William Kilbride

Introduction

It is hard to imagine a more interesting time to work in libraries, nor a more challenging one. In an era of post-truth obfuscation and sinister deletion, the ability to collect, retain and authenticate is suddenly a super-power; in an era of relentless proliferation, the confidence to select and consolidate, with implied permission to relegate and deduplicate, is ubiquitously essential; in an era where data is the 'new oil' of the 'information society', the unassuming librarian holds the keys not only to the past, but now also to the future. One would have thought that this generation more than any other would be the age of the library, an enduring proof of common cause for the common weal: deposit libraries at the summit of our ambition, the record of all we have achieved and source of all we might. Why does it not feel that way?

It's not yet clear whether the digital turn will be the making of the library or its undoing, given many of these opportunities are disruptive, mostly provisional, and largely originate outside the library community. These challenges arise just at a moment where the social and economic context of operations are profoundly unsettled, whether through the continuing dysfunction of economics, the puzzling impasses of public discourse or a global crisis of dislocation and dispossession. With such uncertainty about the times in which we will shortly live, this is no time for an identity crisis. Yet there is little prospect of staying unchanged.

2018 was (another) pivotal year in the development of libraries in the UK and Ireland, a consequence of a review of the legal deposit regime. This has enabled a wider consideration of the place and function of legal deposit libraries, and a deeper dive into the evolving processes and expectations through which their mission, to provide a full and canonical copy of the published record, is fulfilled. So how can libraries help us make sense of these turbulent times and preserve a record that will help us look back on them, too? How can we ensure that legal deposit libraries and their collections will continue to thrive in the second quarter of the 21st century?

The Legal Deposit Libraries Act 2003 made explicit for the first time in the UK provisions for publishers to deposit online and offline publications and about the use and preservation of such publications by the legal deposit libraries. Further regulations published in 2013 implemented the 2003 Act with specific guidance around copying and adapting materials for the purposes of preservation (The Legal Deposit Libraries (Non-Print Works) Regulations 2013; Department for Culture, Media and Sport, 2013). Five years on from this secondary legislation, the UK Department for Digital Culture Media and Sport has initiated a review of the regime. This has provided an opportunity to assess how successfully the legal deposit libraries have implemented all aspects of the regulations and it has inevitably provoked informal discussion on the extent to which the regulations are fit for purpose. In preparation for the review, the legal deposit libraries invited the Digital Preservation Coalition (DPC) to undertake a specific and independent assessment of digital preservation capability for non-print legal deposit collections. This was undertaken throughout 2017 and a full report was published in March 2018 (see Digital Preservation Coalition, 2017). From the perspective of posterity, this assessment is an important measure of the continuing value and presumed role of legal deposit libraries in the future.

This chapter will review five aspects of electronic legal deposit, drawing from the lessons learned in the DPC's assessment of digital preservation capability. It will describe how the legal deposit libraries in the UK and Ireland have addressed the digital preservation challenge; it will summarise the findings of the assessment, identifying the main issues and challenges which the legal deposit libraries have faced; it will explore whether the experience gained so far has prepared them well for the future; it will describe emergent challenges associated with users in which the regulations are seen to be at odds with standards in digital preservation and significantly adrift from current theory in memory institutions; and it will describe an emergent challenge with technology where the regulations assume a false dichotomy between software and data which will become unsustainable. In doing so, this chapter will propose renewal and enhancement to the mission of legal deposit libraries, preparing them for the challenges to come and glimpsing a prospect that may transform them from problem owners uncertain about their role to solution providers that are confident about their purpose.

How have legal deposit libraries addressed the digital preservation challenge?

Libraries have been among the first and most committed champions of digital preservation: and by extension early and steadfast adversaries of obsolescence (see, for example, Hedstrom, 1998; Brindley, 2000; Shenton, 2000; Webb, 2000; Day, 2001). Many of the tools, processes and models of the digital preservation community were developed specifically to support library applications or have improved and advanced beyond recognition when adopted by them. For example, many of the tools and approaches of digital forensics were developed explicitly in the context of legal processes but have found significant and alternative applications in the stabilisation and assessment of digital manuscript collections (John, 2012); many of the technologies of web publishing have been adapted to create robust new methodologies for web archiving (Pennock, 2013); and the outsourced preservation of e-journal content in the context of library collections is in some ways a model for all digital preservation architecture (Beagrie, 2013). Consequently, legal deposit collections are well served with digital preservation capability relative to other sectors and collection types. However, digital preservation is a subtle challenge, emerging from the commercial and technological caprice of social, industrial and economic forces outside libraries' control: what was once good practice may now be insufficient, and what is now robust may soon become uncertain. For example, electronic journals still deploy paper metaphors of files and print but when publishers drop those metaphors and produce truly electronic journals that are complex multimedia interactions of data and syntheses, then a new preservation challenge emerges: in fact, it is already here (Kirchhoff and Morrissey, 2014; Day et al., 2018).

The responsibility to care for digital materials is absorbed within a broader social and cultural mission of legal deposit libraries: to 'make a significant and lasting contribution to global knowledge and the memory of the world' (National Library of Scotland, 2015, 5) whilst ensuring that we can 'guarantee access for future generations' (British Library, 2010, 3). These responsibilities are described more prosaically in the regulations that specify their rights and mandates that shape their processes. In the UK and to a lesser extent also in Ireland this means the UK Legal Deposit Libraries (Non-Print Works) Regulations 2013, which implement the UK Legal Deposit Libraries Act 2003, which, *inter alia*, makes provision for the use and preservation of material deposited for what is termed 'Non-Print Legal Deposit Collections'.

In practical terms implementation of the legal deposit regulations are overseen by the Joint Committee for Legal Deposit, composed of representatives of the publishers and the legal deposit libraries.[1] This committee receives reports on the implementation of the regulations in order that it can evaluate the effectiveness of non-print legal deposit arrangements, assess the application of the regulations in practice and future needs. The committee has gathered evidence in preparation for the UK government's review of the regulations, taking into account the views of specialist groups such as the DPC. The committee convenes a number of task forces and sub-committees from time to time, including a group for overall implementation of the regulations which has digital preservation among its responsibilities.

There are six library partners involved in the legal deposit regime in the UK and Ireland, and each of these have significant digital preservation expertise: for recent and relevant examples, see the National Library of Scotland's work on cloud storage (Hibberd, 2017) or the British Library's work on preservation of diverse media formats (Day et al., 2016). Digital preservation for non-print legal deposit collections is delivered by the British Library, which is effectively a service provider to the other five deposit libraries. This concentration provides economy of scope against a single shared set of challenges. It also means that, of all the different aspects of the legal deposit regime, digital preservation ought to be among the simplest to assess. One question can be posed to one institution: are the digital preservation skills, policies and processes of the British Library sufficient to ensure the non-print legal deposit collections will be accessible for the long term?

Assessment: methodology, scope and findings

There have been numerous attempts in recent years to codify good practice in digital preservation into a series of standards (see Bantin, 2016 for an introduction). The idea of a trusted digital archives was first expressed in 1996 by a joint working party of the Commission for Preservation and Access and the Research Libraries Group which called for an independently administered programme for archival certification (Commission for Preservation and Access/Research Libraries Group, 1996, 9). The concept of the 'trusted digital repository' emerged from that as a core theme at around the same time as the legal deposit regime was expanded to encompass non-print collections (RLG/OCLC Working Group on Digital Archive Attributes, 2002). This has since been developed in a series of related audit and certification standards over the years (e.g. Center for Research Libraries and Online Computer Library Center, 2007; International Standards Organization, 2012).

Given these existing tools, the assessment of what makes a trusted digital repository should be easy to scope, but there is a subtle tension between the concept of the 'trusted repository' as a model of good practice and the force of quasi-judicial regulations. The mismatch between the certification standards in digital preservation, the context of preservation services and the nature of technological change has been reported before (Rosenthal, 2014; Kilbride, 2017b; Duranti, 2016). The public purse is not funding a trusted repository as defined by some abstract standard, but a trusted series of tools, services, procedures and staff, configured around an interpretation of statute and regulation. For example, questions of mandate which are explored at length in the context of the trusted repository audit (such as sections 3.1 3.2, 3.3 and 3.4 of ISO 16363), do not arise, and many aspects of security, staffing and sustainability fall out of scope. In this context the standard metrics of digital preservation capability are more usefully seen as a toolkit in the development of an assessment. Because such organisational metrics were redundant, and because an internal audit using ISO16363 had already been completed (Pennock and Smith, 2016) the opportunity arose for a deeper analysis of operational and governance matters as they related to specific collections.

The details of the resulting Non-Print Legal Deposit Digital Preservation Review, including the metrics, processes and findings, have been published in detail (see Digital Preservation Coalition, 2017, for a complete account). They are summarised here to provide a flavour of the challenges and competences which frame the subsequent discussion.

As well as adapting metrics from the Unified Requirements for Core Certification of Trustworthy Data Repositories (The Core Trust Seal) the review had the luxury of ensuring greater independence, transparency and penetration than might normally be delivered. The DPC was commissioned to examine practice at the British Library by the Joint Committee on Legal Deposit and was ultimately reporting to and accountable to them. Although the British Library is represented on this committee, so are all the other legal deposit libraries and significant representatives of the publishing trade. This guaranteed the independence of the assessment, in contrast to conventional processes for the Core Trust Seal, which is normally awarded after lightweight peer review, carried out by other holders of the Core Trust Seal. The DPC acted as an independent reviewer, requesting information and interviewing staff across legal deposit institutions, and in particular the British Library, to ensure consistency and probe strengths and weaknesses. This process is more exacting, enables a more forensic and detailed analysis of strengths and weaknesses and ensures that there is no inadvertent misunderstanding. It is also more transparent, since there is no conflict of interests between assessor and candidate. The DPC, as an independent not-for-profit organisation which is owned by its members and supports them by delivering the strategic purpose of a secure digital legacy, has engrained expertise in the topic but will not in turn be subjected to the same analysis, thus obtaining no benefit from eroding or amplifying the metrics in its favour.

The assessment included processes, data, staffing, skills, planning and policy (see Digital Preservation Coalition, 2017). Each of the legal deposit libraries was invited to participate and receive reports on progress at key stages in the process. Moreover, the assessment was structured in such a way that it could be repeated, whether by the legal deposit libraries at some later date, or by other institutions seeking validation of their digital preservation activities (see Digital Preservation Coalition, 2017, Appendix One for a list of those interviewed and Appendix Two for the metrics used). It examined three primary non-print legal deposit collections which constitute the vast majority of electronic legal deposit: web archives including both the domain crawl and voluntary deposit; non-print deposit of journals; and non-print deposit of e-books. The review also examined progress with two other content types which are in scope of the regulations but are relatively small in comparison: digital manuscripts of music and cartographic data.

The review progressed iteratively, starting in January 2017 and completing in December 2017. The process consisted of five phases: a period of preparation and initiation; an early assessment phase and report; a period in which recommendations could be acted upon; then a second assessment phase that examined the extent to which recommendations had been followed; and a reporting phase, where all the documents and outcomes were shared and published. It focused on the current state of the preservation capability of non-print legal deposit materials in the UK and Ireland, but also took the opportunity to consider how this capability has changed since the introduction of the Legal Deposit Regulations in 2013, and where current plans may take it by 2023. In this way it assessed and demonstrated responsiveness to a 'moving target'. Significant conclusions from this assessment can be summarised in six key points.

First, it is hard to express the scale and complexity of the challenge which the preservation of digital legal deposit collections has generated. Moreover, it is a constantly changing challenge. In the face of this expansive, challenging and changing workload there is a constant need for renewal of resources, skills and technology. In less than five years the non-print legal deposit collection at the British Library has grown from 365,000 to almost 14,000,000 digital objects, a count which if anything underestimates the abundance of web content, since entire collections of websites are managed as composite WARC file containers.[2] This *38-fold* increase has not been met with an equivalent increase in resources.

Secondly, in order to make progress with this exceptional growth and complexity the British Library has made sensible, clear-cut strategic decisions with respect to the management of resources and skills. Larger content streams – that is, web archives, e-journals and e-books – were prioritised in the early phases of implementation and focus has since moved to the smaller but more complex and interactive streams which are a greater technical challenge.

Thirdly, a number of operational failings were observed in the review, such as technical difficulties with integrity checking and backlogs in accession and replication. Integrity checks are a vital component of digital preservation processes, establishing that the materials currently stored are an exact match to those initially received. These can be time-consuming to process and therefore the question arises as to how frequently such checks should be processed and how long it is necessary to maintain a log of such audits. New non-print legal deposit collections arriving in the British Library were not immediately ingested to the digital library system where they would be automatically replicated to the other legal deposit libraries. A short delay for validation and quality assurance is good practice but lengthy delays mean risks to the content are not fully managed. Challenges in both areas were noted, and in turn revealed difficulties in escalation and oversight. These were reported in the course of the assessment, and subsequent checks verified that actions had been initiated to resolve them. In most cases these were complete by the time of the second review.

Fourthly, these technical challenges turned out to be relatively quick to address: discussion in the preliminary phases made failings and solutions obvious, meaning many were resolved even before they were reported. For example, the Object Authenticity Checker was completely rewritten in the course of the project and a full integrity check was completed, exceeding the reviewers' expectations that this would be possible. The combined problems of integrity checking and backlogs could have resulted in significant loss of NPLD content. But this new integrity check has revealed this not to be the case. Management challenges have been addressed quickly through enhanced reporting to the other legal deposit libraries, and a new specialist task group for the oversight of digital preservation challenges has been established which can report to the Joint Committee. As with many cultural changes, these may take longer to become established norms. Changes to governance should be closely monitored to ensure they remain effective.

Fifthly, it is pleasing to report that the legal deposit libraries, and the British Library in particular, responded positively, effectively and in a timely manner to the Non-Print Legal Deposit Digital Preservation Review. The reviewers came to an independent judgement with detailed knowledge of best practice and standards around the world, and with full access to all relevant documents, processes and staff. This demonstrated a firm commitment to continuous quality improvement.

Finally, and perhaps most importantly, the assessment demonstrated that much of the digital preservation practice at the British Library, on behalf of the legal deposit libraries, has been exemplary. The British Library has been a world leader in many aspects of digital preservation for some time (see e.g. Shenton, 2000; Brindley, 2000; John, 2012; Pennock, 2013). This expertise has been wisely and consistently brought to bear on the non-print legal deposit collections. For example, the proliferation of publisher formats creates significant challenges for characterisation, the act of identifying a file as belonging to a specific format, and validation, the act of confirming that it conforms to the standard or identifying the ways that it fails to conform and the risks that arise. Not only has working practice kept pace with rapid and unpredictable variations, the British Library has engaged actively in pushing forward thoughtful understanding and development of best practice which it has shared and validated in conversation with the global digital preservation community (see e.g. Day et al., 2018). Examples like this enabled the reviewers to describe the British Library as a sector-leading digital preservation institution with global reach.

Future prospects: non-print legal deposit in 2023 and beyond

Five significant challenges emerged from the review which will need to be met to ensure that the legal deposit libraries remain capable to address digital preservation challenges in five years' time:

1 First, the assessment has measured the extent to which collections continue to expand. As publishers move their already published holdings from print to digital, new submissions not only include current publications but also back copies originally published in print. This increase in volume makes planning acquisitions challenging. 42% more content is received from publishers in electronic form than when the same publishers deposited only in print (Digital Preservation Coalition, 2017, 10).
2 Second, digital materials invite revision and correction in ways that are challenging. Revisions ranging from minor correction of punctuation through to significant edits have been requested. In such circumstances deposit and accession processes may need to be carried out several times over.
3 Third, publishing formats and processes are not stable. Publishers and their outputs change over time. This includes business and technical changes such as mergers with other publishers or corporate entities, closing or changing the name of their journal titles. These unpredictable changes result in further complication to established content workflows.
4 Fourth, digital collections are liable to repackaging in ways that physical

collections are not: material previously published in one form can be repackaged and published (otherwise identically) in different granular form; for example, journal articles can be re-published as an e-book.

5 Fifth, digital collections invite richness and interactivity. Sometimes these forms match well with emerging standard data formats, in other cases content becomes tied to proprietary software technology, presenting obstacles to preservation, management and access.

Digital deposits are typically unpredictable, and the simple act of depositing the data can result in challenges itself. A publisher established as a submitter of content to the British Library for preservation typically supplies content in a gradual fashion. However, the successful completion of negotiations with new publishers means that an entire back catalogue may suddenly appear for submission. This unpredictability of the frequency and volume of deposits makes forward planning and the day-to-day management of ingest workflows a continual challenge.

Finally, the increasing volume, complexity and unpredictability of content place considerable strain on digital preservation workflows. Greater volumes (both in numbers of items and sizes of component files) place strains on systems that process them, requiring more resilient software processes and greater automation to enable issues to be resolved without backlogs arising. Backlogs, as noted elsewhere in the assessment, exacerbate risks faced by collections. Evolving complexity requires evaluation and research into new file formats, and new types of digital content. In some cases, this may require new preservation techniques and, most likely, evaluation and implementation of new software applications to handle them. Unpredictability requires greater flexibility to react to changes in content and its supply. Deposited data that doesn't conform to previously encountered norms must be detected, and workflows adapted to process it. The accuracy and completeness of digital preservation activities will be impacted with adaptation to meet these challenges.

Why users matter: making sense of non-print legal deposit

The challenges of preserving non-print legal deposit collections are unpredictable. Unlike physical preservation, the decay of digital materials does not follow predictable chemical or biological vectors which the library may seek to prevent or postpone: the causes of obsolescence and media failure are ultimately typically the result of mercurial economic and business processes that are outside the library's control (I have tried to argue this issue from a historical perspective (Kilbride, 2017c), but for a more succinct technical overview of the causes of obsolescence see Harvey and Weatherburn, 2018, 50–2; Brown, 2013, 200–8). This is why digital preservation experts lay such emphasis on adaptability (see Harvey and Weatherburn, 2018, 204–5 for references). There are two areas where the current regulations appear to constrain this essential flexibility: in relation to users, and in the paper-based definitions of collecting scope.

The 2013 Legal Deposit Regulations are quite specific and restrictive about the contexts in which collections can be accessed: materials can be consulted at a terminal on premises controlled by the deposit library, and moreover the library must ensure that only one computer terminal is available to readers to access the same relevant material at any one time. There seems little doubt that this restriction to access, modelled loosely on restrictions applied to print collections, is a significant constraint on users and the potential impact of non-print legal deposit. There is a case to be made that these constraints to access will have a deleterious effect on preservation. Conservation of physical materials benefits from restricted access and use, while digital materials typically benefit from continued use and the subtle quality assurance this implies.

Digital preservation planning and quality assurance typically revolves around users expressed formally in the design and delivery of 'dissemination information packages', 'representation information' and the 'designated community' (see Lavoie, 2014, for an accessible explanation of these terms and International Standards Organization, 2012, for explicit definitions). To summarise, representation information is a component of an archival information package which holds semantic and structural components, which in turn provide the transparency required to ensure that a 'digital object' can become an 'information object' in the hands of a 'designated community' (Gartner and Lavoie, 2013). Arguably, representation information is the unique characteristic that distinguishes digital preservation from every other kind of content management. In a sort of recursive absurdity, representation information is interpreted using representation information which, at face value, implies that each information package is required to contain or reference the entirety of human knowledge to achieve independent utility. The Open Archival Information System (OAIS) standard avoids this in two ways: by linking representation information into networks; and by accessing an underlying *knowledge base* which can be taken for granted (Lavoie, 2014). For example, a person who has a knowledge base that includes an understanding of English will be able to read, and understand, an English text. So, the requirement for representation information is curtailed when it is mapped against implicit knowledge between two agents within an information exchange. Digital objects are preserved, therefore, through an ongoing configuration of data object, representation information and the implied knowledge of the designated community.

This is self-evidently useful in the face of the alternative infinite regression. However, it implies a significant effort to understand the needs of a designated community and an active engagement to track their changing needs. Archives which fail to do this cannot ultimately deliver long-term preservation. Reading this requirement through the lens of legal deposit regulations creates a tension, since the constraints to access which protect the copyright of publishers undermine the potential for dialogue with the designated community and thus undermine, and ultimately will defeat, the preservation mandate. In the long run preservation and access cannot be completely separated.

There is arguably a third, albeit more abstruse, challenge to be considered in the relationship between access and preservation, derived from deeper cultural and linguistic theory.

Over the last two decades, digital preservation has been configured as a collaborative endeavour that draws from many disciplines, adopting tools and good practice from wherever they can be found. For example, Open Archival Information System (OAIS), which is in many senses the *lingua franca* of digital preservation, is the product of the Consultative Committee for Space Data Systems (Consultative Committee for Space Data Systems Secretariat, 2012). This origin haunts the language and assumptions of digital preservation: the values and norms of space science lurk below the surface of just about every digital preservation conversation.[3] This contribution has been immensely welcome and potent, but it also should be set alongside contemporaneous progress in library, archival and museological theory, which emphasise the difficult and at times contradictory nature of meaning-making. The textual turn of cultural hermeneutics and poststructuralism in particular have been controversial: the former situating cultural studies within wider social and political fields of discourse in which social relations are created and reproduced (see Adorno and Horkheimer, 1972; Hall, 1990; Spivak, 1990); the latter denying the sufficiency of established approaches to meaning-making in structural linguistics (Derrida, 1976; Barthes, 1973). It has been argued that the whole genre of post-truth informatics has some origin in the legacy of postmodernism (D'Ancona, 2017). It has certainly been a mixed blessing for archives, libraries and museums.

On one hand, the recognition that knowledge production is a fundamental tool in the reproduction of unequal power relationships has transformed memory institutions from the gatekeepers of authoritative resilience to the enablers of progressive narrative(s). Derrida equated archives with a sort of house arrest: both as the source and containment of power, arranged to the practical convenience of the authorities, and only shared on asymmetrical terms with the public (Derrida and Prenowitz, 1995, 10). For several decades, anthropologists have traced the machinery of knowledge production and maintenance in explicitly colonial terms, by extension challenging archives and libraries to address concerns of post-colonialism (Sahlins, 1985; Comaroff and Comaroff, 1992). It's no small accomplishment to note that for three decades now any number of disenfranchised communities have taken back control of cultural storehouses to establish new and often conflicting histories that subvert established norms and empower those previously excluded (see Choudry and Vally, 2017 and references for an overview and introduction). Archives, libraries and museums have largely welcomed these new if at times unruly patrons on the assumption that if the epistemology of the institution is not fundamentally about justice then, by default, its purpose is to sustain injustice (O'Neill, 2006).

The tortured history of meaning-making in the late 20th and early 21st century seems strangely at odds with the processes and norms adopted in digital preservation, especially with respect to representation information as described above. If the link to an authoritative definition within a representation network is one of the keys to unlocking meaning, then whoever gets to assign that link or manage the end-point is a very important individual, a dependency that is open to abuse. It's even more problematic when one considers the implied knowledge of the designated community that prevents representation information from spooling out of control. It implies that, if you're not part of the designated community, you're not expected to use or understand the collection, and the library has no explicit responsibility to help you, and no requirement to track your needs. This might be true in the context of academic research such as space science, where a relatively small but expert group of professionals would be expected to use complex datasets and would be motivated enough to cope with opaque documentation and annotations. Arguably this is a risky outcome when identities, actions or meanings are in dispute: where honest misunderstanding may arise, or faux conflicts be engineered and prolonged. It is altogether more concerning for public-facing institutions whose mission statements articulate noble aspirations for global knowledge through the generations.

Thus, best practice in the digital preservation community means that the digital preservation staff are empowered, in fact required, to exercise a kind of intellectual exclusion that seems out of step with just about every other kind of memory institution. Libraries have spent 30 years or more coming to terms with inclusion and polysemy: a challenge which the digital preservation community has largely overlooked.

To summarise, good practice in digital preservation seems to be behind the wider library, museum and archive community with respect to community engagement and meaning-making. It will need to adapt and there are signs that this is beginning to happen. In turn, the legal deposit regime seems several years behind the digital preservation community in making good on the promise of preservation through purposeful and expansive engagement with users. From this perspective, there seems to be quite a lot of catching up required to ensure that the legal deposit regulations will remain fit for purpose in the longer term.

The end and edges of print: what is (are) data and what is software?

The non-print legal deposit regime might be described as a first-generation digital process: the regulations model an analogue process with metaphors and workflows concerning journals and books, publishers, libraries and copies. The archive sector has begun to talk about a disruptive process of second-generation digital archives which recognise that collections are digital by default, that workflows and assumptions should be modelled around digital requirements, and that analogue metaphors will need to be set aside if the archive is to remain relevant and coherent (see e.g. National Archives, 2017). This same disruption seems inevitable and perhaps overdue in the context of legal deposit.

The Legal Deposit Libraries Act 2003 and subsequent regulations are quite explicit about what might be collected and what might not: the libraries have the right to request not only an online publication but any computer program necessary in order to access the work as well as any manual that accompanies it. This is not a blanket permission to collect software, but it does recognise that software and data are often intertwined. But as data, publication and software become more complicated, so these assumptions seem increasingly divergent from the practical reality of digital creativity. It implies a false dichotomy between software and data. By extension the lack of a national deposit collection of software, whether as published objects in their own right or an integrated component of an archival information package, seems likely to become more problematic over the years.

These rather abstract tensions have been apparent for a while but come to a head with the emergence and widespread adoption of the cloud (for an historical account of cloud computing and its relationship to desktop computing see Hu, 2015; for a more accessible description, see Naughton, 2012).

Libraries typically approach cloud computing as a storage platform (see Hibberd, 2017, and references), but storage seems the least important aspect. The cloud is perhaps more important as a utility and service to data creators.

The last decade has witnessed a major architectural change between computing as a product and computing as a service which in turn may render obsolete the current provisions of the legal deposit regime.

In a desktop computing environment, files are more or less self-contained on a disk, and canonical versions of software are provided so that a user can create or alter files in a more or less canonical format in which data is wrapped. Files might be remote and may even be spread over multiple file stores with symbolic references and disks: but there is a byte stream that can be assembled and committed as a file which behaves predictably for all users. Likewise, the software is dynamic, with versions and subversions and service packs supporting them: but there is a single stack and all of them are present at a moment in time in a single grey or beige or black box.

In a cloud environment, everything is a service, accessed through a browser, a web connection and a login. Software is summoned on demand, adapting to suit the configuration of device, browser and user, and it will almost certainly have been updated since it was last used. The software and its execution environment are remote and the stack of applications on which the interaction depends is assembled on demand and differently for each user. The same is true of data: services might use the metaphor of a file, but more likely the file is a series of symbolic links to a highly distributed series of byte streams which can be assembled differently depending on user. It may be possible to save this to a local hard disk: but that is just a neat way of synchronising the local environment with distributed remote storage and is in some sense always a migration from the original. There may never be a file in the conventional sense, nor a self-contained program to run, or a stable format to be rendered, or a fixed user perspective.

Having spotted that platform, software, infrastructure and even data have become services in the cloud, then it becomes quite easy to think of a remote service being compiled from distributed micro-services. And that is what they are: services behaving as services. There's a sort of fractal inclination implicit here, with micro-services drawing on yet smaller services and so on. It may not carry on *ad infinitum* but can continue as long and as far as the business need exists and supply chain can support. And thus, long chains of interdependence emerge in which multiple components have maintenance cycles that are invisible, at least until they go wrong. By implication all of this will fall into the provisions of article 6.2.b of the Legal Deposit Libraries Act 2003.

For the sake of clarity, an example arises in the context of fonts: is a font a necessary component of a published work? They are a simple accessible example of how the gap between application and data can be hard to sustain, and there are a few examples of what happens when fonts and text are separated by virtue of deliberate acts to restrict their distribution or remote updates that fail (see Kilbride, 2017a for three relevant examples in different types of document), underlining a fragility in the current legal deposit regulations. If font and text can be so easily separated, then challenges with relatively well understood formats will certainly be true of complicated ones like geospatial data or multi-user relational databases, which also fall within the purview of legal deposit, not to mention complex personalised interactions with web resources, emerging formats for enhanced e-books, or research data supplied in support of e-journals. If this vulnerability is evident in collections which are accessed every day when people notice unexpected flaws, then it will also be true of preserved collections to which access is restricted and access happens infrequently. If it is true of unexceptional or uncontested data, then it will be even truer of highly contested or high-impact systems.

The questions that arise for the preservation of non-print legal deposit collections are profound. What are the limits of dependency? How can preservation services detect such dependencies confidently, and how can they assess or mitigate the risks such dependencies pose? What are the implications for licensing and is there a potential for orphaned micro-services much as there is for orphan works (Korn, 2009; Hoeren, Kolany-Raiser and Yankova, 2013)? How might we ensure that data is authentic and accessible under reproducible conditions when the underlying services are continuously variable? These are not small questions and they disrupt the print-based and desktop computing assumptions of the current legal deposit regulations.

Digital preservation, legal deposit and the second quarter of the 21st century

This chapter began by questioning the capability of legal deposit libraries in the UK and Ireland to preserve non-print legal deposit collections, finding that, despite a number of flaws, they have risen to the challenge with energy and skill over the last five years, even while the size and nature of that challenge has changed. Moreover, the culture of collaboration and continuous quality improvement are to be commended. The legal deposit libraries' aspirations to be sector-leading internationally has been independently verified. There is much to celebrate and reason to be optimistic, but there is no time to be complacent: on the contrary, the energetic commitment to innovation seems to be the single most important characteristic in delivering this success.

The future is less certain. The legal deposit libraries seem well set to fulfil the requirements of the current regulations, though such statements are inevitably dependent on funding and leadership as well as a clear line of communication with publishers. But the same regulations seem contradictory: how can a digital collection be preserved without also having clear lines of communication and significant feedback from the user community; how can the requirement to preserve supporting software be sustained in an environment where software, platform and even infrastructure are offered as services?

There has seldom been a more interesting time for libraries, nor a more challenging one: there seems little prospect of remaining unchanged. In this context, it would be ungenerous not to offer a number of recommendations that will ensure secure access to our common digital legacy.

Non-print legal deposit collections are dynamic, surprising in scale and changing rapidly in configuration. Up until this point the concentration of expertise and dedication to innovation demonstrated at the British Library on behalf of the other libraries has been exemplary: but this is no excuse to reduce efforts. On the contrary, the lesson from the last five years is that only through an ongoing commitment to continuous quality improvement is there any prospect of preserving and expanding non-print legal deposit collections into the second quarter of the 21st century.

There is an implicit contradiction between preservation and access embedded within the legal deposit regulations in the UK and Ireland. The legal deposit regime, with severe constraints to access, has inhibited the development of a meaningful audience and as a consequence there is precious little dialogue between preservation actions and designated community. If this is ignored the mission to preserve will be defeated: instead of inspiring the next generation the legal deposit regime could well inadvertently disenfranchise them.

There are unresolved tensions between the public role of libraries to enable communities and support meaning-making which, in the context of historic collections, are aggravated by the absence of authorial voice. The digital preservation community, concerned with solutions, has been slow to recognise the extent to which it has diverged from the mainstream of cultural theory. The legal deposit regime exacerbates this, inhibiting access, dissociating collections from designated communities and eroding preservation services.

The technological assumptions underpinning legal deposit place unfortunate emphasis on a false dichotomy between data and software. This distinction has never been viable but is rapidly becoming unsustainable in the advent of cloud computing in which software, application and data can no longer be isolated. A paradigm shift in computing means that specific articles of legal deposit face imminent obsolescence.

This essay asks, in the face of an uncertain present and more uncertain future, what are the prospects that non-print legal deposit collections of the last five years will be available to future generations. There can be no guarantee. But given the energy and dedication exhibited so far, given the open commitment to innovation, confidence in their mission and a willingness to address evident shortcomings in the regulations, the legal deposit libraries have created a favourable environment in which preservation is a distinct prospect.

Acknowledgements

I am grateful to Paul Gooding and Melissa Terras for editorial comments and support in preparing this essay and to Paul Wheatley, Sara Thomson and Sarah Middleton for comments on initial drafts.

Notes

1. For information including terms of reference and membership of this committee see www.bl.uk/legal-deposit/joint-committee.
2. See Pennock, 2013, 17 for an account of the WARC file and its practical deployment.
3. The full title of the Open Archival Information System standard is: Space data and information transfer systems – Open archival information system (OAIS) – Reference model and it is approved by ISO through prior agreement with Consultative Committee for Space Data Systems rather than ISO technical committees.

References

Adorno, T. and Horkheimer, M. (1972) *The Culture Industry as Mass Deception, in Dialectic of Enlightenment*, Herder and Herder.

Bantin, P. (2016) *Building Trustworthy Digital Repositories: Theory and Implementation*, Rowman and Littlefield.

Barthes, R. (1973) *Mythologies*, Granada.

Beagrie, N. (2013) *Preservation, Trust And Continuing Access For E-Journals*, Digital Preservation Coalition Technology Watch Report 13-04, http://dx.doi.org/10.7207/twr13-04.

Brindley, L. (2000) Keynote Address to the Preservation 2000 Conference, *New Review of Academic Librarianship* **6**, 125–38.

British Library (2010) *2020 Vision*, www.bl.uk/aboutus/stratpolprog/2020vision/2020A3.pdf.

Brown, A. (2013) *Practical Digital Preservation: a How-to Guide for Organizations of Any Size*, Facet Publishing.

Commission for Preservation and Access/Research Libraries Group (1996) *Preserving Digital Information*, www.clir.org/wp-content/uploads/sites/6/pub63watersgarrett.pdf.

Center for Research Libraries and Online Computer Library Center (2007) *TRAC, Trustworthy Repositories Audit & Certification: Criteria and Checklist*, www.crl.edu/PDF/trac.pdf.

Choudry, A. and Vally, S. (2017) History's Schools: Past Struggles and Present Realities. In Choudry, A. and Vally, S. (eds), *Reflections on Knowledge, Learning and Social Movements: History's Schools*, Routledge, 1–19.

Comaroff, J. and Comaroff J. (1992) *Ethnography and the Historical Imagination*, Westview.

Consultative Committee for Space Data Systems Secretariat (2012) *Reference Model for an Open Archival Information System (OAIS): Recommended Practice* (CCSDS 650.0-M-2: Magenta Book), http://public.ccsds.org/publications/archive/650x0m2.pdf.

D'Ancona, M. (2017) *Post Truth: The New War on Truth and How to Fight Back*, Ebury.

Day, M. (2001) Preservation 2000, *Ariadne*, **26**, www.ariadne.ac.uk/issue26/metadata.

Day, M., Pennock, M., May, P., Davies, K., Whibley, S., Halvarsson, E. and Kimura, A. (2016) The Preservation of Disk-based Content at the British Library: Lessons from the Flashback Project, *Alexandria*, **26**, 216–34.

Day, M., Pennock, M., Smith, C., Cooke, I. and Jenkins, J. (2018) Preservation Planning for Emerging Formats at the British Library. In *Proceedings of the Fifteenth International Conference on the Preservation of Digital Materials (iPres)*, https://osf.io/65p7m.

Department for Culture, Media and Sport (2013) *Guidance on the Legal Deposit Libraries (Non-Print Works) Regulations 2013*, https://assets.publishing.service.gov.uk/government/uploads/system/uploads/attachment_data/file/182339/NPLD_Guidance_April_2013.pdf.

Derrida, J. (1976) *Of Grammatology*, Johns Hopkins University Press.

Derrida, J. and Prenowitz, E. (1995) Archive Fever: a Freudian Impression, *Diacritics* **25**, 9–63.

Digital Preservation Coalition (2017) *Non-Print Legal Deposit Digital Preservation Review: Final Report*, https://www.bl.uk/britishlibrary/~/media/bl/global/digital%20preservation/non-print-lega-deposit-digital-preservation-review.

Duranti, L. (2016) What Will Trustworthy Systems Look Like in the Future? In Bantin, P. (ed.) *Building Trustworthy Digital Repositories: Theory and Implementation*, Rowman and Littlefield, 337–8.

Gartner, R. and Lavoie, B. (2013) *Preservation Metadata*, 2nd edn, Digital Preservation Coalition Technology Watch Report 13-3, http://dx.doi.org/10.7207/twr13-03.

Hall, S. (1990) *Culture, Media, Language*, Unwin.

Harvey, R. and Weatherburn, J. (2018) *Preserving Digital Materials*, 3rd edn, Rowman and Littlefield.

Hedstrom, M. (1998) Digital Preservation: A Time Bomb for Digital Libraries, *Computers and the Humanities*, **31**, 189–202.

Hibberd, L. (2017) Cloudy Culture: Preserving Digital Culture in the Cloud, *DPC Blog*, November, www.dpconline.org/blog/cloudy-culture-part-4.

Hoeren, T., Kolany-Raiser, B. and Yankova, S. (2013) *Legal Aspects of Digital Preservation*, Edward Elgar.

Hu, T.-H. (2015) *A Prehistory of the Cloud*, MIT Press.

International Standards Organization (2012) *Space Data and Information Transfer Systems – Audit and Certification of Trustworthy Digital Repositories*, ISO 16363:2012/CCSDS 652.0-R-1.

John, J. L. (2012) *Digital Forensics and Preservation*, Digital Preservation Coalition Technology Watch Report 12-03, http://dx.doi.org/10.7207/twr12-03.

Kilbride, W. (2017a) The Data Vanishes, *DPC Blog*, August, www.dpconline.org/blog/the-data-vanishes.

Kilbride, W. (2017b) No End of History, *DPC Blog*, June, www.dpconline.org/blog/no-end-of-history.

Kilbride, W. (2017c) Obsolescence 2.0: Digital Preservation by People for People, *DPC Blog*, 2 May, www.dpconline.org/blog/obsolescence-2-0-digital-preservation-by-people-for-people.

Kirchhoff, A. and Morrissey, S. (2014) *Preserving E-books*, Digital Preservation Coalition Technology Watch Report 14-01, http://dx.doi.org/10.7207/twr13-04.

Korn, N. (2009) *In From the Cold: An Assessment of the Scope of Orphan Works and its Impact on the Delivery of Services to the Public*, Strategic Content Alliance, www.djsresearch.co.uk/Free/published/infromthecoldv1.pdf.

Lavoie, B. F. (2014) *The Open Archival Information System (OAIS) Reference Model: Introductory Guide*, Digital Preservation Coalition, https://www.dpconline.org/docs/technology-watch-reports/1359-dpctw14-02/file.

Legal Deposit Libraries Act 2003 c.28, www.legislation.gov.uk/ukpga/2003/28/contents.

National Archives (2017) *Digital Strategy*, www.nationalarchives.gov.uk/documents/the-national-archives-digital-strategy-2017-19.pdf.

National Library of Scotland (2015) *The Way Forward: Library Strategy 2015–2020*, www.nls.uk/media/1190455/2015-strategy.pdf.

Naughton, J. (2012) *From Gutenberg to Zuckerberg: What You Really Need to Know About the Internet*, Quercus.

O'Neill, M. (2006) Essentialism, Adaptation and Justice: Towards a New Epistemology of Museums, *Museum Management and Curatorship*, **21**, 95–116.

Pennock, M. (2013) *Web-Archiving*, Digital Preservation Coalition Technology Watch Report 13-01, http://dx.doi.org/10.7207/twr13-01.

Pennock, M. and Smith, C. (2016) *Managing an ISO 16363 Self-Assessment: A How To Guide*, 11th International Digital Curation Conference, www.dcc.ac.uk/sites/default/files/documents/IDCC16/18_Managing_ISO16363.pdf.

RLG/OCLC Working Group on Digital Archive Attributes (2002) *Trusted Digital Repositories: Attributes and Responsibilities*, RLG-OCLC Report, www.oclc.org/content/dam/research/activities/trustedrep/repositories.pdf.

Rosenthal, D. (2014) TRAC Certification of the CLOCKSS Archive, *DSHR Blog*, https://blog.dshr.org/2014/07/trac-certification-of-clockss-archive.html.

Sahlins, M. (1985) *Islands of History*, University of Chicago Press.

Shenton, H. (2000) From Talking to Doing: Digital Preservation at the British Library, *New Review of Academic Librarianship*, **6**, 163–78.

Spivak, G. (1990) *The Post-Colonial Critique: Interviews, Dialogues Strategies*, Routledge.

The Legal Deposit Libraries (Non-Print Works) Regulations 2013 (S.I. 2013/777), www.legislation.gov.uk/uksi/2013/777/contents/made.

Webb, C. (2000) Towards a Preserved National Collection of Selected Australian Digital Publications, *New Review of Academic Librarianship*, **6**, 179–219.

CHAPTER 8

Giving with one click, taking with the other: electronic legal deposit, web archives and researcher access

Jane Winters

Introduction

If people are familiar with web archives at all, they will most often have heard of the Internet Archive (IA), a non-profit organisation based in San Francisco, California. This is perhaps only to be expected. The IA is 'amongst the earliest systematic attempts at web archiving, operates at a global scale, and gives unrestricted access to its content via the Wayback Machine' (Webster, 2017, 176). It has been archiving the web since late 1996, and at the time of writing makes available more than 325 billion historical web pages for browsing and limited searching (Internet Archive, n.d.).[1] Much less well known is that archives and libraries around the world, from Iceland to Australia, are also busy archiving the web. The nature, scale and scope of this archiving activity varies enormously, but unlike the IA these institutions are concerned either solely or primarily with national web domains (usually delimited by a 'country code Top Level Domain', or ccTLD, such as .fr or .uk) rather than with the web as a whole. This chapter will outline the different legal frameworks within which this national web archiving takes places, focusing on the impact of electronic legal deposit. It will discuss the vitally important enabling role of e-legal deposit, but also describe the challenges posed by the legislation – to access, use, reuse and publication. It concludes by suggesting why researchers should concern themselves with sometimes complex legal issues, and how they might contribute their voices to ongoing discussions about access to our digital cultural heritage.

Web archives around the world

The situation in the UK is complicated by Crown Copyright (more of which below), but in general national web archives fall into two main categories: those which are created under a legal deposit regime and those which collect on a permissions or fair-use basis. The International Internet Preservation Consortium's (IIPC) list of countries or regions in which some form of domain-based archiving takes place includes 17 countries in the former category and 12 in the latter (International Internet Preservation Consortium, n.d.).[2] Permissions-based and ad hoc archiving is characterised by diversity, but so too is the web archiving that takes place within the framework of legal deposit legislation.

A quick glance at the IIPC list reveals a fractured international timeline for archiving the web, and a bewildering array of access arrangements. Iceland, for example, introduced legal deposit legislation in 1997, which was extended to incorporate digital materials in 2002, and web archiving commenced at the National and University Library of Iceland two years later in 2004. Access to the archive of the .is ccTLD is open online to researchers anywhere in the world (Icelandic Web Archive, n.d.). Legal deposit in Denmark, by contrast, dates back to 1697 (Royal Danish Library, n.d. (b)). It was revised in 1997 to include audiovisual material (CDs and video cassettes, etc.) and 'static web documents', and again in 2004 to take in radio, television and 'the dynamic internet', giving Denmark 'one of the most advanced and comprehensive legal deposit laws in the world' (Schostag and Fønss-Jørgensen, 2012, 110). Despite this advanced legislation, however, offsite access to the Danish Web Archive is restricted to researchers with a specific project, who are required to submit an application to the Royal Danish Library (Royal Danish Library, n.d. (a)). In France, legal deposit dates back to the Ordonnance de Montpellier introduced by François I. Legislation was extended to include 'multimedia, software and databases' in 1992, and websites falling within the .fr domain in 2006. Access is even more restricted than in Denmark, however, with the archive only available onsite at the Bibliothèque nationale de France (BNF) and in 25 French regional libraries (Stirling et al., 2011, 2–7).[3] Finally, in Sweden, legislation relating to the legal deposit of digital materials was enacted in 2012, but there is as yet no researcher access, either off- or onsite, to web archives at the National Library of Sweden (Hjerpe, 2014; International Internet Preservation Consortium, n.d.). In the majority of institutions where legal deposit web archiving takes place, there is also a degree of selective, permissions-based archiving, often focused on particular events or anniversaries deemed to be significant for national cultural heritage. These open collections serve as a useful taster for the larger domain archives, but currently no more than that.

UK web archives

Turning to the UK, if anything the landscape becomes even more complicated.[4] There are two main organisations which have responsibility for archiving the web: The National Archives (TNA), which harvests and preserves the online presence of UK central government; and the British Library, which is charged with archiving the entire .uk ccTLD. The legislation which governs their respective web archiving activities is very different. The National Archives began to archive government websites in 2003, under the terms of the Public Records Act. The definition of what constituted 'public records' was sufficiently broad to require no changes to the Act in order to accommodate born-digital data; and archived websites, as Crown Copyright material, may be freely reused under the terms of the Open Government Licence.[5] The result is the open UK Government Web Archive, which is accessible onsite at The National Archives in Kew, but can also be searched online, either as a standalone service or through TNA's main Discovery catalogue.

The British Library began archiving UK websites in 2004 (British Library, 2004), but selectively and on a permissions basis. At the time of writing, 59 of these open special collections are available through the public UK Web Archive. In order to move beyond this time-consuming and limiting approach to archiving the web and harvest data at the domain level, it was necessary, as elsewhere, for legal deposit to be extended to include digital publications, broadly defined. The Library has been undertaking an annual crawl of the .uk domain since April 2013. This first crawl took 70 days to complete and resulted in the collection of 1.9 billion web pages and other assets, amounting to 31TB of data (Webster, 2013), and the scale of the task increases every year. In just five years, the annual domain harvest has generated an extraordinarily rich and diverse primary source for historical research, combining many different types of media, from the records of government to personal blogs to online newspapers. It has the potential to provide unique insights into life in the UK in the early 21st century, to preserve official voices alongside the words of ordinary people – bloggers, citizen journalists, teenagers – who are so often absent from the historical record. And this potential is mirrored in the domain collections being developed by other national memory institutions. As Webster notes:

> The user of web archives has reason to be thankful for the existence of a network of national libraries with a mission to preserve published heritage at a large scale. Without this network, with its long-established channels of communication and co-operation, users would be even more reliant on the Internet Archive than they already are.
>
> (Webster, 2017, 179)

The challenge of web archiving

The work of the Internet Archive has been both ground-breaking and foundational, but the IA does not have a statutory responsibility to preserve the outputs of a nation's culture; nor is it able to draw on, in some cases, centuries of experience in adapting to changes in the technologies of publishing and reading. In so far as it is possible to guarantee the long-term preservation and sustainability of digital cultural heritage, national libraries and archives are exceptionally well placed at least to try.

The extension of legal deposit to include the archiving of various national web domains has, however, proven to be something of a double-edged sword for researchers, and indeed for libraries and archives (Milligan, 2015). There can be no doubt that it underpins the collection, preservation, (partial) curation and republication of the archived web in a stable form.[6] But legal deposit also builds in barriers to the use and reuse of web archives by researchers, and even more by the wider public. Some of these barriers are there by design; others fall under the heading of unintended consequences.

The first difficulty posed by the archiving of the web on the basis of legal deposit arises from the national nature of the relevant legislative traditions and frameworks. The live web is (relatively) open, networked and international, but national web archives are primarily defined by a ccTLD.[7] They are explicitly, and necessarily, national in focus. This is not to say that some material from one national domain is not 'accidentally' harvested during a web crawl for another, but that is not the purpose of the exercise. Artificial geographical boundaries are imposed on web archives which are simply not present on the live web. This is problematic for most kinds of research. Even if the object of study is the web presence of a single UK institution, it is likely that the researcher will come across links to websites and web pages which lie within a different national domain and therefore have not been archived by the British Library. They will hit a virtual brick wall. In this example, the fact that a handful of web pages are not accessible is more of an annoyance than an insurmountable barrier, but what of the researcher who is interested in tracing an international phenomenon? The UK Web Archive holds a large amount of material for a historian interested in the growth of Euroscepticism in Britain (Deswarte, 2015), but reactions to that Euroscepticism in other European countries will not be present; nor will it be possible to gain much insight into parallel movements and trends in other countries.[8]

The scattering of primary sources across different archives and countries is far from a new challenge for researchers, but it has not generally been deliberate.[9] It may even be useful for the historian. The final archival destination of a manuscript, document or book can shed fascinating light on the movement of people, knowledge, money and influence over time. Web archives, however, are artificially segmented by the requirements of legal deposit, and thus become further removed from the live web of which they will be our only record. This is in striking contrast to the ways in which libraries and archives have used digital technologies to remove geographical barriers to access for their analogue holdings, by digitising some of their collections and publishing them on the web. There are numerous examples of projects and initiatives which have gone a step further and virtually reunited physically dispersed corpora.[10] Digitisation and the web have transformed access to much archival material, but counterintuitively, access to born-digital and readily accessible primary sources is closed off by archiving processes.

The obvious solution to this problem would be to aggregate the national domain collections in some way, perhaps even to develop, as a first step, a service which would allow cross-searching of European web archives.[11] Options for regional rather than national web archiving initiatives have also been explored, for example among the Nordic countries (Hallgrímsson and Bang, 2003). But as noted above, many of these national web archives are not accessible online even to the citizens of the countries whose history they record. And once again, this is a function of legal deposit. Some national domain archives which rely on legal deposit are, in fact, open by default, for example the Croatian Web Archive at the National and University Library in Zagreb; but they are the exception rather than the rule. In the UK, access to the domain crawl archive is restricted to reading rooms in the UK's six legal deposit libraries.[12] An open, selective archive is publicly accessible offsite, but it contains only a fraction of the content collected under legal deposit.[13] Even onsite, the user experience is far from seamless, as recounted by Milligan (2015). A new search interface has been launched since Milligan reported, but the key points remain the same: it is not possible (or rather, not legal) to take photographs of information on the computer screen (whether or not that might be useful in practice); intrusive copyright warning messages interfere with browsing; all dynamic content is disabled; and it is not possible to cut and paste text or images. As Milligan notes, 'My research process would be slower using this archive than any other traditional archive that allowed digital photography'. In essence, an archive of born-digital data has been rendered less easy to use than a collection of medieval manuscripts or early modern printed books held in the same library. Functionality that is taken for granted on the live web has been stripped away in order to comply with legal deposit restrictions.

It is the disjuncture between browsing and searching the live web and the web archive that is so disconcerting to a researcher. Some of this results from the archiving process itself: 'the fundamental characteristic of the archived website is that it is a reconstructed and unique version of what was once online, rather than a copy of it'; it is 're-born digital' and does not have the same functionality as a live website (Brügger, 2012a, 758). Some of it, however, is imposed by the legislation. One of the most obviously peculiar effects of the legal framework which allows the archiving of the web in the UK is the *de facto* treatment of a web page as akin to a printed book. From that starting point, it follows that no two people in the same legal deposit library can simultaneously view the same instance of a captured web page.[14] In order to make sure that this does not happen, the web archiving team at the British Library has had to devise and implement a technical solution that automatically refers the user to a different instance of the desired web page, archived as close in time as possible to the originally selected date. If this remains the case, it will be exceptionally difficult to use the UK Web Archive in a teaching context. Students would be unable to explore and critique the same archived website as a group, for example, unless they crowded round a single monitor – behaviour which is not exactly encouraged in a library reading room. Similar problems will face anyone wishing to undertake collaborative research.

The restrictions on use, however, are even more serious than this. As Milligan (2015) discovered, the locked-down nature of the legal deposit collection means that researchers are prevented from accessing the source code for a web page. They cannot see or analyse the underlying html. Critical code studies is an emerging field of research, and is already playing an important role in web historiography:

> Focusing on the archived source code of websites does not only enable analysing web technologies used to construct them, which can tell us something about the web's underlying infrastructure, providing insights into how the web is built and how websites are connected, but can also serve as a means to investigate the web's economic underpinnings, to understand the business models of websites and third parties and trace the economically valuable data flowing between them.
>
> (Helmond, 2017, 139)

This is an enormously promising mode of investigation, but one to which the UK Web Archive is not, and is unlikely to be, susceptible – at least until researcher access is transformed. This is a clear example of unintended consequences. At no point in the drafting of the non-print legal deposit legislation was there a formal decision to allow researchers only to read and analyse the visible text of a web page, but that is the practical effect of the current wording of the law.[15] Policy makers and legislators cannot be expected to anticipate the future directions of research in the humanities and social sciences, but care should be taken not to close off opportunities; to limit the kinds of research questions that can be asked; even to distort whole disciplines and fields of enquiry. This will only happen if researchers collectively feed in to conversations about the development and evolution of legal deposit in relation to born digital archives.

Analysing web archives at scale

The freedom of researchers to develop their own methodologies, to choose what and how they research, is crucial for the national research base and the strength of the university sector as a whole. The risk of undermining this in relation to web historiography is clear. Nowhere is this more apparent than when it comes to analysing web archives at scale. There are currently two clear trends in research drawing on web archives: qualitative, case-study approaches to the history and development of particular websites or web spheres[16] (see, for example, Raffal, 2018; Chakraborty and Nanni, 2017; Dougherty, 2017); and quantitative analyses either of text corpora or of derived data, for example link analysis (see, for example, Ben-David and Amram, 2018; Hale et al., 2014; Milligan, 2017). Researchers wishing to work with the UK Web Archive, or legal deposit collections in other countries, are forced into adopting a qualitative approach. They can, laboriously, work through the archived pages of an organisation or search for pages related to an event such as the London 2012 Olympics. The British Library's curated special collections similarly encourage this kind of research. What researchers cannot do is create their own web corpora, download all of the images associated with a particular event, analyse links between websites in a .uk subdomain, for example .ac.uk or .police.uk. The archived web is a source of enormous potential value for linguistic study, for example in relation to the emergence and take-up of neologisms (see, for example, Winters, 2018), but at present the archive can neither be brought to the appropriate analytical tools, nor the appropriate analytical tools brought to the archive. This creates difficulties for researchers, but it also poses present and future challenges for archiving institutions. If their web archives are to be used at all, they will have no option but to develop at least some of the necessary tools themselves. In some cases they will be forced to reinvent the wheel because of legal restrictions that may well not persist. In straitened times, this is an enormous waste of resources – human, financial and technical.

This does not mean that there will be no quantitative research using web archives – there is a burgeoning literature to the contrary[17] – but it may well mean that those interested in quantitative analysis will simply bypass legal deposit collections. Those responsible for web archiving in national memory institutions are all too aware of this risk. Paul Koerbin, the Assistant Director for Web Archiving and Government Publications at the National Library of Australia, argues that national libraries are in a good position to archive the web because to do so effectively 'requires a strategic purpose with a long term objective' – this is something that national libraries know how to do. But:

> There is much that is required in terms of technologies, systems, policies, procedures and resources to make archiving more than merely harvesting and storing. Not the least is the *sine qua non* purpose of archiving and preservation: sustainable long-term access. Without access preservation is little more than a costly and meaningless storage burden.
>
> (Koerbin, 2017, 195)

Legal deposit, web archives and the wider public

Legal deposit legislation does not only hamper those whose research calls for quantitative, big-data approaches; it also prevents a range of non-academic users from engaging with these collections. The British Library is, of course, open to anyone over the age of 18 'who has a need to see specific items in our collection' (British Library, n.d. (a)), but travelling to the Library or to one of the other legal deposit libraries in the UK in order to register for a reader pass is a significant hurdle, and one that the majority of people will never overcome (or indeed even consider overcoming). If they are interested in reading a particular book or journal article though, they might just consider ordering a copy using British Library On Demand (formerly the BL Document Supply Service), which at the time of writing provides access to approximately 87.5 million items, with publisher agreement (British Library, n.d. (b)). There is as yet no option to request a print-out of an archived web page. There is a hierarchy of access in place, and web archives are firmly at the bottom of the pyramid.

The effects of these restrictive access arrangements are becoming increasingly obvious, particularly in the media. As I have noted elsewhere, 2016 was something of a breakthrough year for the visibility of web archives in the mainstream media (Winters, 2017b, 175–6). Journalists began to turn to the archived web as a source of evidence when information disappeared from the live web or was thought to have been altered in some way.[18] In the overwhelming majority of cases, it is content archived by the IA to which these newspaper and magazine articles refer; information which is readily available to journalists at their desks and to which readers will also have seamless access. You would not expect a reporter from a US newspaper to consult, or even know about, the archived collections of the British Library or the Bibliothèque nationale de France, but these vast national legal deposit collections are also being overlooked by journalists in the UK, France and elsewhere. This has potentially very damaging implications for memory institutions with responsibility for archiving the web, who are at a significant disadvantage when it comes to promoting and encouraging awareness about and use of their digital holdings. This was demonstrated very clearly when the BBC announced in May 2016 that it would be taking down its much-loved BBC Food website. There was a great deal of news coverage in the UK media, a lot of it pointing to the Internet Archive as the place where people would still be able to find their favourite recipes. The team at the UK Web Archive responded with a blog post announcing that they had 'instigated a … crawl of the BBC website with the specific aim of ensuring that we save the recipes from the food pages', but with no content to link to the message was easy to overlook (Winters, 2017b, 175–6; Webber, 2016a). The relative inaccessibility of the legal deposit web archive stands in stark contrast to the readily available live web, and to archived content on that live web. The (more or less) public has become (more or less) private.

Web archives and open access

The severity of the restrictions imposed by legal deposit legislation on the use and reuse of web archives is, moreover, increasingly at odds with current trends in academic research and publishing worldwide. In the UK, all journal articles and conference proceedings published after 1 April 2016 have been required to comply with an open access mandate in order to be considered in national research evaluation processes (specifically the Research Excellence Framework or REF) (Higher Education Funding Council for England, 2016).[19] This mandate will be extended, in one form or another, to monographs after the 2021 REF (Hill, 2018). Researchers are also encouraged, wherever possible, not only to publish articles and comparable works on an open access basis, but to share the data that underpins their research findings in a similarly open fashion. The European Commission, for example, launched an Open Research Data pilot which was extended to cover 'all thematic areas of Horizon 2020 from the start of the 2017 work programme', instituting a regime in which 'open access becomes the default setting for research data' (European Commission, 2017, 8–9). It is permissible for researchers to opt out of publishing their data openly, either wholly or partially, and this will necessarily be the default position for researchers who work with web archives. In many instances, the open publication of research data places new or previously hidden information into the public sphere; users of the archived web, by contrast, are forced to restrict access to data which was previously open. Uncertainty about what is and is not permissible with regard to the republication of data from legal deposit web archives places a significant burden on individuals to engage with a complex legal framework, and potentially encourages an unnecessarily risk-averse approach. Best-practice guidance and publication norms will undoubtedly emerge as users begin to test what is acceptable, but for the moment it remains easier to include a textual description of a web archive screenshot in a research article than to publish even a thumbnail image.[20]

Faced with this litany of problems and challenges, it would be all too easy to throw up one's hands in exasperation and decide to study only publicly accessible web archives, or even choose to work with alternative primary source materials. This is not, however, either a reasonable or a desirable position for researchers to adopt. Web archives developed under a legal deposit regime are inherently more stable, comprehensive and sustainable than those generated by individuals, collectives, businesses or philanthropic organisations, whatever their motivation, commitment or degree of financial investment. We may rail against the failure of legislation to keep up with developments in both technology and research, to adapt sufficiently swiftly to new ways of living and working, but it is that same legislation which both makes possible the harvest of national web domains and assigns responsibility for the task. The long-term preservation of our digital cultural heritage is not left to chance, made vulnerable to privatisation or commercialisation, or to creeping changes in 'terms and conditions'. Like other national libraries and archives, 'The British Library's mission is to make [the UK's] intellectual heritage accessible to everyone for research, inspiration and enjoyment'. Its duties and functions are defined by law, which may be slow to change but is also slow to overturn (British Library, n.d. (c)). Legal deposit brings undoubted problems, but it also brings unique benefits.

Web archives have all the characteristics of a black box; indeed 'understanding a Web archive implies opening several black boxes, the first being that of its collection' (Schafer, Musiani and Borelli, 2016, 3). But the archives collected by national memory institutions, in line with electronic legal deposit, are far more likely than other kinds of web archive to have been documented to the level of detail required by researchers if their analyses are to be sufficiently robust. Historians in particular have always needed to consider the archival context for their primary sources – why did a manuscript end up in one collection rather than another? – but this is particularly true for web archives. History and provenance are vital, but also exceptionally hard to establish. Failure to take into account the different sources of data in a superficially coherent web archive, or to acknowledge the impact of changes in the technologies of web crawling over time, can distort or even fatally undermine research findings (see, for example, Winters, 2017a). An example of good practice in this area is the publicly available documentation for the UK Government Web Archive (UKGWA), which clearly sets out scope and selection policy (National Archives, 2014).[21] The UKGWA is not a legal deposit collection, but it similarly has a basis in statute (National Archives, n.d. (c)). The team behind the UK Web Archive at the British Library had documented its processes on a public blog, which has itself been archived (Webber, 2016b), and more detailed information still will become available to researchers as it falls within the remit of the BL Corporate Archive Policy (British Library, 2012). Initiatives like the IA and the Common Crawl have established themselves as important parts of digital research infrastructure in the early 21st century, but they do not face the same imperative to explain or account for the ways in which they have worked in the past, or how they will work in the future.[22]

To date, web archiving has been characterised by an extraordinary degree of collaboration between archiving institutions and researchers to explore the full potential of legal deposit archives, to open them up to a wide contemporary audience and to try to account for the kinds of access that future historians will need and expect. These collaborations demonstrate what is already possible within the constraints of present legislation and point the way to future innovation. In France, 'Web90: patrimoine, mémoires et histoire du Web dans les années 1990' has combined the study of web archives at the BNF with an exploration of the material culture of the web and internet; in the UK, the BUDDAH project has demonstrated the diversity of the research that can be conducted using web archives, from the investigation of disability action groups online (Millward, 2015) to an ethnosemiotic study of the French in London (Huc-Hepher, 2016). A long-term collaboration between researchers at Aarhus University and the Royal Danish Library has produced ground-breaking research illuminating the shape of a national web domain and provides a model for research in other countries (Laursen and Møldrup-Dalum, 2017). Others, notably Ian Milligan, have shown what can be achieved when historians and computer scientists work together to explore unrestricted web archives (see, for example, Milligan, 2016; 2017). It is to be hoped that the tools and methods Milligan and his colleagues at Waterloo University are developing will be applicable to legal deposit materials at some point in the future. And we know that there is a good chance that those collections will remain available to us in decades to come because of, not despite, electronic legal deposit. We simply need the legislation to develop, to empower national memory institutions to share the digital materials that they are collecting with the widest possible audience, and to allow us easily to access our own digital stories and histories. Electronic legal deposit has laid the groundwork, but more still needs to be done if the full potential of this new type of primary source is to be realised.

A call to arms

As an individual researcher, it is easy to feel rather helpless in the face of legal deposit restrictions. After all, more than 15 years elapsed between the first discussions about extending legal deposit to include non-print material and the implementation of the new legislation (Webster, 2017, 180). What can one person do to influence change? One person probably cannot achieve very much, but researchers who work with the archived web, or would like to do so in the future, can find ways to influence national discussions. We can produce case studies that will help libraries and archives to demonstrate the value of the data that they hold and argue for improved access conditions – and we can publish them openly so that they are accessible to journalists and policy makers. We can talk (and listen) to librarians and archivists about those areas where we are most likely to be able to make progress, so that energy is not wasted on the (for now) unachievable. Privileged research access, for example, might be a first step towards wider openness in the long term. Over time, we can produce an evidence base and build collaborations that will help to bring about legislative evolution. We can afford to wait a little – the data, thanks to legal deposit and the work of national memory institutions, will not be going anywhere. But we cannot afford to wait too long, or research and teaching will be held back, and opportunities missed.

Notes

1. For most of its history, it was only possible to search the Wayback Machine by URL. This meant that researchers were only able to find web pages about which they already knew, or with a URL which could be inferred. In 2016, however, a beta search service was launched which offered full-text searching of website home pages (Goel, 2016). This functionality was subsequently rolled out to the public Wayback Machine.
2. It should be noted that this list does not include the Portuguese Web Archive (Arquivo.pt), which unusually does not fall into either category. Legal deposit legislation in Portugal 'created a framework to support selective archiving of online publications', but Arquivo.pt does not archive the Portuguese web on this basis (Gomes et al., 2008).
3. Responsibility for archiving the French web is divided between the BNF and the Institut national de l'audiovisuel, with the latter dealing with online audiovisual materials (Bibliothèque nationale de France, n.d.).

4. For a more detailed description of the history and development of web archiving in the UK, see Winters, 2018.
5. 'Crown copyright is defined under section 163 of the Copyrights, Designs and Patents Act 1988 as works made by officers or servants of the Crown in the course of their duties' (National Archives, n.d. (a)). The default licence for Crown copyright material is the Open Government Licence, which, with a handful of exemptions, allows both commercial and non-commercial copying, publication, distribution, transmission, adaptation and exploitation of data.
6. The Internet Archive developed the ARC file format for its Heritrix web crawler (Library of Congress, 2008), but the majority of national libraries and archives now use the improved WARC file format (Library of Congress, 2009).
7. In most countries, the legislation does allow national memory institutions limited freedom to look beyond the appropriate ccTLD. In the UK, for example, a web page falls within scope if it is 'made available to the public by a person and any of that person's activities relating to the creation or the publication of the work take place within the United Kingdom' (Bodleian Libraries, n.d.). The Danish Act on Legal Deposit of Published Material mandates that 'Material published in electronic communication networks are [*sic*] considered to be Danish when . . . it is published from other internet domains etc. and is directed at a public in Denmark' (Royal Danish Library, n.d. (a)).
8. This case study is one of 10 produced for the Big UK Domain Data for the Arts and Humanities (BUDDAH) project, funded by the UK Arts and Humanities Research Council (AHRC) as part of its Digital Transformations in the Arts and Humanities theme (grant reference AH/L009854/1). A synthesis of all 10 case studies is available in Cowls, 2017.
9. Archives are sometimes subject to structural separation, as is immediately apparent to anyone researching the history of the British Empire at The National Archives of the UK. TNA's Discovery catalogue, for example, notes in relation to 'Correspondence with the colonies, entry books and registers of correspondence' that 'Domestic records of colonial governments do not normally form part of the Colonial Office records, being kept by those governments in their own archives' (National Archives, n.d. (b)). The profit motive has also come into play on occasion, as archives and individual manuscripts have deliberately been broken up for sale (see, for example, Cummings, 2015; I am grateful to Melissa Terras for suggesting this comparison). Some of these issues fall within the useful concept of 'archival diaspora' (see Punzalan, 2014).
10. See, for example, Early English Laws (grant reference AH/F019394/1), which digitised and made available online 81 manuscripts from 25 libraries and archives in three different countries.

11. Exploring the possibilities for just this kind of research infrastructure inspired the European network RESAW: A Research Infrastructure for the Study of Archived Web Materials.
12. The British Library undertakes the crawls of the .uk domain on behalf of the wider consortium, which includes the National Library of Scotland, the National Library of Wales, the Bodleian Libraries, Oxford, the University Library, Cambridge and the Library of Trinity College, Dublin.
13. This selective archive remains accessible as a standalone service (still referred to as the UK Web Archive at the time of writing), but in late 2017 the British Library launched an expanded beta version of the UK Web Archive, which for the first time allows users to search across both open and restricted content. This successfully removes one barrier to access – the requirement for researchers to use different interfaces to explore web archives depending on the terms by which they were collected – but it makes more prominent the problem of onsite access. The vast majority of search results are flagged with a notice in red that the archived website is 'Viewable only on Library premises'.
14. 'A deposit library must ensure that only one computer terminal is available to readers to access the same relevant material at any one time' (The Legal Deposit Libraries (Non-Print Works) Regulations 2013, no. 777, part 4, regulation 23); and 'a deposit library must ensure that only one reader uses an accessible copy of the same relevant material made under this regulation at any one time (The Legal Deposit Libraries (Non-Print Works) Regulations 2013, no. 777, part 4, regulation 26). I am grateful to Andy Jackson at the British Library for clarifying that the simultaneous access restriction applies on a library-by-library basis.
15. See The Legal Deposit Libraries (Non-Print Works) Regulations 2013, no. 777, part 4, 'Permitted activities'.
16. Brügger (2012b, 2) defines a web sphere as 'web activity related to an event, a theme or the like (for instance political elections, catastrophes, etc.).'
17. The journal *Internet Histories: Digital Technology, Culture and Society* is a good place to start, and particularly the bumper launch issue (1–2, 2017). See also Meyer et al., 2017; Hale et al., 2014; Cowls and Bright, 2017; Helmond, 2017; Milligan, Ruest and St Onge, 2016.
18. Notable examples from that year include the removal of information from the website of the EU Referendum Leave campaign in the UK shortly after the vote on 23 June; and coverage in the USA of the taking down of Melania Trump's website amid disputed claims about her education (Kamen, 2016; Revesz, 2016; and see Winters, 2017b, 176).
19. In a striking example of the value of web archives generally, but particularly of open and accessible web archives, at the time of writing the web page which links to the relevant HEFCE policy document contains a note that, as a result of changes to the structure of UK higher education, 'The HEFCE domain –

www.hefce.ac.uk – will continue to function until September 2018. At this point we will close the site entirely and all its information will only be available from the National Web Archive [*sic*]' (Higher Education Funding Council for England, 2016). The misnamed 'National Web Archive' is, in fact, the open UKGWA.

20. Researchers working with web archives are, of course, not the only ones to face difficulties when it comes to the publication of images in particular. The challenges for art historians, for example, are well rehearsed (see, e.g., Moore, 2017). Web archives, however, stand apart from other materials in legal deposit collections in being uniquely restricted from reproduction. It might be necessary to pay a fee to reproduce a page from an early modern incunable, but at least it may be reproduced, and the permission processes are both known and tested.
21. Rather less good practice is evident in the disappearance from the live TNA website of a useful narrative history of the construction of the UKGWA. It does, however, remain publicly available in archived form at http://webarchive.nationalarchives.gov.uk/20170608213215/www.nationalarchives.gov.uk/webarchive/information.htm.
22. The problems arising from a relative lack of transparency are raised by Leetaru, 2015a and 2015b, albeit unduly critically.

References

Ben-David, A. and Amram, A. (2018) The Internet Archive and the Socio-technical Construction of Historical Facts, *Internet Histories: Digital Technology, Culture and Society*, DOI: 10.1080/24701475.(2018)1455412.

Bibliothèque nationale de France (BNF) (n.d.) *Digital Legal Deposit: Four Questions About Web Archiving at the BNF*, www.bnf.fr/en/professionals/digital_legal_deposit/a.digital_legal_deposit_web_archiving.html.

British Library (n.d.) (a) *Get a Reader Pass*, www.bl.uk/help/how-to-get-a-reader-pass.

British Library (n.d.) (b) *On Demand*, www.bl.uk/on-demand.

British Library (n.d.) (c) *British Library – Statement of Public Task*, www.bl.uk/aboutus/stratpolprog/pubsect-info-regulations/faq/bl_psi_public_task_statement.pdf.

British Library (2004) UK Web Archive, www.webarchive.org.uk/ukwa.

British Library (2012) *British Library Corporate Archive Policy*, www.bl.uk/aboutus/foi/pubsch/pubscheme5/20130124%20BLCA%20Policy.pdf.

Bodleian Libraries, (n.d.) *Identifying UK Websites and Electronic Publications*, www.bodleian.ox.ac.uk/our-work/legal-deposit/information-for-publishers/identifying-uk-websites-and-electronic-publications.

Brügger, N. (2012a) Web Historiography and Internet Studies: Challenges and Perspectives, *New Media and Society*, **15** (5), 752–64, DOI: 10.1177/1461444812462852.

Brügger, N. (2012b) Web History and the Web as a Historical Source, *Zeithistorische Forschungen/Studies in Contemporary History*, **9** (2), 1–11, www.zeithistorische-forschungen.de/2-2012/id=4426.

Chakraborty, A. and Nanni, F. (2017) The Changing Digital Faces of Science Museums: a Diachronic Analysis of Museum Websites. In Brügger, N. (ed.) *Web 25: Histories from the First 25 Years of the World Wide Web*, Peter Lang Publishing, 157–72.

Cowls, J. (2017) Cultures of the UK Web. In Brügger, N. and Schroeder, R. (eds), *The Web as History: Using Web Archives to Understand the Past and the Present*, UCL Press, 220–37, http://discovery.ucl.ac.uk/1542998/1/The-Web-as-History.pdf.

Cowls, J. and Bright, J. (2017) International Hyperlinks in Online News Media. In Brügger, N. and Schroeder, R. (eds), *The Web as History: Using Web Archives to Understand the Past and the Present*, UCL Press, 101–16, http://discovery.ucl.ac.uk/1542998/1/The-Web-as-History.pdf.

Cummings, M. (2015) Beinecke Library Acquires 'Treasure Trove' of Medieval Manuscripts from a Famed 'Book Breaker', *YaleNews*, https://news.yale.edu/2015/11/15/beinecke-library-acquires-treasure-trove-medieval-manuscripts-famed-book-breaker.

Deswarte, R. (2015) Revealing British Euroscepticism in the UK Web Domain and Archive Case Study, *Web Archives as Big Data*, http://sas-space.sas.ac.uk/6103.

Dougherty, M. (2017) 'Taqwacore is Dead. Long Live Taqwacore' or Punk's not Dead? Studying the Online Evolution of the Islamic Punk Scene. In Brügger, N. and Schroeder, R. (eds), *The Web as History: Using Web Archives to Understand the Past and the Present*, UCL Press, 204–19, http://discovery.ucl.ac.uk/1542998/1/The-Web-as-History.pdf.

European Commission (2017) *H2020 Programme: Guidelines to the Rules on Open Access to Scientific Publications and Open Access to Research Data in Horizon 2020*, http://ec.europa.eu/research/participants/data/ref/h2020/grants_manual/hi/oa_pilot/h2020-hi-oa-pilot-guide_en.pdf.

Goel, V. (2016) Beta Wayback Machine – Now With Site Search! *Internet Archive Blogs*, https://blog.archive.org/2016/10/24/beta-wayback-machine-now-with-site-search.

Gomes, D., Nogueira, A., Miranda, J. and Costa, M. (2008) Introducing the Portuguese Web Archiving Initiative, 8th International Web Archiving Workshop, Aarhus, Denmark, http://sobre.arquivo.pt/wp-content/uploads/introducing-the-portuguese-web-archive-initiative.pdf.

Hale, S., Yasseri, T., Cowls, J., Meyer, E. T., Schroeder, R. and Margetts, H. (2014) Mapping the UK Webspace: Fifteen Years of British Universities on the Web. In

Proceedings of the 2014 ACM Conference on Web Science, 62–70, https://dl.acm.org/citation.cfm?id=2615691.

Hallgrímsson, Þ. and Bang, S. (2003) *Nordic Web Archive*, http://nwatoolset.sourceforge.net/docs/nwa@ecdl2003.pdf.

Helmond, A. (2017) Historical Website Ecology: Analyzing Past States of the Web Using Archived Source Code. In Brügger, N. (ed.) *Web 25: Histories from the First 25 Years of the World Wide Web*, Peter Lang Publishing, 139–55.

Higher Education Funding Council for England (HEFCE) (2016) *Policy for Open Access in the Next Research Excellence Framework: Updated November 2016*, www.hefce.ac.uk/pubs/year/2016/201635.

Hill, S. (2018) Open Access Monographs in the REF, *HEFCE Research Policy blog*, http://blog.hefce.ac.uk/2018/02/23/open-access-monographs-ref-2027.

Hjerpe, A. (2014) Detailed Digital Deposits, *Scandinavian Library Quarterly*, **47** (2), http://slq.nu/?article=volume-47-no-2-2014-7.

Huc-Hepher, S. (2016) Searching for Home in the Historic Web: An Ethnosemiotic Study of London-French Habitus as Displayed in Blogs, *Web Archives as Big Data*, http://sas-space.sas.ac.uk/6252.

Icelandic Web Archive (n.d.) *Um íslenska vefsafnið*, http://vefsafn.is/index.php?page=um-vefsafnid.

International Internet Preservation Consortium (IIPC) (n.d.) *Legal deposit*, http://netpreserve.org/web-archiving/legal-deposit.

Internet Archive (n.d.) *Wayback Machine*, http://web.archive.org.

Kamen, M. (2016) Vote Leave Wipes Homepage after Brexit Result, *Wired*, www.wired.co.uk/article/vote-leave-wipes-website-after-brexit.

Koerbin, P. (2017) Revisiting the World Wide Web as Artefact: Case Studies in Archiving Small Data for the National Library of Australia's PANDORA Archive. In Brügger, N. (ed.) *Web 25: Histories from the First 25 Years of the World Wide Web*, Peter Lang Publishing, 191–206.

Laursen, D. and Møldrup-Dalum, P. (2017) Looking Back, Looking Forward: 10 Years of Development to Collect, Preserve, and Access the Danish Web. In Brügger, N. (ed.) *Web 25: Histories from the First 25 Years of the World Wide Web*, Peter Lang Publishing, 207–27.

Leetaru, K. (2015a) How Much of the Internet does the Wayback Machine Really Archive?, *Forbes*, www.forbes.com/sites/kalevleetaru/2015/11/16/how-much-of-the-internet-does-the-wayback-machine-really-archive.

Leetaru, K. (2015b) Why It's So Important to Understand What's in Our Web Archives, *Forbes*, www.forbes.com/sites/kalevleetaru/2015/11/25/why-its-so-important-to-understand-whats-in-our-web-archives.

Library of Congress (LOC) (2008) *ARC_IA, Internet Archive ARC File Format*, www.loc.gov/preservation/digital/formats/fdd/fdd000235.shtml.

Library of Congress (LOC) (2009) *WARC, Web Archive File Format*, www.loc.gov/preservation/digital/formats/fdd/fdd000236.shtml.

Meyer, E. T., Yasseri, T., Hale, S. A., Cowls, J., Schroeder, R. and Margetts, H. (2017) Analysing the UK Web Domain and Exploring 15 Years of UK Universities on the Web. In Brügger, N. and Schroeder, R. (eds) *The Web as History: Using Web Archives to Understand the Past and the Present*, UCL Press, 23–44, http://discovery.ucl.ac.uk/1542998/1/The-Web-as-History.pdf.

Milligan, I. (2015) Web Archive Legal Deposit: a Double-Edged Sword, *Ian Milligan: Digital History, Web Archives, and Contemporary History*, https://ianmilligan.ca/2015/07/14/web-archive-legal-deposit-a-double-edged-sword.

Milligan, I. (2016) Lost in the Infinite Archive: the Promise and Pitfalls of Web Archives, *International Journal of Humanities and Arts Computing*, **10** (1-2), 78–94.

Milligan, I. (2017) Welcome to the Web: the Online Community of GeoCities During the Early Years of the World Wide Web. In Brügger, N. and Schroeder, R. (eds), *The Web as History: Using Web Archives to Understand the Past and the Present*, UCL Press, 137–58, http://discovery.ucl.ac.uk/1542998/1/The-Web-as-History.pdf.

Milligan, I., Ruest, N. and St Onge, A. (2016) The Great WARC Adventure: Using SIPS, AIPS, and DIPS to Document SLAPPs, *Digital Studies/ Le champ numérique*, DOI: 10.16995/dscn.18.

Millward, G. (2015) Digital Barriers and the Accessible Web: Disabled People, Information and the Internet, *Web Archives as Big Data*, http://sas-space.sas.ac.uk/6104.

Moore, M. (2017) Museum Fees Are Killing Art History, Say Academics, *The Times*, www.thetimes.co.uk/edition/news/museum-fees-are-killing-art-history-say-academics-qhfwmdws6.

National Archives (n.d.) (a) *Crown Copyright*, www.nationalarchives.gov.uk/information-management/re-using-public-sector-information/uk-government-licensing-framework/crown-copyright.

National Archives (n.d.) (b), Correspondence with the Colonies, Entry Books and Registers of Correspondence, http://discovery.nationalarchives.gov.uk/details/r/C433.

National Archives of the UK (n.d.) (c) *UK Government Web Archive*, www.nationalarchives.gov.uk/webarchive.

National Archives (2014) *Operational Selection Policy OSP27: UK Central Government Web Estate*, www.nationalarchives.gov.uk/documents/information-management/osp27.pdf.

Punzalan, R. L. (2014) Digital Diasporas: a Framework for Understanding the Complexities and Challenges of Dispersed Photographic Collections, *American Archivist*, **77** (2), 326–49, DOI: 10.17723/aarc.77.2.729766v886w16007.

Raffal, H. (2018) Tracing the Online Development of the Ministry of Defence and Armed Forces Through the UK Web Archive, *Internet Histories: Digital Technology, Culture and Society*, DOI: 10.1080/24701475.2018.1456739.

Revesz, R. (2016) Melania Trump's Website Vanishes from Internet as Rumours Swirl Over Her University Degree, *The Independent*, www.independent.co.uk/news/world/americas/melania-trump-vanishes-biography-website-online-disappears-rumours-plagiarised-speech-education-a7160856.html.

Royal Danish Library (n.d.) (a) *Netarchive*, https://en.statsbiblioteket.dk/national-library-division/netarchive.

Royal Danish Library (n.d.) (b) *Act on Legal Deposit of Published Material (Translation)*, www.kb.dk/en/kb/service/pligtaflevering-ISSN/lov.html.

Schafer, V., Musiani, F. and Borelli, M. (2016) Negotiating the Web of the Past, *French Journal for Media Research, La Toile Négociée/Negotiating the Web*, http://frenchjournalformediaresearch.com/lodel/index.php?id=963.

Schostag, S. and Fønss-Jørgensen, E. (2012) Webarchiving: Legal Deposit of Internet in Denmark. A Curatorial Perspective, *Microform & Digitization Review*, **41**, 110–20.

Stirling, P., Illien, G., Sanz, P. and Sepetjan, S. (2011) The State of E-legal Deposit in France: Looking Back at Five Years of Putting New Legislation into Practice and Envisioning the Future. In *World Library and Information Congress: 77th IFLA General Conference and Assembly*, 1-27, www.ifla.org/past-wlic/2011/193-stirling-en.pdf.

Webber, J. (2016a) Saving BBC Recipes website, *UK Web Archive Blog*, http://blogs.bl.uk/webarchive/2016/05/saving-bbc-recipes-website.html.

Webber, J. (ed.) (2016b) *UK Web Archive Blog*, http://blogs.bl.uk/webarchive/index.html.

Webster, P. (2013) Crawling the UK Web Domain, *UK Web Archive Blog*, http://blogs.bl.uk/webarchive/2013/09/domaincrawl.html.

Webster, P. (2017) Users, Technologies, Organisations: Towards a Cultural History of World Web Archiving. In Brügger, N. (ed.) *Web 25: Histories from the First 25 Years of the World Wide Web*, Peter Lang Publishing, 175–90.

Winters, J. (2017a) Tackling Complexity in Humanities Big Data: from Parliamentary Proceedings to the Archived Web. In Hiltunen, T., McVeigh, J. and Säily, T. (eds), *Big and Rich Data in English Corpus Linguistics: Methods and Explorations*, Varieng, www.helsinki.fi/varieng/series/volumes/19/winters.

Winters, J. (2017b) Breaking in to the Mainstream: Demonstrating the Value of Internet (and Web) Histories, *Internet Histories: Digital Technology, Culture and Society*, **1** (1–2), 173–9, DOI: 10.1080/24701475.2017.1305713.

Winters, J. (2018) Negotiating the Archives of UK Web Space. In Brügger, N. and Laursen, D. (eds), *The Historical Web and Digital Humanities: the Case of National Web Domains*, Routledge.

Online resources

Big UK Domain Data for the Arts and Humanities, https://buddah.projects.history.ac.uk.

British Library (2017) UK Web Archive (beta version), https://beta.webarchive.org.uk.

Common Crawl, http://commoncrawl.org.

Early English Laws, www.earlyenglishlaws.ac.uk.

RESAW: A Research Infrastructure for the Study of Archived Web Materials, http://resaw.eu.

Web90: Patrimoine, Mémoires et Histoire du Web dans les Années 1990, https://web90.hypotheses.org.

CHAPTER 9

Follow the users: assessing UK non-print legal deposit within the academic discovery environment

Linda Berube and Frankie Wilson

Introduction

It is a truth universally acknowledged that the lone search box is what all users prefer. It simplifies information seeking and retrieval by freeing users from restrictive terminology or 'library-speak' and by unifying a thundering herd of disparate resources, all accessible, into a single result list (Boyd et al., 2006; Lown, Sierra and Boyer, 2013; Guajardo, Brett and Young, 2017). Information seeking is simplified in the sense that users do not have to navigate different interfaces or think too deeply about search terms and search strings. Businesses developing software and especially web-based products have heeded the popularity of the apparent simplicity of search afforded by the likes of Google. They, and those they sell to, have become more data-driven, or in a mostly numeric sense, user-driven (Rodden, Hutchinson and Fu, 2010; Fabijan et al., 2017). The more customers discover and interact with their content and services, the more data gleaned, and the more competitive, profitable and responsive these companies can be (Fabijan et al., 2017). Within the discovery-access-assessment environment, this process describes a continuous feedback loop of systems-based communication – inputs and outputs – among customers, staff, and managers (Markey, Reichheld and Dullweber, 2009).

Academic libraries, in their turn, have pursued the web-based unified search environment. They have added discovery layers to local library catalogue and management systems, providing access to both popular and research resources, as well as esoteric collections. However, academic library resources and collections are not all completely web-based. Moreover, some digital collections may not be able to compete with subscription-based digital resources in 'the familiar metrics of user experience', including page views, repeat unique users (Rodden, Hutchinson and Fu, 2010, 2395), and more specifically for libraries, usage metrics. These metrics can range from 'basic user surveys to the usage tracking of physical journal issues and monographs to library loan statistics' (Glanzel and Gorraiz, 2014, 2161). Some resources, such as the UK Non-Print Legal Deposit (NPLD) collections, come with access and use restrictions that run counter to digital discovery and academic user expectation of it, proving a challenge for UK academic legal deposit libraries (Gooding, Terras and Berube, 2019). The challenge in part has been identifying their place in the unified digital discovery environment. And, if they do not figure in any significant way in this environment, is there a place for them in library assessment based on use metrics?

These challenges stem partly from an initial emphasis on NPLD technical implementation across the six legal deposit libraries. Evaluating UK NPLD access and use has admittedly not been a priority of legal deposit libraries. Since The Legal Deposit Libraries (Non-Print Works) Regulations 2013, mandating the collection of electronic resources, they have focused more on technical and procedural implementation, of necessity at the beginning of this complicated process (Gibby and Brazier, 2012), but at the expense of collecting and analysing quantitative and qualitative data that focus on access and use (Gooding, Terras and Berube, 2019). For example, the Bodleian Libraries at Oxford University, an academic legal deposit library whose discovery environment and full programme of library user assessment illustrate various points in this chapter, has concentrated on NPLD-focused user assessment predominantly through its participation in the AHRC-funded project in 2017–19, 'Digital Library Futures (DLF): the impact of e-legal deposit in the academic sector' (Gooding, Terras and Berube, 2019, see also elegaldeposit.org, n.d.). DLF was the first user-focused study which analysed how NPLD e-books, e-journals and a UK web archive are accessed and used by researchers through a mixed methodology of qualitative and quantitative data collection.

In this chapter we explore the role that NPLD collections play or can play in library discovery and its assessment. What NPLD collections demonstrate is that a purely numeric or metrics approach to library use provides a limited view of user interaction with library resources, electronic and otherwise. The academic library digital environment is wholly distinct from the consumer or business web environment. It more truly represents discovery, in that users are not just confined to simple search, but are also able to seek information and ideas, from resources as well as colleagues, without the interference of intrusive personalisation, advertisement, all the noise and distraction of the wider web (Schofield, 2015). It is a 'digital third space' (Pinfield, Cox and Rutter, 2017, 52). In this distinct electronic environment combined with the physical library space, essentially a 'hybridised information environment' (Schmersal, 2018), academic libraries offer their user communities the full range of resources from print to electronic, and some, such as NPLD, which fall somewhere in between. Moreover, there is no single method of information seeking: users have their own individual ways of searching and discovering, their own priorities and values, as well as the kinds of resources, print or electronic, they prefer (Guajardo, Brett and Young 2017). In a library 'culture of assessment', a regular and flexible mixed methodological approach can track users in their journey from discovery to assessment. The librarians play their part by feeding the results of assessment back into this library feedback loop, a process critical to understanding how staff, users and collections work together (Lakos and Phipps, 2004; Farkas, Hinchliffe and Houk, 2015). This loop provides a rich understanding of the whole information space and consequently the value that NPLD collections can bring to it. A place can be found in the library feedback loop if NPLD collections are viewed through the lens of the hybridised information space; a more varied methodological approach to quantitative and qualitative analysis; and a recognition of what makes these resources a truly unique offering.

In pursuit of discovery: NPLD in the library search environment

Library discovery: from card catalogues to library service platforms

A search that will return NPLD e-books and e-journals[1] begins with the library catalogue or search portal. Local and third-party search in academic libraries has undergone radical transformation: from the days of the card catalogue through to one large local database of content on an electronic catalogue to the current digital environment consisting of web- and cloud-based library systems providing access to a range of institutionally owned and third-party resources. Users no longer expect to move to different terminals in order to access commercial databases. Now, a range of content is available from one library dedicated terminal or even from personal laptops in and outside the library. And, in the midst of all these digital resources, print materials (whether archival, reference or circulating) are still important to study and research. Indeed, academic users access a diverse range of materials, especially when studying in libraries (Lopatovska and Regalado, 2016).

Whether referring to the retro card file or the integrated library system (ILS),[2] the library catalogue, the foundation of locally owned content, is designed mainly for the look-up search: searching for known items or precise bits of information from a central server. However, 'library technology [tracking] alongside the prevailing technologies available in the general business and consumer sectors' (Breeding, 2015, 6) has expanded from simple search of locally owned resources to unified information seeking and retrieval across a diverse range of purchased, licensed and repository publications, oftentimes necessitating separate underlying systems (Dempsey, 2008). For example, in common with most academic libraries, the Bodleian Libraries provides access to the catalogue of printed holdings and to its electronic resources via a resource discovery platform, known as SOLO (Search Oxford Libraries Online), comprised of two Ex Libris products: its Integrated Library System (ILS), Aleph, and discovery platform, Primo. Most of the college and non-Bodleian University libraries also provide access to their catalogue holdings via SOLO, so it functions as a 'one-stop shop' for readers to locate physical and electronic resources in the collegiate University. SOLO also provides a circulation system for the lending stock and enables readers to request books from the offsite storage facility to a reading room. All readers can click through to electronic books and journals from a SOLO search on a library computer in a reading room; members of the University can also access electronic resources from anywhere with an internet connection using their 'Single Sign On' (Shibboleth).[3]

In addition to full computers for readers, 'quick-check kiosks' are also provided in each library. These limited-access terminals are intended to function as a public access catalogue so that readers who just want to locate a physical book in the library can find the relevant shelf mark without needing to log in to a computer. These computers do not allow click-through access to electronic resources and time out after a period of inactivity.

SOLO is an example of the library service platform (LSP),[4] the result of a combination of supplier feedback, beta testing, early implementation and development *in partnership* with academic libraries. This development builds on the customisable solutions offered to academic libraries which combine library and third-party resource access along with unified search, such as OpenURL Link Resolvers and Electronic Resource Management Systems (ERMS) (Breeding, 2015; Thomsett-Scott and Reese, 2012). In addition, Google offers libraries a way of making their resources discoverable through Google Scholar with its Google Scholar Library Links tool.[5]

This unified digital environment provides the single search box that users presumably prefer. However, the discovery platforms used by academic libraries also offer advanced and faceted or filtered search reflecting the range of library collections and pitched at the information-seeking capabilities of the academic user (Sadeh, 2015; Kim, 2011a). For this reason, academic libraries have sought a search environment conducive to the more exploratory requirements of research: in other words the acquisition of knowledge, as opposed to basic information on any given subject (Athukorala et al., 2015). LSPs combined with discovery tools, from the same or different vendors, provide just this kind of environment for exploratory search, with options for skimming through titles and abstracts, and reading more deeply across resources and over extended periods to acquire knowledge and mastery of a subject. The effort extended by the Bodleian and other academic libraries to provide access to a wide range of resources illustrates their response to user expectations in the digital environment. Indeed, the Digital Library Futures (DLF) research with Bodleian users revealed their appreciation of ease of use, convenient access, and storage for repeat uses (Gooding, Terras and Berube, 2019).

UK non-print legal deposit in the academic discovery environment

In this digital discovery environment, what happens to unique collections perhaps hidden within the crowd of content? Collections that, while for the most part discoverable remotely, are not retrievable outside physical library premises? The UK Non-Print Legal Deposit (NPLD) collections are one such example: e-journals and e-books are collected, and websites are harvested, as part of a regulation that also prescribes for access and use.

In practice, what this has produced is a divergence between how this material is searched, accessed and used relative to the 'bought' or subscription collections of the legal deposit libraries. The metadata for NPLD e-journals and e-books is discoverable through a search in the library catalogue within the library and remotely, regardless of device. However, they cannot be accessed or retrieved remotely; users must not only be at the library but also at a designated terminal to have access.[6] Moreover, there is the further limitation of one user per title per designated library terminal (HM Government, 2013, regulation 23, part 4). However, in terms of discoverability, it is a collection that is integrated with other collections of e-books and e-journals in the library catalogue.

The UK Legal Deposit Web Archive, however, differs from NPLD e-books and e-journals in some significant ways. It is a unique collection of millions of websites automatically harvested from the UK web. It differs from what was once known as the Open UK Web Archive, launched in 2004, which is a permissions-based collection of about 50,000 sites which can be remotely searched and accessed.[7] The UK Legal Deposit Web Archive, by comparison, contains over 500TB of data (Gooding et al., 2019). Both archives can be searched from a single web interface.

Unlike NPLD e-books and e-journals, metadata for the UK Legal Deposit Web Archive's sites is not integrated with other collections in the legal deposit libraries' LSP: it is accessed via a separate interface. Without an obvious (to the user) link to this website, as well as a description of this unique resource, it cannot be considered discoverable. Moreover, depending upon the library, the link is not always visible to the remote user, who may not realise it is another option for research within the library. The exception to these strictures is the British Library (BL), where web archive metadata has been added to the BL LSP, enabling remote search and discovery, although not remote access. Whether the academic user can discover web archive materials through remote or onsite library searching, lack of access means that there is no opportunity to learn about and use this unique collection. These restrictions, as well as others such as print-only use, are dictated by legislation (HM Government, 2013) and so no matter how much effort is put in by libraries to unify search, access and retrieval, this collection will, for the foreseeable future, remain separate from the results of that effort.

In the case of electronic resources, the user expects not just remote discovery but also remote access (Gooding, Terras and Berube, 2019; Kim, 2011a). Ultimately, digital discovery of non-print legal deposit materials fails at the first hurdle of discovery systems: the promise of quick and easy access and use. By regarding them almost exclusively through the use of metrics of page views, accesses and print requests, perhaps necessary for proving return on investment (ROI) (Murray, Ireland and Hackathorn, 2016), legal deposit libraries leave NPLD collections out of the routine local library user and service assessment, and consequently out of the feedback loop.

Follow the users: library assessment in the discovery environment

Library discovery by the numbers

Rodden, Hutchinson and Fu (2010) discuss the analytical tools available to the human-computer interaction (HCI) community to measure use of software and products. However, they do caution that these 'standard web analytics metrics may be too generic to apply to a particular product goal or research question' (p. 2396). Academic library user assessment has followed the same pattern, afforded by the more advanced systems that can supply large-scale metrics at the touch of a button.

Library assessment or performance measurement has traditionally been data-driven in its own way, even in the olden days before electronic systems, through the collection of such quantitative data or library use statistics as books circulated, number of registered users, footfall, enquiries made, all to support internal evaluation of services, collections and performance (Nicholas, 1997; Glanzel and Gorraiz, 2014). Electronic and especially web-based systems and resources have provided more data, for example users' interaction with the systems and resources, as well as tools for quantitative analysis. The investment in these systems, combined with budget considerations and competition with web-based information resources, means that assessment increasingly focuses on proving value to academic administrations, primarily in the form of contribution to student academic success (Chen et al., 2015), as well as 'their parent institutions' teaching, learning, and research missions' (Hurst et al., 2016, 571).

In terms of ROI, the results of gathering systems-based access and use statistics, even when basic user surveys are included, have not necessarily been encouraging. Some studies reporting the lack of use of academic library website resources have questioned whether library investment in discovery has been worthwhile, especially if interfaces remain difficult to use (faceted search v. single search box again) (Kim, 2011a). One supplier of library management systems remarks on the lack of development in the most important areas, one being the flexibility to handle non-bibliographic content. He attributes this to the librarian's penchant for the inflexible MARC tags and a preoccupation with back-office customisation (Beastall, 2015). As if these challenges were not enough, research suggests that academic libraries are not necessarily the first port of call for their users, whether they be undergraduates or researchers. In *Does Discovery Still Happen in Libraries?*, Roger Schonfeld summarises results from a 2014 Ithaka S+R Survey, which asked US academic library directors to respond to the following statement: 'It is strategically important that my library be seen by its users as the first place they go to discover scholarly content' (Schonfeld, 2014, 3). Schonfeld points out that the number agreeing to this statement has been in decline (albeit modest) since 2010, although 'library directors seem to perceive continuing value in being seen to serve as the starting point' (p. 3). Those in agreement have continued to decline in a more recent Ithaka Survey in 2016. In fact, 'library directors are increasingly recognizing that discovery does not and should not always happen in the library' (Wolff-Eisenberg, 2017). Both Schonfeld and Wolff-Eisenberg observe that library directors' attitudes to discovery are evolving and that they understand how important commercial resources and peer networks are, sometimes quicker and less restrictive. Indeed, these findings confirm ongoing research on user expectation and information-seeking behaviour, originating from human-computer interaction (HCI) studies (Marchionini, 1997; Agarwal and Poo, 2007; Savolainen, 2018).

There are no surprises, though, for where discovery is happening, or at least where it begins. Schonfeld is not alone in reporting that a preponderance of research starts with a browser search. Google not only provides apparently unfettered search and access across resources, bibliographic and non-bibliographic, but it is more responsive to a basic approach to searching. This approach reflects how users actually search or want to search: 'rather than expecting the user to develop search strategies, Google accommodates a trial-and-error approach' (Sadeh, 2015, 215) which matches the user's own method of searching. So, while vendors and librarians alike grapple with making library systems more responsive to library and user expectation, users and especially academic research users are heading straight for Google and Google Scholar, which now offers direct access back to library resources without reference to library discovery tools or platforms (another type of feedback loop?).

In this 'return on investment' climate driven by data collected by web-based systems, NPLD collections and their access restrictions would appear to be resistant to 'proving value' during assessment. Indeed, prior to the DLF project, only systems-based data in the form of library use (number of items accessed) had been collected across the six legal deposit libraries and disseminated by the British Library for the NPLD collections. The general feeling among staff had been that the numbers were low (Gooding, Terras and Berube, 2019, 18). It can be argued that NPLD collections after all are not much different from print reference or archive collections in terms of discoverability and accessibility: findable through catalogues remotely but only accessible onsite. Because they are electronic, though, user expectations are raised to the level of all electronic resources available on the web and indeed through the library's own digital environment.

The more users interact with content in the discovery environment, the more data libraries have upon which to base decisions about technology tools and content, even library space (Chen et al., 2015, 1). NPLD collections, with their access and use restrictions, are left out of this quantitative feedback loop because of comparatively low access numbers (Gooding, Terras and Berube, 2019). The propensity by library staff to not look beyond the numbers and consequently not grapple with the distinct nature of the NPLD collections means that their users do not know what to make of them. The current routine assessment process for NPLD collections, consisting solely of systems-based access and use statistics, certainly does not support an understanding of the value of these resources.

Not just a numbers game: library user assessment in the hybridised academic environment

Library assessment by users

If discovery is not happening solely in libraries, or if they are not the first port of call for researchers, then does that mean the investment in discovery has not been worth it? Has Google really '[broken] libraries' information monopoly' (Kim, 2011b, 9). A different kind of assessment is required to understand that, while libraries may no longer have a monopoly, they can still be considered major players in the information economy. This different kind of assessment is more user-focused, not dismissing quantitative data but that it 'should be triangulated with findings from other sources, such as usability studies and field studies, which leads to better decision-making' (Rodden, Hutchinson and Fu, 2010, 2396). Moreover, and especially for NPLD collections, quantitative data collection should move beyond the out-of-the-box library use metrics.

The growth in number and types of academic users suggests that academic libraries still have a significant stake in the information environment. The Bodleian Libraries, for example, supports the learning and research needs of 7,000 academic staff, 12,000 undergraduates and 12,000 postgraduates (following both taught and research programmes). The 28 libraries that form the Bodleian Libraries comprise most (though not all) of the centrally provided University libraries, and include major research libraries, libraries attached to faculties and departments, and the historic Bodleian Library. There are also libraries in all of the 38 colleges.[8] All libraries in the collegiate University provide physical resources and study space, but the Bodleian Libraries provides electronic resources for the whole system. As a National Research Library, the Bodleian Libraries provides access for academically affiliated and independent researchers to its printed collections, archives and manuscripts, and electronic resources, in its reading rooms. Half of the 60,000 readers who use the Libraries each year are external library card holders, comprising those formerly affiliated with the University as well as a significant number from the wider community.

This number and range of distinct user communities with access to library resources require an understanding beyond basic use metrics. To try to quantify these communities and their interactions with library resources not only misrepresents library use, but also misses the unique offering of academic libraries. These metrics also do not provide an understanding of the academic user, whose information-seeking behaviour cannot be reduced to a single metric. Remote access is important, but academic users frequent and use their libraries for multiple reasons. Providing users with 'quick-check kiosks' for searching locally owned print books for example, as does the Bodleian Libraries, indicates a basic acknowledgement of varied information-seeking behaviours on library premises.

The hybridised third space

Libraries have begun to recognise the value of looking beyond numbers, being more user-driven by employing user experience techniques (Killick and Wilson, 2019). In the process, they have developed a more nuanced view of what is happening in their physical as well as digital spaces. Indeed, a careful study of information seeking on library premises reveals more complexity. In a study of user behaviour in four academic libraries in New York City, Lopatovska and Regalado (2016) observed 'students [using] a wide variety of print and digital resources and tools often simultaneously' (p. 393). This behaviour combined with the more social aspects conducive to the library space resulted in users 'spending considerable amounts of time in their libraries' (p. 395). In other words, it is not just the space: if it were, students would all be in cafés, internet and otherwise. A study by the second author of the use of the physical Bodleian Libraries (Wilson and Ovenden, 2016) revealed that, yes, in a 21st Century research-intensive university, even when consumption, production and dissemination of information is electronic (such as in the disciplines of science, technology, engineering, mathematics and medicine) there is a need for a physical library to support teaching, learning and research. The research underscored students' dependence on the library to provide a space that was safe, with no distractions, little noise, and with books. Not only were books, and specifically textbooks, used within the space, but a range of other resources, including electronic resources, course notes, grey literature and, for medical students, anatomical models. The student wish list for the science library included:

> Be quiet, Be welcoming, Be comfortable (temperature, light, ventilation, ergonomic furniture, water, nice toilets), Have desks appropriate for work (large desks usually; small individual desks for revision), Have excellent IT, Facilitate working alongside peers – companionable silence, Enable them to stay all day (café, lockers, lounge), Be accessible (wheelchair use; standing desks).
>
> (Wilson, 2018, Slide 20)

This list demonstrates users truly invested in a space that is most conducive to research and study. It is also important to note here not just the range of resources required, but the specificity depending upon discipline. Other studies have confirmed different patterns of use as well as resources across academic environments (Gooding et al., 2019; Kim, 2011b). For example, one study reports that humanities users have a preference for print and therefore are more inclined to use library resources than business users, who required more timely resources and so used commercial websites (Kim, 2011b).

The range of resources and information-seeking behaviours points to what Schmersal (2018, 62) identifies as a 'hybridized information environment'. In his singular comparison of information-seeking theological students to pastoral nomads, Schmersal recounts observations similar to the aforementioned studies about the library space as distinct:

> the physical library space also facilitates direct, unmediated, face-to-face interactions between scholars and librarians. Moreover, the design of the physical library itself, the 'aura' of a formal, quiet space with minimal distractions, is itself an important part of the service we provide.
>
> (Schmersal, 2018, 68)

It is probably not surprising, given that his subject is theology libraries and students, that he goes on to describe the 'solemnity and sacredness' that physical books confer upon an environment. However, his words echo the desire expressed in this study as well as the Bodleian study (Wilson and Ovenden, 2016) and others for a place devoid of distraction, which academic libraries are able to provide both in their physical and digital spaces. In addition, Schmersal (2018, 63) points out that the digital discovery environments of academic libraries are particularly adept at allowing students 'to most fully and efficiently exploit an overabundance of resources within the confines of limited time and attention'.

What has the physical library space to do with NPLD materials? If assessment is purely based on access and use in the digital discovery environment, then NPLD collections do not meet users' expectations of what electronic resources are and how they should behave. If the academic library is then to be regarded purely as the sum of its electronic resources and systems, then NPLD collections cannot figure in proving return on investment. However, if the academic library is understood to provide a discovery environment that is both digital and physical, if library users do indeed value the library for the variety of resources it provides onsite, then NPLD collections, a hybrid resource, do have a place in this hybridised, third space. But libraries must be willing to expand their user assessment programmes, their routine feedback loops, to include not only a range of qualitative and quantitative methods but also to delve deeper into the datasets they own. This approach provides for a more substantial knowledge, a 'better [understanding of] how students, faculty, and other researchers adapt to our dimorphic information environment and suggest ways we might assist them in doing so' (Schmersal, 2018, 63).

Library assessment: mixing the methods

Understanding how their users behave not just in the digital environment but within this hybridised environment can only be achieved through a more mixed methodological approach to user assessment. For example, Lopatovska and Regalado (2016, 384) used a variety of methods, including 'ethnographic methods to collect data on the directly observable artifacts and behaviour of the library users'. 'Naturalistic observations' were combined with semi-structured interviews with students of the participating institutions.

This kind of adaptation of methods to user behaviour can inform all levels of library offering and provides an understanding that highlights the library's value to the university. By choosing to use this data as a basis for decision making, libraries can allocate and assess with a degree of confidence.

All libraries, not only academic libraries, are helped by statistical gathering, as it can prove value and return on investment or proof against 'intensified contextual pressures' as a recent SCONUL report stated (Pinfield, Cox and Rutter, 2017, 4; see also Aabø, 2009). It is therefore not surprising that libraries have concentrated considerable resources in systems specifically designed to furnish this proof (Schonfeld, 2014). User-focused assessment, however, seeks to learn what users are doing not only inside the library discovery environment, but more importantly outside it. In other words, libraries must engage with the larger digital environment to be better informed about activity, or the activity they would like to foster, within their own digital walls. In this 'culture of assessment' (Lakos and Phipps, 2004; Farkas, Hinchliffe and Houk, 2015), librarians and users are not just stakeholders, but partners in according instrumental value[9] to resources and services.

For example, the Bodleian Libraries undertakes assessment for three standard reasons: to drive service improvements; to inform decision making; and to underpin advocacy (Bodleian Libraries, n.d.). As the University library, the Bodleian Libraries started to build a user assessment culture in 2012, with the creation of a new post, Head of Assessment, a position created to develop a culture and processes for measuring the effectiveness of library services and for supporting data-driven, evidence-based decision-making related to services, collections, technology, and facilities.

A wide range of mixed assessment tools and techniques are used to gather data (both qualitative and quantitative), measure performance and understand user needs and experiences. In the last three years, assessment activities have included:

- a triennial Reader Survey for all members of the collegiate University and external Bodleian Card holders, using the LibQUAL+ protocol
- exploration of usage trends over the last five years of all services provided by the Libraries
- usability testing of interfaces of Bodleian Libraries' provided online services, such as the Institutional Repository
- focus groups with undergraduates, postgraduates and academic staff on their needs from physical library spaces
- return-on-investment analysis to communicate the value of the Libraries

- co-design with students of a new interface for the Libraries' resource discovery system
- local surveys of preferences for extending opening hours of a library
- diary study of new postgraduate research students in their first term on their doctoral programme
- evaluation of the impact of public engagement activities, such as exhibitions and museum education programmes, on those who participate
- committees on library provision and strategy (CLiPS), the formal mechanism for gathering feedback. These subject- or Library-focused committees meet every term, and comprise representatives from academic staff, students and librarians.

This mixture of methods that incorporates various feedback helps the Bodleian in identifying its user communities and their distinct information behaviours. Moreover, the results of all the completed assessment activities have prompted change in policies, procedures and practices at the Bodleian Libraries, either directly or as a result of combining a number of results in order to synthesise a holistic understanding of the library's research environment.

For example, the Radcliffe Science Library research employed a mixture of research methods, both quantitative and qualitative, to understand whether or not there was a requirement for a physical specialist library. A range of research methods were employed, including: 'Entry data and headcount, Free-text LibQual+ comments,[10] Literature review, Survey, Focus groups, UX' (Wilson, 2018, Slide 5). The UX methods[11] focused on 'how people actually behave in a space and their emotional response to the space' and included 'Anthropological techniques: Observation (14 periods over 8 locations), Journey mapping, Touchstone tours, Love letters / break-up letters, Interviews – structured and unstructured' (Slide 21).

The use of quantitative data in this research as a way of adding context to other qualitative data harks back to Rodden, Hutchinson and Fu (2010) and their 'triangulation' of data types (p. 2396) in order to arrive at a truer picture of what users make of products. However, while libraries may have branched out in terms of their user assessment techniques, quantitative methods have been relatively confined to out-of-the-box technology tools supplied by discovery and systems vendors. Library datasets, including NPLD collections, are not just a source of numeric information, but can also provide a way of 'observing' users in their information-seeking and retrieval behaviour, supplying another view of library use. For example, library systems log analysis and web analytics, including the appropriate measures for personal data protection, are the digital equivalent of observational research methods in reading rooms: counting and categorising books requested, books left on desks at the end of the day, books checked out of the library. Using an 'automatic classification matching tool', Gooding et al. (2019, 1) looked at 'what insights into users of digital library collections [including the Bodleian Libraries] can be derived from automatic classification matching'. This tool illuminated how retrieval data classified by subject can be used in conjunction with other related information about users and libraries to develop profiles or personas of behaviour.

The Bodleian culture of assessment as well as the studies cited point not only to the various ways users access library resources, but also to the diverse methods that can inform academic libraries of their information-seeking and retrieval behaviours. These methods reveal and highlight the academic library as a 'hybridized information environment' (Schmersal, 2018), not just a digital third space, but simply a third space spanning the analogue and digital worlds. It provides an arguably neutral (or at least non-commercial) environment for research, collaboration and socialisation (Codispoti and Frey, 2007). This way of understanding users' behaviour would suggest that NPLD collections can have a place in both the physical and digital academic library discovery environment. Not only do the collections provide a different type of resource, but they can also support academic legal deposit libraries in their drive to understand and serve their distinct communities of users.

NPLD: a hybrid resource for a hybrid environment

In order for academic users to appreciate the contribution of NPLD collections to the discovery environment, librarians must first understand that contribution. This understanding can be developed by using the various methods of collecting and analysing data in the library feedback loop as part of a culture of assessment as described by Lakos and Phipps (2004). In such an environment, librarians can see the value of NPLD collections through an analysis of space and collections, as well as the appropriate and flexible data gathering methods.

NPLD and the third space

The NPLD collections of e-journals, e-books and web archive exemplify an in-between or a hybrid resource: looking like electronic material but acting like archival or reference print resources, with attending access and use restrictions. Taking these properties on board in combination with the various user behaviours pointed out by Lopatovska and Regalado (2016), Warwick et al. (2008) and Schmersal (2018), there is much that NPLD collections have to offer academic users. What they require, as highlighted by Schmersal, is assistance and direction from librarians in order to perceive the value of such singular collections.

For example, studies confirm a preference in general for printed or print materials among academic users, especially for extended, concentrated reading that is free of distractions (Aharony and Bar-Ilan, 2016; Lopatovska and Regalado, 2016; Wilson, 2018). The fact that NPLD collections, especially e-journals, allow for printing matches this reading behaviour. Indeed, according to Gooding, Terras and Berube, certain valuable use cases are supported once access restrictions are overcome:

> For those willing to travel to libraries, NPLD does support certain aspects of what researchers want to do: respondents said that when they discovered sources they preferred to print, save, or read them right away. NPLD resources are designed to allow reading and printing, and it is therefore likely that researchers who overcome their unwillingness to use fixed terminals are reasonably well served in this regard.
>
> (Gooding, Terras and Berube, 2019, 21)

Academic users routinely inhabiting the library space where, as with the Bodleian Libraries, NPLD access is spread across most public access terminals, will serendipitously find these collections. They may initially be using their laptops, but if the NPLD resource meets their requirements they have ready access. Indeed, the success of this multiple terminal access is demonstrated in the systems-based use statistics across all six legal deposit libraries, where the Bodleian Libraries ranks second after the British Library for use of NPLD e-journals and e-books (Gooding, Terras and Berube, 2019, 19).

NPLD as a unique offering

One user requirement may be the importance of the material factor as discovered by Warwick et al. (2008). When a resource is seminal or even the only copy available, discovery and format restrictions do not apply and academic users will go to extreme lengths to access restricted resources, whether they be print or NPLD. NPLD collections are a third option here, available in digital form and printable, if a resource is neither available in print or from the electronic subscription collection. Lopatovska and Regalado (2016, 393) go so far as to state that 'libraries should continue providing access to print and digital collections to satisfy students' needs in both types of resources'.

Indeed, NPLD collections support the identification of academic libraries as that third space, analogue and digital. According to Delaney and Bates:

> The library should focus on what people aspire to not the tools. Instead of saying 'the library has 40 databases which you can access via the catalogue,' they could be saying, 'we provide you with information Google cannot find,' because this is where the value lies.
>
> (Delaney and Bates , 2015, 35)

Primarily, librarians should focus on what is unique in their collections, not just in promotion but also in user assessment, which can often serve as a form of promotion of those collections. As demonstrated in the DLF findings, the UK Legal Deposit Web Archive is just such a unique collection, in its breadth and depth of UK holdings. In DLF staff interviews it was described as 'a crown jewel' and a 'gold standard' (Gooding, Terras and Berube, 2019, 17). However, research survey respondents reported never having heard of the Web Archive and never having used it (p. 20). Part of this response is certainly attributable to the fact that it cannot be accessed through a simple catalogue search, either onsite or remotely at the academic legal deposit libraries. Indeed, the Web Archive is a prime example of how a unified search environment, the single search box, cannot always represent the complexity of academic library print and electronic collections (Boyd et al., 2006; Lown, Sierra and Boyer, 2013).

However, the fact that respondents reported rarely using any web archive at all for research or otherwise demonstrates that the limited use of the UKLD Web Archive cannot be explained entirely by access and interface problems and restrictions. When these responses are cross-referenced with the literature on web archives, a wider issue for the academic community emerges: researchers do not regard web archives as a resource for their work (Winters, 2017; Gooding, Terras and Berube, 2019). In this instance, widening the feedback loop to include consulting the wider research community as well as routine horizon scanning provides an understanding of the use of web archives and how the UK Legal Deposit Web Archive fits into the wider digital research environment. This understanding in turn supports the development of a more targeted promotion of the Web Archive to support 'researchers... to acquire new skills and develop new methodologies if they are to get to grips with web archives as a source' (Winters, 2017, 240).

NPLD as a user assessment dataset

As noted by Gooding, Terras and Berube (2019), there have been other consequences of excluding NPLD collections from holistic usage reporting:

> NPLD collections were not embedded into the culture of institutions in the same way as other resources: not only did librarians not feel they could recommend them but did not have the same robust knowledge base about NPLD collections as the rest of the services that fell under each library's remit.
>
> (Gooding, Terras and Berube, 2019, 26)

We have maintained throughout this chapter that the purpose of user assessment for libraries is not just to produce quantifiable data, but to produce data that creates a holistic understanding of how and why academic users seek and retrieve information. Because NPLD collections have not been part of this process, information services librarians cannot see how the materials could relate to users seeking information. An assessment culture that encompasses a flexible and mixed methods approach affects not only users but librarians as well. It teaches librarians that whatever enters 'the system', a new collection for instance, must immediately be recognised and evaluated. In this way, 'learning environments' are created for librarians where 'customer "feedback loops" ... and appreciation of the need for assessment as an everyday, reflective, systematic activity are commonplace' (Lakos and Phipps, 2004, 358).

In this assessment culture, librarians have the opportunity to adopt more creative approaches and methods, ones that can unlock the value of NPLD collections. For example, NPLD e-books and e-journals comprise discrete datasets that can illustrate larger themes and issues within information seeking and retrieving. In the previous section we discussed their analysis through automatic classification matching by the DLF project using the Python-based tool, Subjectify (Gooding et al., 2019). In this research not only have NPLD collections been useful in illustrating academic domain-specific information seeking, but they also demonstrated with the aid of Subjectify 'user behaviour at scale' (p. 5). In a library setting, this information can be used along with other data to support library collection development and management, as well as bibliographic training, strategy, and policy making. For example, domain-specific use data, gathered from subscription and NPLD collections, can contribute towards library training modules, matching course materials and recommendations from lecturers and instructors (Kim, 2011b). Moreover, as a subject of 'methodological approaches', NPLD collections can 'contribute directly to our understanding of information sources in the digital humanities' (Gooding et al., 2019, 1).

Conclusion

While it may be true that the academic library no longer has an information monopoly, ceding ground to the likes of Google Scholar, it still has a critical role to play for its varied communities of users. Investment in digital discovery tools has meant that it can offer a non-commercial scholarly digital environment for research. But the academic library is more than its digital environment. The academic library environment can be considered a unique hybridised information space, an information space which cannot always be approached by way of the single search box.

Because of their regulatory access and use restrictions, NPLD collections appear at first glance, and indeed according to the numerical usage statistics across all legal deposit libraries provided by the British Library, as if they have little to offer academic users. However, this is to approach their assessment in too narrow a way. As regulatory access and use restrictions may not change in the foreseeable future, legal deposit librarians must guide users in an understanding of what role NPLD collections can play in their research.

The academic third space is dependent upon its users and librarians to give it definition and value, as well as to demonstrate return on investment to academic senior management. The Oxford University Radcliffe Science Library's users directly addressed the doubts over whether a physical library is just as important as a digital library (Wilson and Ovenden, 2016). However, these voices would not have been heard were it not for a holistic user assessment culture:

- following the users through discovery and access of the unique range of academic resources
- identifying the specific communities, their information preferences and behaviours when interacting with the resources
- using the data from these activities to plan and deliver services 'in ways that maximize[s] positive outcomes and impacts for customers and stakeholders' (Lakos and Phipps, 2004, 352).

This culture allows for a greater understanding of users, in order that allocation of resources and services can be customised on the basis of user needs and not of broad assumptions. Assessment must have a purpose derived not only from the generic academic library environment, but also from the individual academic library's environment. The use and efficiency of collections and services are to be measured against that purpose (Farkas, Hinchliffe and Houk, 2015). This purpose, as followed through the feedback loop tracking discovery, access and assessment, offers librarians a better understanding of how collections and services, especially NPLD material with its access and use restrictions, can be promoted to users. In describing the assessment feedback loop, Lakos and Phipps (2004, 358) advise: 'it is imperative for libraries and librarians to be educated about "systems thinking", about the dynamic relationships between expectations and inputs, about seeing the big picture, about thinking outside the box'. NPLD collections, as demonstrated in this chapter, certainly benefit from 'thinking outside the box'.

Instead of waiting for the regulations to change or for time to pass, librarians themselves can learn through targeted assessment how and where to be more proactive in developing ways for the collections to be exploited for the users' benefit in the present. In this way, they can mould user expectation of NPLD collections, demonstrating that they are a resource which exemplifies the third space and illustrates that library collections are indeed richer than a single search box can convey.

Notes

1. The Legal Deposit UK Web Archive, which is considered separately in this chapter, cannot be searched through the discovery portals at the academic legal deposit libraries.
2. 'An automated library system usually consists of a number of functional modules, such as acquisitions, circulation, cataloging, serials, and an OPAC (Online Public Access Catalog). An "integrated" library system is an automated system... in which all of the functional modules share a common bibliographic database' (Lopata, 1995).
3. https://help.it.ox.ac.uk/internal/sld/shibboleth.
4. 'The library services platform includes knowledge bases and bibliographic service from which local collections are drawn or defined. The model of the integrated library system assumes a reliance on external resources for the metadata involved in collection description and management.' (Breeding, 2015, 9).
5. 'Library links are article-level links to subscription full text for patrons affiliated with a library. This program works best for electronic resources, such as journal and conference articles. To sign up, you'll need an OpenURL-compatible link resolver, such as SFX from Ex Libris, 360 Link from Serials Solutions, LinkSource from EBSCO, or WebBridge from Innovative Interfaces... The vendor [of link resolver] will normally ask you to fill a registration form that contains your subscriber IPs and the text of the link. They will then augment this information with your electronic holdings, and make this data available to our automatic indexing system.' (Google Scholar Library Links, https://scholar.google.co.uk/intl/en/scholar/libraries.html).
6. Some legal deposit libraries have restricted access to a limited number of designated terminals, while others, like the Bodleian, have provided designated access through most reader access terminals in the library.

7. Both the Legal Deposit Web Archive and the Open UK Web Archive have been combined to form the UK Web Archive (www.webarchive.org.uk).
8. For more information about the organisational structure of the University of Oxford, see www.ox.ac.uk/about/organisation.
9. 'The question of impact in cultural heritage generally distinguishes between intrinsic value (the value something has in and of itself), and instrumental value (the value something has because it helps to achieve or get something)' (Gooding, Terras and Berube, 2019, 15).
10. 'LibQUAL+ is a web-based survey offered by the Association of Research Libraries that helps libraries assess and improve library services, change organisational culture, and market the library. The survey instrument measures library users' minimum, perceived, and desired levels of service quality across three dimensions: Affect of Service, Information Control, and Library as Place.' (www.libqual.org).
11. For more information about UX techniques, see uxlib.org and Killick and Wilson, 2019.

References

Aabø, S. (2009) Libraries and Return on Investment (ROI): a Meta-analysis, *New Library World*, **110** (7/8), 311–24, https://oda.hioa.no/en/libraries-and-return-on-investment-roi-a-meta-analysis/asset/dspace:942/475260.pdf.

Agarwal, N. K. and Poo, D. C. C. (2007) HCI and Information Search: Capturing Task and Searcher Characteristics Through User Ability to Specify Information Need. In Smith, M. J. and Salvendy, G. (eds), *Human Interface and the Management of Information. Methods, Techniques and Tools in Information Design. Human Interface* 2007. *Lecture Notes in Computer Science*, v. 4557, 373–82, Springer, http://dx.doi.org/10.1007/978-3-540-73345-4_43.

Aharony, N. and Bar-Ilan, J. (2016) Students Academic Reading Preferences: An Exploratory Study, *Journal of Librarianship and Information Science*, **50** (1), 3–13, (Article first published online 6 July, 2016; issue published 1 March 2018), https://doi.org/10.1177%2F0961000616656044.

Athukorala, K., Glowacka, D., Jacucci, G., Oulasvirta, A. and Vreeken, J. (2015) Is Exploratory Search Different? A Comparison of Information Search Behavior for Exploratory and Lookup Tasks, *Journal of the Association for Information Science and Technology*, **67** (11), 2635–51, https://doi.org/10.1002/asi.23617.

Beastall, G. (2015) Library Management Systems, Past, Present, and Future, *Industry News, Soutron Blog*, 24 August, www.soutron.com/library-management-systems-past-present-future.

Bodleian Libraries (n.d.) *Performance and Feedback*, www.bodleian.ox.ac.uk/our-work/performance, [accessed 21 January 2020].

Boyd, J., Hampton, M., Morrison, P., Pugh, P. and Cervone, F. (2006) The One-box Challenge: Providing a Federated Search That Benefits the Research Process, *Serials Review*, **32** (4), 247–54, DOI 10.1080/00987913.2006.10765074.

Breeding, M. (2015) Library Service Platforms: a Maturing Genre of Products, *ALA Tech Source: Library Technology Reports*, **51** (4), May/June, Chapter 1: Introduction and Concepts, 5–19, http://dx.doi.org/10.5860/ltr.51n4.

Chen, H., Doty, P., Mollman, C., Niu, Xi., Yu, J. and Zhang, T. (2015) Library Assessment and Data Analytics in the Big Data Era: Practice and Policies. In *ASIST 15 Proceedings of the 78th ASIS&T Annual Meeting: Information Science with Impact: Research in and for the Community*, St. Louis Missouri 6–10 November, **52** (1), 1–4, https://doi.org/10.1002/pra2.2015.14505201002.

Codispoti, M., and Frey, S. (2007) The Library as Third Place in Academe: Fulfilling a Need for Community in the Digital Age. In *Conference: Thirty-seventh Popular Culture Association, and twenty-ninth American Culture Association national joint conference*, April, Boston, Massachusetts, http://scholars.indstate.edu/handle/10484/909.

Delaney, G. and Bates, J. (2015) Envisioning the Academic Library: a Reflection on Roles, Relevancy and Relationships, *New Review of Academic Librarianship*, **21** (1), 30–51, DOI 10.1080/13614533.2014.911194.

Dempsey, D. (2008) Reconfiguring the Library Systems Environment, Guest editorial, *portal: Libraries and the Academy*, **8** (2), April, 1–18, www.oclc.org/content/dam/research/publications/library/2008/dempsey-portal.pdf.

elegaldeposit.org (n.d.) *Digital Library Futures: the Impact of E-legal Deposit in the Academic Sector.*

Fabijan, A., Dmitriev, P., Olsson, H. H. and Bosch, J. (2017) The Evolution of Continuous Experimentation in Software Product Development. In *2017 IEEE/ACM 39th International Conference on Software Engineering (ICSE)*, Buenos Aires, 770–80, DOI 10.1109/ICSE.2017.76, http://muep.mau.se/bitstream/handle/2043/24149/2017-05%20ICSE2017_EvolutionOfExP.pdf?sequence=2&isAllowed=y.

Farkas, M., Hinchliffe, J. and Houk, A. (2015) Bridges and Barriers: Factors Influencing a Culture of Assessment in Academic Libraries, *College & Research Libraries*, **76** (2), 150–69, https://doi.org/10.5860/crl.76.2.150.

Gibby, R. and Brazier, C. (2012) Observations on the Development of Non-print Legal Deposit in the UK, *Library Review*, **61** (5), 362–77, https://doi.org/10.1108/00242531211280487.

Glanzel, W. and Gorraiz, J. (2014) Usage Metrics Versus Altmetrics, *Scientometrics*, **102** (3), 2161–4, https://link.springer.com/article/10.1007/s11192-014-1472-7.

Gooding, P., Terras, M. and Berube, L. (2019) *Towards User-Centric Evaluation of UK Non-Print Legal Deposit: a Digital Library Futures White Paper*, http://eprints.gla.ac.uk/186755.

Gooding, P., Terras, M., Berube, L., Bennett, M. and Hadden, R. (2019) Subjectifying Library Users to the Macroscope Using Automatic Classification Matching. In *Digital Humanities 2019*, Utrecht, The Netherlands, 9–12 July, http://eprints.gla.ac.uk/189049.

Guajardo, R., Brett, K. and Young, F. (2017) The Evolution of Discovery Systems in Academic Libraries: a Case Study at the University of Houston Libraries, *Journal of Electronic Resources Librarianship*, **29** (1), 16–23, https://doi.org/10.1080/1941126X.2017.1270097.

Hurst, M., Madsen, C., Wilson, F., Smith, M. and Garrity, W. (2016) All Your Data Displayed in One Place: Preliminary Research and Planning for a Library Assessment Dashboard and Toolkit. In *2016 Library Assessment Conference: Building Effective, Sustainable, Practical Assessment*, Arlington, Virginia, 31 October–2 November, 568–73, http://old.libraryassessment.org/bm~doc/91-wilson-2016.pdf.

Killick, S. and Wilson, F. (2019) *Putting Library Assessment Data to Work*, Facet Publishing.

Kim, Y. (2011a) Users' Perceptions of University Library Websites: a Unifying View, *Library & Information Science Research*, **33** (1), 63–72, https://doi.org/10.1016/j.lisr.2010.04.007.

Kim, Y. (2011b) Why Should I Use University Library Website Resources? Discipline Differences, *Journal of Academic Librarianship*, **37** (1), January, 9–18, https://doi.org/10.1016/j.acalib.2010.10.002.

Lakos, A. and Phipps, S. (2004) Creating a Culture of Assessment: a Catalyst for Organizational Change, *portal: Libraries and the Academy*, **4** (3), 345–61, http://muse.jhu.edu/article/170684/pdf.

Lopata, C. (1995) *Integrated Library Systems, Eric Digests, Eric Clearinghouse on Information and Technology*, www.ericdigests.org/1996-1/library.htm.

Lopatovska, I. and Regalado, M. (2016) How Students Use Their Libraries: a Case Study of Four Academic Libraries, *College & Undergraduate Libraries*, **23** (4), 381–99, https://doi.org/10.1080/10691316.2015.1039742.

Lown, C., Sierra, T. and Boyer, J. (2013) How Users Search the Library From a Single Search Box, *College & Research Libraries*, **74** (3), 227–41, https://crl.acrl.org/index.php/crl/article/view/16303.

Marchionini, G. (1997) *Information Seeking in Electronic Environments*, Cambridge University Press.

Markey, R., Reichheld, F. and Dullweber, A. (2009) Closing the Customer Feedback Loop, *Harvard Business Review*, **87** (12), December, 43–7, https://hbr.org/2009/12/closing-the-customer-feedback-loop.

Murray, A., Ireland, A. and Hackathorn, J. (2016) The Value of Academic Libraries: Library Services as a Predictor of Student Retention, *College & Research Libraries*, **77** (5), September, 631–42, https://crl.acrl.org/index.php/crl/article/view/16541.

Nicholas, D. (1997) The Information Needs Interview: a Long Way From Library-Use Statistics, *Education for Information: Libraries without Number*, **15** (4), 343–9, https://content.iospress.com/articles/education-for-information/efi15-4-07.

Pinfield, S., Cox, A. and Rutter, S. (2017) *Mapping the Future of Academic Libraries: a Report for SCONUL*, Society of College, National and University Libraries (SCONUL), http://eprints.whiterose.ac.uk/125508.

Rodden, K., Hutchinson, H., and Fu, X. (2010) Measuring the User Experience On a Large Scale: User-Centered Metrics for Web Applications. In *CHI 10 Proceedings of the SIGCHI Conference on Human Factors in Computing Systems*, 2395–8, https://storage.googleapis.com/pub-tools-public-publication-data/pdf/36299.pdf.

Sadeh, T. (2015) From Search to Discovery, *Bibliothek–Forschung und Praxis*, **39** (2), 212–24, www.degruyter.com/view/j/bfup.2015.39.issue-2/bfp-2015-0028/bfp-2015-0028.xml.

Savolainen, R. (2018) Pioneering Models for Information Interaction in the Context of Information Seeking and Retrieval, *Journal of Documentation*, **74** (5) 966–86, https://doi.org/10.1108/JD-11-2017-0154.

Schmersal, D. (2018) Dimorphism as a Metaphor for Information Seeking Behavior. In *2018 Seventy-second Annual Conference of the American Theological Library Association (ATLA)*, Indianapolis, Indiana, June, 62–85, https://doi.org/10.31046/proceedings.2018.79.

Schofield, M. (2015) Does the Best Library Web Design Eliminate Choice? *ART + marketing*, https://artplusmarketing.com/does-the-best-library-web-design-eliminate-choice-4f1920c3f79.

Schonfeld, R. (2014) Does Discovery Still Happen in Libraries?, *Ithaka S+R Issue Brief*, 28 September, https://doi.org/10.18665/sr.24914. See full report at www.lib.umd.edu/binaries/content/assets/public/architecturelibrary/sr_briefing_discovery_20140924_0.pdf.

The Legal Deposit Libraries (Non-Print Works) Regulations 2013 (S.I. 2013/777), www.legislation.gov.uk/uksi/2013/777/contents/made.

Thomsett-Scott, B. and Reese, P. (2012) Academic Libraries and Discovery Tools: a Survey of the Literature, *College & Undergraduate Libraries*, **19** (2–4), 123–43, https://doi.org/10.1080/10691316.2012.697009.

Warwick, C., Terras, M., Huntington, P. and Pappa, N. (2008) If You Build It Will They Come? The LAIRAH Study: Quantifying the Use of Online Resources in the Arts and Humanities, *Literary and Linguistic Computing*, **23** (1), 85–102, http://dro.dur.ac.uk/13505/1/13505.pdf?DDD11+d700tmt.

Wilson, F. (2018) The Illusory Holy Grail: Comprehensive Mixed-Methodology Assessment Is No Better Than Using a Single Method; a Case-Study On the 21st-

Century Science Library. *Presentation given at 2018 Library Assessment Conference: Building Effective, Sustainable, Practical Assessment. Houston, Texas, 5–7 December,* 27 slides,
http://old.libraryassessment.org/bm~doc/wilson-illusoryholygrail.pdf.

Wilson, F. and Ovenden, R. (2016) *The 21st Century Library: Spaces for Effective Learning and Research.* https://www.bodleian.ox.ac.uk/__data/assets/pdf_file/0018/247221/2017-The-21st-Century-Library-FINAL.pdf.

Winters, J. (2017) Coda: Web Archives for Humanities Research – Some Reflections. In Brügger, N. and Schroeder, R. (eds), *The Web as History: Using Web Archives to Understand the Past and the Present,* UCL Press, 238–48.

Wolff-Eisenberg, C. (2017) US Library Survey 2016, *Ithaka Research Report,* 3 April , https://doi.org/10.18665/sr.303066.

CHAPTER 10

'An ark to save learning from deluge'? Reconceptualising legal deposit after the digital turn

Paul Gooding and Melissa Terras

Introduction

Despite the introduction of non-print legal deposit (NPLD), the concept of legal deposit is still viewed primarily as a function of print modes of publishing and consumption. This chapter will argue that the print era notions that influence the NPLD access and reuse regulations are increasingly out of step with broader developments in publishing, information technology and broader socio-political trends in access to information. We will explore case studies relating to archives of web materials, in order to demonstrate the ways that innovative research, publishing, and copyright are changing our understanding of what constitutes an archive. The digital archive is a space where innovation is occurring, and where the role of the library is evolving, yet NPLD regulations largely close down options for innovative approaches to digital materials.

This chapter will use two case studies which encounter digital materials as a new media form, with their own functions and affordances. First, we will look at the Internet Archive (IA), a non-profit organisation that provides a suite of services to support national library and public-facing web archives. We will discuss how the IA's approach to copyright, and its openness to data-driven methods, allow it to provide web archival services that go far beyond those allowed under legal deposit. Second, we will review Common Crawl, another non-profit organisation that provides web archival content for non-commercial text and data mining. Through these case studies, we will demonstrate that web archives can provide a space for computational research. Innovation with digital materials is occurring within national library labs in particular, and we will conclude by applying the lessons learned from web archives to understand the challenges of innovative reuse of the NPLD e-book and e-journal collections. Similar change is occurring in relation to scholarly publishing, and yet digital scholarship is similarly closed off in each subset of NPLD collections. For scholarly publishing and use, NPLD's remediation of print services leaves it out of step with changing approaches to digital materiality elsewhere. The significance of this chapter is twofold: first, it advocates a new understanding of access to legal deposit in relation to the textuality of digital media, which we label the 'datafication' of the legal deposit library; and second, it recognises that unlike print media, where legal deposit materials were often not the only copy available, many non-print collections will be unique to the legal deposit libraries. We will conclude by suggesting ways in which NPLD regulations could support new approaches to digital materials in a variety of formats, based on aligning legal deposit to UK copyright regulations, but within the confines of the library reading rooms. This process will assist us to understand how to promote innovative reuse of the unique and vulnerable collections preserved by legal deposit, without undermining the commercial viability of publications through unfettered open access.

The historical context for legal deposit

Sir Thomas Bodley (1545–1613) casts a long shadow over the history of legal deposit in the UK. His influence began in 1598, when he wrote to the Vice-Chancellor of the University of Oxford with an offer to redevelop the University Library, with the following words:

> Where there hath been heretofore a publike library in Oxford: which you know is apparent by the rome itself remaining, and by your statute records I will take the charge and cost upon me, to reduce it again to its former use.
>
> (Quoted in Philip, 1983, 1)

By 1602, the fruits of his work were evident, as the Library reopened under the leadership of Thomas James (c.1573–1629). James was the first Librarian of the Bodleian Library, with the institution renamed in honour of its founder. The significance of Bodley's act of patronage was recognised by his contemporaries. Francis Bacon, for instance, praised him in 1605 for 'having built an ark to save learning from Deluge' (quoted in Spedding, 1861, 253).

Legal deposit has existed in various forms, in various nations, for roughly 500 years. This lineage shows that successive generations have keenly valued the idea that national memory can be protected through the capture and preservation of our published history. With the introduction of NPLD in the UK, and similar regulations elsewhere, it is evident that the value of regulations for formal deposit remains broadly recognised by government, librarians, publishers and researchers alike. These stakeholders broadly recognise the wide prestige and posterity value of NPLD, which associate it with the same intrinsic value as print legal deposit collections (Gooding, Terras and Berube, 2019, 17). Iain Sproat MP, for instance, noted in a 1997 parliamentary debate on extending legal deposit to non-print materials that 'the main purpose of legal deposit is to establish as comprehensive an archive as possible of our national published output for use by future generations' (Hansard, 1997). Yet this is not its only purpose. Larivière (2000), for example, considers legal deposit to be the foundation of a national policy to support freedom of expression and access to information, while Brazier (2016, 42) points out that the resultant collections form the basis for the world's 'great research libraries'. De Beer et al. (2016) further outline several ways in which the creation of comprehensive legal deposit collections can support the national interest:

> It is important to provide citizens as well as researchers (within the country as well as abroad) with access to a research collection of the country's published material, it supports bibliographic control and it makes it possible to monitor the growth of the publishing industry.
>
> (De Beer et al., 2016, 88)

In many respects, then, Bacon's 'Ark to save learning' appears as deft a metaphor for contemporary legal deposit as it was for Bodley's acts of patronage over 400 years before. Bacon's words hint at the public service remit of the regulations, the effort to capture at least some of the modern data deluge, and the focus on long-term preservation through which we understand legal deposit. On the other hand, the contemporary metaphor of the 'digital universe' (National Library of Scotland, 2013) that greeted the introduction of NPLD in the UK recalls those utopian visions of the universal library that have permeated our thinking all the way from the Renaissance through to the mission of the Internet Archive (Kahle, 2007). Gantz and Reinsel describe the true breadth of the so-called universe:

> Images and videos on mobile phones uploaded to YouTube, digital movies populating the pixels of our high-definition TVs, banking data swiped in an ATM, security footage at airports and major events such as the Olympic Games, subatomic collisions recorded by the Large Hadron Collider at CERN, transponders recording highway tolls, voice calls zipping through digital phone lines, and texting as a widespread means of communication.
>
> (Gantz and Reinsel, 2012)

Legal deposit, by comparison, preserves a razor-narrow subsection of this flood of digital information: e-books, e-journals, electronic mapping, CD-ROMS, newspapers and websites are all included, whereas the data deluge described by Gantz and Reinsel contains nothing that falls under legal deposit. Whether these data are *worth* preserving is a different matter, but for now it is enough to be clear that they are *not* preserved, at least not systematically for the public good. For this reason, we intend to focus solely on digital forms that come under NPLD, in order to explore how concepts of digital materiality inform our thinking around the scope of the regulations.

It is foundational to this line of thinking to understand that digital materialities offer different affordances from those offered by printed media. Indeed, N. Katherine Hayles argues that:

> Our notions of textuality are shot through with assumptions specific to print, although they have not been generally recognized as such. The advent of electronic textuality presents us with an unparalleled opportunity to reformulate fundamental ideas about texts.
>
> (Hayles, 2005, 89)

One way in which she understands this is through the 'work as assemblage' (Hayles, 2005, 104–9), a notion that echoes Lev Manovich's (2001) description of the modularity of digital media. The automation of tasks, and the ability to apply computational methods to digital data, are based upon the ability of digital texts to be described formally, and to be understood as assemblages of their constituent elements. Hayles argues that the context and presentation of a text is key to its meaning, and that there is therefore a spectrum of similarity and difference, with clusters of similar textual embodiments of a specific work emerging. Texts can therefore be discussed both in terms of their content and their physical embodiment. This approach to digital textuality supports the idea that archived websites are formally unique from the original website because they draw on modular components to create an interpretation rather than a facsimile copy:

> The archived website is a reconstruction in the sense that it has to be assembled by the use of all the archived bits and pieces, first when they are archived, and later when the material has to be displayed for the user of the archive. Thus, it could be argued that the archived website did not exist before it entered the archive, and in this respect it differs significantly from other media types.
>
> (Brügger, 2012)

Shifting forms of digital textuality have implications for historians engaged in researching the late 20th and early 21st century, an era for which digital media are primary resources. Winters (2017) notes that search and discovery tools are not adequate for the kinds of analysis that are required of web archival sources, thereby distancing research from print-era discovery and reading models:

> The dominance of (a particular type of) search as a digital research method quickly becomes problematic for web archives where, quite apart from difficulties arising from scale, the scope of a particular archive is unknown and the process of creation largely undocumented. Discovering what might be in the archive is often the primary objective – and this is not well served by keyword searching which produces a list of results unordered by anything other than date.
>
> (Winters, 2017, 243)

We can thus begin to see an emerging understanding of digital textuality, based on the separability of content or data, from the physical embodiment of the text. These multiple layers of meaning require different methods, analytical frameworks and discovery tools from those of print resources. One defining feature of digital media is that they can be understood as both data *and* text. As a result, scholars have increasingly begun to engage with digital scholarship, excavating meaning through analysis, synthesis and visualisation.

The library sector was slow to move beyond an understanding of digital materials as mere carriers of information, arguing that content matters more than format (e.g. Quint, 2001) while continuing to understand new media forms through the language of print. The same logic has been applied to the NPLD regulations, which embody a belief that access to digital materials should mirror the affordances offered by print. Such thinking ignores material shifts, other than where preservation of content might be affected: Seadle (2001, 302), for instance, asserts that 'for digital materials, it makes no sense to write rules for legal deposit based on the medium. Increasingly the medium on which a digital work exists matters less than what mark-up format it uses, what external links it requires, and what technological protection it has'. He is correct, but only insofar as it would be impractical to develop regulations that respond directly to individual digital forms. However, since Quint and Seadle asserted the primacy of content over form in 2001, there has been a reassertion of the importance of textuality in the digital age. The assumptions of print are explicitly incorporated into NPLD regulations, although they are not always recognised as such.

The doors to the Ark: access to UK NPLD materials

It is necessary for legal deposit regulations to define boundaries that make it feasible for libraries to undertake collection and preservation activities, given their limited funding and often small operational staffing. However, the print-based assumptions of legal deposit in the UK are important precisely because they continue to define NPLD; indeed, the broad scope of the digital universe stands in stark contrast to the access model that applies to NPLD materials.[1] The NPLD regulations were introduced in 2013 to address a twofold challenge: a decrease in the number of print publications being collected under legal deposit; and a dramatic increase in the amount of born-digital content that, due to its publishing format, would no longer fall under legal deposit regulations. Print intake under legal deposit has steadily fallen, and indeed, given the huge success of NPLD in collecting other materials, it can be easily surmised that print materials now form an ever-smaller subset of published materials. As long ago as 1998, the working party on non-print legal deposit concluded that it was necessary to extend statutory deposit in order to secure a comprehensive national collection (British Library, 1998). The working group paved the way for an interim voluntary arrangement, which was introduced in 2003 and allowed the UK deposit libraries to make significant progress in archiving non-print materials. This voluntary arrangement was underpinned by the Legal Deposit Libraries Act 2003, which established the principle of electronic legal deposit and provided legal protection to the deposit libraries to allow them to collect electronic materials at scale; however, it also required a further piece of subordinate legislation to enact its provisions fully in law. In order to establish a consensus, the Legal Deposit Advisory Panel (LDAP) was convened from 2005 to 2010. In 2009, LDAP submitted recommendations for the legal deposit of offline media, and the harvesting and archiving of web materials. In 2010, it made further recommendations, covering paywalled electronic materials, structured datasets such as railway timetables, and content which is pushed to the user by electronic means (Gibby and Brazier, 2012). After a period of consultation, the introduction of The Legal Deposit Libraries (Non-Print Works) Regulations 2013 formalised arrangements for collection, preservation and providing access to NPLD materials.

These regulations were the result of many years of careful negotiation and thought, and have been a huge benefit to the legal deposit libraries over the last five years, but it is worth exploring how the assumptions that underpinned their introduction may be problematic when we view deposited works as data (Padilla et al., 2019). The current interpretation of NPLD exists as a print-era regulation adapted for a prescribed range of digital materials, without mechanisms to deal with changing material, formal and structural considerations. Nowhere is this more evident than in the formulation of access in the regulations. There are two layers to the access criteria: first, the broad wording of the regulations that define access and use; and second, the way that legal deposit libraries have interpreted and implemented those stipulations. In this respect, little has changed since Bodley's time, with the reference-only policy of the Bodleian Library seeing just a few users each day using its resources (Bodleian Libraries, 2017). Access is still defined in respect to the single copy deposited under print legal deposit, which due to its format could only ever be accessed by one individual at a time. Indeed, when Lord Gardiner of Kimble reported to the House of Lords in 2013, he explained that reader access to NPLD materials had been regulated 'in order to mirror the level of access to printed publications' (Hansard, 2013). The regulations (HM Government, 2013) state strict rules for how materials may be accessed:

- Reader access to NPLD materials is limited to computer terminals on premises controlled by the legal deposit libraries (Part 1, Regulation 2).
- Each legal deposit library must ensure that material is only accessible to readers via one computer at a time (Part 4, Regulation 23).
- For materials published online, at least seven days must elapse between the date of delivery of that material and the date on which it is made available to readers (Part 4, Regulation 24).
- A copyright owner may request in writing that access is withheld for a specific period of time. Deposit libraries are bound to comply with such requests, provided that:
  - the period for which materials are withheld does not exceed three years from the date on which the request is made;
  - the deposit library is satisfied that, for the specified period, viewing of the relevant material by readers would, or would be likely to, 'unreasonably prejudice the interests of the person making the request' (Part 4, Regulation 25).

In some respects, the deposit libraries adopt a consistent interpretation of the regulations. The agreed technical solution for preserving NPLD materials is based on a 'Shared Technical Infrastructure' (British Library, 2013), housed in a secure environment with no public access.[2] Each of the national libraries stores a full copy of all NPLD materials at a local node, based in St Pancras (London), Boston Spa, Aberystwyth and Edinburgh, while the academic legal deposit libraries each connect to the British Library nodes. The system is designed to be secure, to protect against unauthorised use and to be resilient enough to ensure long-term preservation of assets. The nodes are also responsible for managing access to ensure only one copy of each unique item is used concurrently. All libraries share a technical solution called ERICOM that delivers digital materials through a 'secured remote desktop browser system' which ensures that files are not stored locally: it is to all intents and purposes streamed remotely, to protect against the proliferation of illegal copies (British Library, 2013). This is a solution agreed on by publishers and libraries, as appropriate to ensure the security of deposited materials.

The UK's legal deposit libraries have each been responsible for working out how these regulations would be implemented locally, and so the extent of access for users is further defined by the location of computer terminals. The British Library provides fixed terminals only within its reading rooms, for instance, as does the Cambridge University Library, limiting access to a specific subset of fixed terminals within each library.[3] The Bodleian Libraries, on the other hand, allow access via any fixed terminal, as long as the IP address is recognised to reside within the library's walls. The National Library of Scotland (NLS) has gone further still, creating a digital reading room in Glasgow's Kelvin Hall that expands fixed terminal access to its digital collections beyond its historic home in Edinburgh (National Library of Scotland, 2016).

The NLS decision to allow users outside Edinburgh to access electronic materials closer to home emphasises how competing conceptual frameworks can come to influence the scope and effectiveness of the 2013 regulations. It is a matter of public record that models for access to NPLD materials are shaped largely upon the level of access to print publications. Here, we make the less obvious point that those access models are built on assumptions that are specific to the print medium but have been transplanted over centuries to become foundational tenets of legal deposit. These tenets, now in the process of being reformulated, are largely responsible for ensuring that the textuality of digital media is ignored in a legal deposit environment.

NPLD regulations, and the interpretation of them at local level, artificially mimic the inherent scarcity of the printed form. This mimicry is intended to protect the commercial interests of rights holders, but problems arise when defining access to digital materials in terms that relate specifically to printed texts. Print works most conveniently lend themselves to traditional models of scholarship developed around information discovery via catalogue searching, followed by reading or browsing of specific volumes. These traditional models grew up alongside print, in order to make the most of the affordances of the available materials; however, digital materials have become increasingly understood in terms of their own textuality. As we have argued in the past (Gooding, 2016), it is important to recognise that digital materials are different: they provide a different experience to users that is nevertheless rich when understood on its own terms. Digital materials allow us to make new links between resources, to search huge amounts of material with a few key presses, to develop new forms of scholarship, and to make derivative and public-domain works available online. These are all vital functions of digital materiality that are unavailable to users of NPLD materials, who have increasing expectations of open access to data, remote access to library resources , and the ability to perform text and data mining (Winters, 2017, 46; Gooding, Terras and Berube, 2019, 18–23).

New media, new users, new services

This is not to say that libraries have been totally unable to provide innovative services to their users. In recent years, libraries have been experimenting with services that have allowed them to respond to the needs of users of digital materials. Like many other national libraries, the British Library has responded by developing a digital scholarship team with direct responsibility for collection areas with a strong digital practice focus, internal digital skills training and dissemination, and knowledge exchange with researchers. This has led to training programmes in digital research methods (McGregor and Farquhar, 2013), new staff roles, and particularly the emergence of library 'Labs' initiatives (Gooding, 2017, 100–1). Brooks, Heller and Phetteplace (2013, 186) define library labs as 'any library program, physical or digital (or a hybrid) in which innovative approaches to library services, tools, or materials are tested in some structured way before being made part of regular workflows, programs, or mission'. Labs emerged from a culture of experimentation with supporting digital research methods. For instance, the British Library Dataset Programme saw the creation of DataCite, the international data citation initiative which assigns Digital Object Identifiers to datasets. These services were then leveraged to promote dataset discovery services (Wilkinson, Pollard and Farquhar, 2010). Other organisations, such as the National Library of Wales, also developed digital research teams to provide core expertise and knowledge exchange, and to undertake in-house research. These activities demonstrate a willingness among libraries to engage with their digital collections, to make them available to users, and to provide innovative services that facilitate computational research with library collections (Gooding, 2017, 103).

By providing a defined space, and often dedicated staff with specific expertise in programming, digital collections, and digital research, library labs can help foster a culture of innovation and experimentation. For instance, the British Library (Kremerskothen, 2013) and the National Library of Wales (Pugh, 2010) have experimented with releasing digitised images to the commons via Flickr, to great success (Scholz and Miles, 2015), while the

National Library of Scotland recently launched its Digital Foundry as an online repository of data for researchers (National Library of Scotland, 2019). The success of labs, usually on limited project funding, has led to their widespread adoption and the emergence of an international library labs network via workshops hosted by BL Labs (Mahey, 2018). It is therefore certainly the case that libraries are developing creative, innovative and inspiring new ways of working with their collections. However, these activities must generally exclude legal deposit materials, due to restrictions on their use. When it comes to legal deposit, then, we must look towards non-governmental organisations for examples of services that are emerging around new forms of digital media such as web archives.

The following case studies will address two key risks to stakeholders as a result of the framing of access within NPLD: first, to libraries, which risk being left behind by non-governmental innovators in the sector because of the lopsided nature of limitations on access and reuse; and second, to publishers, which risk pushing users away from libraries and towards less tightly regulated services in an otherwise understandable attempt to protect their commercial interests. Larsen (2005, 86) notes that 'in the paper world legal deposit and preservation of printed heritage are almost synonymous with libraries. In the digital world it is not a matter of course that libraries are best suited to perform these tasks'. This is evident in the way that non-profit organisations now fulfil traditional library roles without being subject to legal deposit regulations or the need to adopt risk-averse approaches in order to maintain positive publisher-library relationships. As a result, they can bypass certain protections entirely by exploring the boundaries of copyright and intellectual property regulations and experimenting with key exceptions. The high-profile Internet Archive, for instance, uses exceptions to copyright law to allow users far more liberal access to archived web materials than is possible via legal deposit. The less famous Common Crawl leverages the particular strengths of digital textuality in providing a representative sample of global web archival data for text and data mining.

We will conclude by proposing that NPLD regulations must find a balance between protecting publishers' rights and adapting to contemporary innovations in data science and digital scholarship. While some have argued that NPLD should avoid a media-centric approach, on the basis that the material carrier of information is increasingly irrelevant (Seadle, 2001), we will argue that an awareness of the textuality of digital sources is in fact vital for how they are interpreted, accessed and reused. The NPLD regulations are not media-agnostic: on the contrary, they are fundamentally rooted in structures that deliberately remediate print codes as closely as possible; by artificially recreating the scarcity of the printed form, but also by recreating the inherent limitations to reading that are imposed by print. This important reconceptualisation of legal deposit, which we call the 'datafication of the legal deposit library,' will assist in preserving the precious relationship between publishers, libraries and researchers that has evolved around our national memory over the last five centuries. As the following case studies will show, innovation of this type is already happening outwith the legal deposit libraries.

The Internet Archive: access, copyright, and the limits of legal deposit

The Internet Archive is a non-profit organisation based in San Francisco, USA. Founded in 1996, its institutional mission is to 'provide Universal Access to All Knowledge,' an ambitious agenda described by Brewster Kahle as one of the greatest possible contributions to humanity:

> Universal access to all knowledge is possible, and I'd say it could be measured as one of the great achievements of humankind, along with putting a man on the moon or assembling the Library of Alexandria. I think our generation could bring universal access to all knowledge, and that's something we'd be proud of for centuries.
>
> (Kahle, 2007, 31)

The institutional mission of the IA is hugely ambitious, but it is more specific in positioning itself as a 'provider of web archiving technologies and services' (Hockx-Yu, 2016, 3), incorporating:

- open-source software for crawling and public access
- a global web archiving service for the general public
- Archive-It, a subscription service for creating, managing, accessing and storing web archive collections, and
- a tailored broad crawling service for national libraries (Hockx-Yu, 2016, 3).

The UK Legal Deposit Web Archive (UKLDWA) is supported by IA software, with the organisation's Wayback Machine providing the basis for its search interface; however, the IA also makes the Wayback Machine service freely available online to the general public. It has been hugely successful, attracting over 600,000 visitors per day in 2016 (Hockx-Yu, 2016), compared to an average of just 226 visitors per month to the UK Legal Deposit Web Archive (Gooding, Terras and Berube, 2018). Additionally, the IA offers various application programming interfaces (APIs) that allow users to access and build additional services that are able to utilise the IA dataset. Its collections are broader than those of national libraries, being global rather than national in scope, leading Meyer, Yasseri and Hale (2017, 27) to remind us that 'while the IA is the *most* comprehensive archive available of web materials, this should not be confused with thinking that the IA crawls represent a *fully* comprehensive record of the web'. Unlike the UKLDWA, the IA is also freely available online. For these reasons, and because the UKLDWA is relatively inaccessible by comparison, the IA has become the go-to source for academic researchers interested in accessing historical web content. Brügger and Schroeder's edited volume, for instance, contains regular citations of the IA as a data source or service provider for academic research (Hale, Blank and Alexander, 2017, 45–61; Meyer, Yasseri and Hale, 2017, 28; Weber, 2017, 83–100), whereas the UKLDWA is presented solely as an object for critique (Meyer, Yasseri and Hale, 2017; Winters, 2017). The reliance of UK-based researchers on the IA is evident beyond the confines of this single volume, with the notable exception of studies based on the JISC UK Web Domain dataset. As such the IA, not the UKLDWA, is the *de facto* research service for scholars of the UK web. This is based on the following two key points of difference between the IA and national library legal deposit services.

1. The Internet Archive provides free access to its collections via the web

Unlike legal deposit libraries, which are subject to maintaining restrictive access conditions, the IA undertakes its work under the purview of copyright law, as an independent non-governmental organisation. This allows them to take a more liberal approach to copyright, as can be seen in the case of the 'Sonny Bono Memorial Collection', which was digitised by Elizabeth Townsend Gard, a copyright scholar at Tulane University. Townsend Gard explains that the so-called Last Twenty exception, Section 108(h) of the US Copyright Act, allows published works in the USA to be digitised and distributed by libraries, archives and museums, as long as there is no continuing commercial sale of the work, nor availability of reasonably priced copies (Townsend Gard, 2017). With the help of her students, Elizabeth Townsend Gard utilised the exception to digitise a collection of eligible out-of-print books, naming the subsequent collection after 'the author of the bill making this necessary'[4] (Kahle, 2017). The existence of the collection shows that the IA is willing to explore the boundaries of copyright law to enable access to collections in its care. While there are problems in viewing global archival collections solely through the lens of US copyright law, it is certainly true that the resulting IA services are enabling new forms of research on a global basis. The alternative, as Martin Eve (2016) points out, is that researchers interested in text and data mining in the UK are often forced to either illegally break digital rights management software, or digitise texts themselves. The systems that underpin access to NPLD make this impossible.

2. The Internet Archive makes it possible for researchers to build services that allow for large-scale computational analysis of web resources

As a result of its lack of restrictions, the IA has been able to experiment with allowing researchers to undertake computational analysis on web archive resources. Ian Milligan, for instance, points to the 'Wide Web Scrape' (Milligan, 2016), a 2012 experiment by the IA to collect around 80TB of WARC files containing around 2.7 billion URIs. The resultant dataset is not freely available online, but is managed through direct queries to the IA in the spirit of supporting non-commercial research (Rossi, 2012). Libraries have partly been left behind for technological reasons, although the growth of Library Labs outlined above points to a way forward. Coyle, for instance, makes it clear that innovation in organisation technology has often occurred within libraries in the past. However, she argues that several factors have had a negative impact on relative levels of innovation in library and information services in comparison to other industries:

> Looking at the relative timelines, those of the overall information technology space and that of the library technology space, it becomes clear that libraries have failed to make the same changes that were happening in the other communities making use of computing. The reasons behind this are undoubtedly many, from issues of budget limitations, institutional conservatism, and the historicity of the library mission.
>
> (Coyle, 2017)

The innovation gap is partly forced upon libraries by the retrograde assumptions that run through the legal deposit regulations. This is a risk when we bear in mind that web users are often agnostic about their sources, using those that will support retrieval of information or data with as little friction as possible (Warwick et al., 2008; Tanner, 2013) but, despite this, government and the scholarly community still entrust national collections to the library and archival sector due to their trusted role in society and long-term view of custodianship. This is important because it distinguishes the ongoing value of the legal deposit libraries as trusted, broad and deep repositories of our printed national record. However, libraries are being left behind in comparison to key newcomers in the library space in terms of access, usability and provision of tools and datasets. The IA's Wayback Machine is more accessible and comprehensive than any publicly available web archive, while users of the UKLDWA face major barriers in accessing NPLD materials for data-driven purposes. As a result, libraries risk the erosion of this trusted position because other providers can respond proactively to changing user needs, take into account regulatory shifts, and take an organisational view on risk.

Common Crawl: the changing needs of researchers

Common Crawl is more explicitly targeted to the needs of data scientists and computational researchers than the Internet Archive. Its approach to web materials raises important questions about our concepts of digital textuality, and how this affects the needs of researchers. Common Crawl was founded in the USA as a non-profit organisation in 2011 with the mission to crawl the web and provide a representative sample of web domains at no cost for non-commercial analysis and research. The organisation undertakes a monthly web crawl which it makes freely available to download as WARC files.[5] Its compliance with copyright regulations is predicated on the US concept of fair use: it argues that websites are intended for human consumption one at a time, whereas Common Crawl undertakes a transformative process by bundling billions of pages together into specialised formats that include text, metadata, and raw data. Furthermore, it explicitly aims to provide a representative sample of roughly 3 billion web pages rather than a comprehensive archive of the global web; in this respect, its mission is very different to that of either the Internet Archive or the national libraries.

The entire data collection model for Common Crawl emphasises that digital materials, and specifically web pages, are data files underneath their representational form. In separating data from form, the organisation is better able to meet the needs of researchers. Winters (2017, 246), for instance, emphasises that 'it is the portability of data, its separability from an easy-to-use but necessarily limiting interface, which underpins much of the most exciting work in the digital humanities'. Fields that adopt digital approaches to materials rely upon open access to portable datasets that will allow analysis via computational tools. That legal deposit materials are neither easy to use, nor portable, means that libraries are unable to support these researchers in either the short or the long term. As a result, it is easy for libraries to be presented as unwilling to update their practices. Sara Crouse, Director of Common Crawl, does exactly this when she draws attention to:

> The risk averse nature of the web archiving community as a whole (historically many adhered to and still adhere to a strict 'opt-in' policy requiring prior approval before crawling a site) and the unwillingness of many archives to modernize their thinking on copyright and to engage more closely with their legal community in ways that could help them expand fair use horizons.
>
> (Quoted in Leetaru, 2017)

While there is an element of truth to this, Crouse misses the extent to which the hands of librarians and archivists are tied by regulations that do not apply to non-governmental content holders. National libraries have released public domain material to the Commons when possible (Pugh, 2010; Kremerskothen, 2013), and they have experimented with open licensing to support research and creative reuse. The independence of Common Crawl and IA is exactly what allows them to innovate, removing them from the problematic print paradigm at the heart of NPLD. However, some NPLD materials are unique, unlike most print legal deposit items, and there will come a time that some digital materials are only available through the legal deposit libraries. It is at this point, in the short to medium term, that an impoverished position on digital textuality could become a barrier to research.

Web materials have been collected under formal legal deposit for just five years but provide a clear example of the differing textuality of digital media. Users are unable to access legal deposit collections in the way that they expect, and in this respect, it could be argued that NPLD is working as intended. It is right and proper that libraries protect the interest of publishers and other rights holders, and the current regulations are designed to reassure publishers that legal deposit will not undermine their legitimate interests. In this sense, user expectations are less relevant than the fact that users are denied the opportunity to exercise their legitimate rights under copyright law, in relation to legal deposit materials. This is starkly evident for web archival materials, where it is effectively impossible for users to treat the UKLDWA as a dataset. However, the implications of this print paradigm are felt elsewhere. In particular, even the simple task of accessing open access materials is complicated by the framing of NPLD.

Open access and copyright

The NPLD regulations aim to mirror levels of access to print legal deposit collections, to reassure publishers that their legitimate interests will not be undermined. However, the digital turn has precipitated not only a reassessment of how we view textuality, but a shift in attitudes towards access that are keenly visible in the open access movement in academic publishing.

As Adrienne Muir notes elsewhere, the importance of open science, and open access, has been ascribed increased importance in government policy and the scholarly community in the past decade. The UK Research Councils have had policies on open access since 2005, and the RCUK Open Access policy of 2013 recognises that free and open access to publicly funded research is a societal good (UK Research and Innovation, 2013). The open access requirement adopted for the 2021 Research Excellence Framework formalised an expectation that researchers in higher education should increasingly publish in the most open formats possible (UK Research and Innovation, 2013). Most recently, 11 national research funding organisations, with the support of the European Commission and the European Research Council, announced the launch of cOAlition S,[6] built around the ambitious Plan S, which was described as follows:

> By 2020 scientific publications that result from research funded by public grants provided by participating national and European research councils and funding bodies, must be published in compliant Open Access Journals or on compliant Open Access Platforms.
>
> (Science Europe, 2018)

The key principles of compliance with cOAlition S include: authors retaining their copyright; incentives for establishing new journals and platforms; institution and funder support for OA fees, alongside a capping of those fees; and a longer-term aim to make monographs and books available via open access (Science Europe, 2018). These developments map the start of a trajectory towards a culture of open access by default for academic research.

Shifts in UK copyright law further reinforce the exceptional nature of academic research in the regulatory environment, as they embed specific exceptions for non-commercial research. UK copyright law already contains explicit exceptions that allow limited reuse of some copyrighted materials for non-commercial research, or genuine private study. This reuse falls under the UK concept of 'fair dealing,' although the UK Intellectual Property Office makes it clear that 'there is no statutory definition of fair dealing – it will always be a matter of fact, degree and impression in each case' (Intellectual Property Office, 2014). Tests for legitimate fair dealing include whether the market for the original work would be affected by a proposed use, and whether the amount of copyrighted work to be taken would be considered reasonable and appropriate. In 2015, the government introduced a further exception that allows researchers to make copies, without specific permission, of whole copyright works to which they have access, for the purpose of computational analysis for non-commercial research (Intellectual Property

Office, 2014). This exception does not apply to users of NPLD materials (Gooding, Terras and Berube, 2019, 23–4).

As a result of the digital turn, not only are users increasingly interested in the data that sits underneath our digital materials, but open access to publications and data is increasingly common. Open access journals commonly use Creative Commons licences that explicitly allow others to legally build upon, share, and create derivative works under explicit but generous conditions (Eve, 2014, 12). For material published under these licences, publishers will no longer hold rights in the same way as in the past, especially in situations where copyright is not transferred from the author. Furthermore, a publishing model has emerged that is reliant on upfront payment of article or book processing charges to cover costs and provide profits. These APCs and BPCs often cost up to a few thousand pounds in high-impact journals, and £10,000 or more for OA books. In this respect, publishers have no legitimate rights as owners of openly licensed content: indeed, in cases where scholars retain their own copyright, there is a convincing argument that restrictive legal deposit of OA materials in fact infringes upon the legitimate rights of authors to ensure the openness of their publications (Gooding, Terras and Berube, 2019).

The shift towards ubiquitous open access in academic publishing has important implications for NPLD, which continues to limit access based on publishing paradigms that are increasingly outdated. Indeed, the phrasing of the regulations introduced a form of 'perpetual copyright' (Gibby and Brazier, 2012) because the legal deposit access restrictions remain in force forever, including after the expiry of copyright. Not only are legal deposit materials not accessible to new forms of research while under copyright, but they will effectively never enter the public domain. This perpetual copyright is a function of the Legal Deposit Act 2003, which by default excludes all uses of deposit materials unless explicitly permitted by legal deposit regulations (Legal Deposit Act 2003, Section 7). This in effect delinks legal deposit from copyright and IP legislation, so that to vary the terms of access it would be necessary to vary the legal deposit regulations. As a result, the restrictions become indefinite, other than by variation through explicit acts of parliament. In the scholarly space, at least, the problem of perpetual copyright allows publishers to demand permanent control over NPLD materials even in cases where they hold no legitimate interests. Users are unable to access legal deposit materials in several important ways that are otherwise enabled by the digital turn: via remote access arrangements; for the purposes of text and data mining; or under open access licences. The effect is twofold; first, libraries are unable to serve their contemporary users in accessing digital materials in ways which take advantage of the digital textuality of NPLD materials; and second, users are pushed towards non-governmental organisations which are already providing the precise kinds of data collection and access from which NPLD is supposed to protect the publishing industry.

The different textual and formal affordances of digital texts are contributory factors in a cultural shift towards open access, and towards an understanding of digital media not only as a formal representation of a text, but also as computational data (Padilla et al., 2019). These changes have realigned how researchers and government view access to digital materials, and national policy has recognised the significance of open access and computational methods via a series of exceptions that enable their use across the majority of publications. User expectations are thus being shaped by services such as the IA and Common Crawl. They increasingly want information in portable datasets and on demand. In the UK, though, NPLD restrains users from accessing materials via legal deposit collections, and libraries from providing innovative responses to emerging trends in research and user behaviour, while non-governmental organisations are free to engage in these activities without the responsibility of acting as trusted national repositories. The conceptual fixity of legal deposit, which explicitly informs non-print regulations, does not allow these trusted repositories to evolve in line with broader social, political, and technical trends.

Discussion

We have drawn attention to areas where NPLD has already disadvantaged libraries and contributed to publishers losing control of the data they are trying to control. It is certainly true that the problem caused by perpetual copyright has been recognised[7] but there seems little urgency to address it in the short term. In fact, the response to concerns about the inadequacy of NPLD for contemporary users has been to emphasise the posterity-driven mission of legal deposit. Lord Gardiner, for instance, addressed the issue in the House of Lords:

> The Government recognise that the scenario of restrictions on access to content following the expiration of copyright is a concern for the research community. This is an important issue, but will only arise once the copyright term of 70 years has ceased, so in practice the issue will not affect legal deposit for many years to come.
>
> (Hansard, 2013)

However, perpetual copyright is just one problem that affects legal deposit; the challenge of open access, and the growth in data-driven research, both call into question the print paradigm that underpins the regulations. The result is not just that legal deposit regulations begin to seem anachronistic, but that the protectionist ethos is actively undermined by broader regulatory shifts. Publications that NPLD is tasked with protecting, such as web pages, books and journals, are already available elsewhere, legally, without the continuity that is assumed of national libraries. The services that legal deposit libraries cannot provide for web archives are already being provided by other organisations that operate outside existing legal deposit frameworks.

As a result, the UKLDWA is largely ignored by researchers in favour of resources such as the Internet Archive and Common Crawl. Menell makes a strong case that public access to accurate digital records is an important public good:

> Democracy-enhancing spillovers are particularly important in the digital age. While the rise of the internet has opened up communications channels to a much greater diversity of speakers, it has, at times, also produced a polarizing cacophony. Expanding access to the most authoritative sources of information and enabling much more accurate and efficient search capability holds the potential to improve the quality of information available. Better information has the power to sharpen and clarify discourse.
>
> (Menell, 2007, 1042–3)

The reference-only core of NPLD is an important factor in maintaining publisher support for exactly such authoritative collections, but the great challenge for legal deposit is that the logic at the core of this negotiated compromise has been eroded by changes in copyright, academic publishing, data science, and digital research. Because of this, the challenges to legal deposit cannot simply be passed onto future generations to solve but must instead necessitate a rethinking of the way that reference access is provided. We argue here that the solution is for the 'datafication of the legal deposit library,' which is built on the understanding that key legal deposit reference collections, including the UKLDWA, have been impacted by the digital turn in ways that undermine the assumptions that underpin their protections. This datafication is evident in the labs model that many national and research libraries have adopted. The labs allow users to engage with library collections not only as information, or as artefacts, but as data. To address this need, two key areas of legal deposit require addressing:

1. Alignment with copyright

Legal deposit libraries face huge challenges because legal deposit regulations are decoupled from copyright. This has created the problem of perpetual copyright and has left libraries behind non-governmental organisations in their ability to provide innovative services to their users. We propose that legal deposit could be more closely aligned to copyright, by specifying exemptions in legal deposit based on access location, rather than access model. In other words, libraries could, if they wish, develop 'Legal Deposit Labs' which allow reuse of legal deposit materials for non-commercial purposes within the physical confines of their reading rooms, or in trusted data safe havens which provide access to computational infrastructure. This would allow libraries to respond proactively to future developments, applied through the prism of reference-only services within libraries.

2. Open access and changing IP rights

As the trend towards OA publishing continues to grow, the idea that legal deposit limitations are in place to protect rights holders' legitimate interests becomes increasingly difficult to defend in the academic publishing space. However, Seadle's (2001) point that the regulations should not be media-centric but general and adaptable requires this to be addressed at the rights level rather than the content level. Exceptions that allow legal deposit libraries to provide access to genuine OA materials would allow legitimate publisher interests to be defended, while ensuring that openly licensed materials are made available in line with rights holders' wishes. It is particularly important to differentiate between material that is open access, and that which is only freely available; a particular challenge for the UKLDWA, where advertising models often support free access to copyrighted materials. We are also aware that this would place a burden on libraries to create and police differentiated access and reuse systems: this issue would need to be addressed through the implementation stages but would truly allow us to enter an era where legal deposit reference materials are viewed as both content and data.

Conclusion

We have argued in this chapter that the current conception of legal deposit in the UK relies upon a framework explicitly drawn up to mirror the norms of print legal deposit collections. These norms remediate the textuality of print, with its inherent scarcity, and its suitability to particular forms of information behaviour, defining access to NPLD materials. Libraries and librarians have tended to downplay the significance of digital materiality in defining usage, while often being blind to the fact that print norms can define library services to the detriment of other forms. It is the dual nature of digital media – as content, and as data – that requires us to understand that print is not a neutral form. First, the digital turn has led to a shift towards open access for academic publishing, which raises important questions about how the legitimate rights of publishers are interpreted in legal deposit. Second, regulatory exceptions that support data-driven research are incompatible with an access model that privileges reading above other forms of access. Third, the replicability of digital materials means that NPLD stops only the legal deposit libraries in making certain materials available; non-governmental organisations have already provided innovative services that make huge swathes of contemporary materials available.

Given these overlapping points, the current restrictive access arrangements only limit access for users of legal deposit libraries, thereby eroding the ability of these libraries to provide innovative services. This creates a gap between trusted repositories, which are tied to legal deposit regulations, and non-governmental organisations. Our proposed 'datafication of the legal deposit library' is a response to these problems that recognises the changing nature of our cultural outputs, while understanding the fundamental importance of reference-only access to legal deposit collections. This proposal would be supported by two complementary priorities for legal deposit: first, closer alignment with copyright regulations, to support reading rooms to develop innovative services; and second, allowing differentiation between OA and non-OA materials to replicate the use originally intended by rights holders. The importance of these suggestions lies in the fact that NPLD collections promise to contain unique materials in quantities that are unprecedented in the history of legal deposit, and that libraries will thus become the sole source for access.

The deluge noted by Francis Bacon was the rapid growth of print sources following the invention of the printing press. To the world after the digital turn, however, it evokes images of information overload through online proliferation. This proliferation has changed user expectations, scholarly publishing models, and primary regulations; it has also allowed data-driven research and re-centralised the importance of understanding the textuality of our cultural sources. We must respond by interrogating legal deposit in a new light, so that our non-print collections are not permanently affected by the legacies of print media.

Notes

1. See the first chapter in this book, by Linda Arnold-Stratford and Richard Ovenden, for further elaboration on the development and implementation of access arrangements for non-print legal deposit in the UK.
2. For further details of the technical implementation, see Chapter 1 of this book.

3. The Digital Library Futures White Paper (Gooding, Terras and Berube, 2019, 13) contains a photo from the Cambridge University Library, which demonstrates the appearance and layout of the NPLD terminals in the Library.
4. The Bill that Kahle refers to is the Copyright Term Extension Act (CTEA) of 1998, which extended copyright to the life of the author plus 70 years. It was informally named after the deceased singer and congressman Sonny Bono, who was one of 12 sponsors of a similar bill. High-profile lobbyists also included Disney, leading it to be derisively billed 'The Mickey Mouse Protection Act,' due to the proximity of the copyright term extension to the point at which the rights to Mickey Mouse would have entered the public domain.
5. WARC is the Web ARCHive file format, which specifies a method for combining multiple digital resources into an aggregate archival file with related information. It consists of metadata fields to support the retrieval of each harvested resource, and allows the storage of content blocks to store resources in any format: this can include binary image or audiovisual files that may be embedded in HTML pages (Library of Congress, 2009).
6. While at first glance this looks like a spelling mistake, cOAlition S is the official name of a declaration of commitment to open access. Further details are available at www.scienceeurope.org/coalition-s.
7. The issue of perpetual copyright was, for instance, brought up as a key concern by the library submission to the recent Post-Implementation Review of Non-Print Legal Deposit. For further discussion see Annex A of the DCMS review (Department for Digital, Culture, Media and Sport, 2019).

References

Bodleian Libraries (2017) *History of the Bodleian*, www.bodleian.ox.ac.uk/bodley/about-us/history.

Brazier, C. (2016) Great Libraries? Good Libraries? Digital Collection Development and What it Means for Our Great Research Collections, in Baker, D. and Evans, W. (eds), *Digital Information Strategies: From Applications and Content to Libraries and People*, Chandos Publishing, 41–56.

British Library (1998) *Report of the Working Party on Legal Deposit*, www.bl.uk/aboutus/stratpolprog/legaldep/report/index.html.

British Library (2013) *Security for Electronic Publications*, www.bl.uk/aboutus/legaldeposit/websites/security.

Brooks, M., Heller, M. and Phetteplace, E. (2013) Library Labs, *Reference & User Services Quarterly*, **52** (3), 186–190.

Brügger, N. (2012) Web History and the Web as a Historical Source, *Studies in Contemporary History*, **2**, www.zeithistorische-forschungen.de/site/40209295/default.aspx .

Coyle, K. (2017) Creating the Catalog, Before and After FRBR, *Encuentro di Catalogacion y Metadatos*, Universidad Nacional Autonoma de Mexico, 9 December, http://kcoyle.net/mexico.html .

De Beer, M., Van der Merwe, M., Ball, L. and Fourie, I. (2016) Legal Deposit of Electronic Books – A Review of Challenges Faced by National Libraries, *Library Hi Tech*, **34** (1), 87–103.

Department for Digital, Culture, Media and Sport (2019) *Post-Implementation Review of the Legal Deposit Libraries (Non-Print Works) Regulations 2013*, www.gov.uk/government/publications/post-implementation-review-of-the-legal-deposit-libraries-non-print-works-regulations-2013 .

Eve, M. P. (2014) *Open Access and the Humanities: Contexts, Controversies and the Future*, Cambridge University Press.

Eve, M. P. (2016) The UK Copyright Exemption for Text and Data Mining vs. the DMCA and EUCD, *Martin Paul Eve blog*, www.martineve.com/2016/01/07/the-uk-copyright-exemption-for-text-and-data-mining-vs-the-dmca.

Gantz, J. and Reinsel, D. (2012) *The Digital Universe in 2020: Big Data, Bigger Digital Shadows, and Biggest Growth in the Far East*, IDC Go-to-Market Services.

Gibby, R. and Brazier, C. (2012) Observations on the Development of Non-Print Legal Deposit in the UK, *Library Review*, **61** (5), 362–77.

Gooding, P. (2016) Exploring the Information Behaviour of Users of Welsh Newspapers Online Through Web Log Analysis, *Journal of Documentation*, **72** (2), 232–46.

Gooding, P. (2017) *Historic Newspapers in the Digital Age: 'Search All About It'*, Routledge.

Gooding, P., Terras, M. and Berube, L. (2018) Legal Deposit Web Archives and the Digital Humanities: a Universe of Lost Opportunity?, *Digital Humanities*, http://doi.org/10.5281/zenodo.1300011.

Gooding, P., Terras, M. and Berube, L. (2019) *Towards User-Centric Evaluation of Non-Print Legal Deposit: a Digital Library Futures White Paper*, University of Glasgow, http://elegaldeposit.org/resources.

Hale, S. A., Blank, G. and Alexander, V. D. (2017) Live Versus Archive: Comparing a Web Archive to a Population of Web Pages. In Brügger, N. and Schroeder, R. (eds), *The Web as History: Using Web Archives to Understand the Past and Present*, UCL Press, http://discovery.ucl.ac.uk/1542998/1/The-Web-as-History.pdf .

Hansard (1997) *Non-Print Publications (Legal Deposit), HC Deb 1997*, Vol. 290, Col. 15563, https://hansard.parliament.uk/Commons/1997-02-11/debates/609493dd-462b-4560-9110-3cf9f53c7aec/Non-PrintPublications(LegalDeposit)?highlight=%22legal%20deposit%22#contribution-29c1ed93-bf71-4c27-81e7-066affed5975.

Hansard (2013) *HL Deb (2013)*, https://hansard.parliament.uk/Lords/2013-03-06/debates/13030683000250/LegalDepositLibraries(Non-PrintWorks)Regulations2013?highlight=%22legal%20deposit%22#contribution-13030683000082.

Hayles, N. K. (2005) *My Mother Was a Computer: Digital Subjects and Literary Texts*, University of Chicago Press.

Hockx-Yu, H. (2016) *Web Archiving at National Libraries: Findings of Stakeholders' Consultation by the Internet Archive*, Internet Archive, https://ia800405.us.archive.org/12/items/InternetArchiveStakeholders ConsultationFindingsPublic/InternetArchiveStakeholdersConsultation-Findings_ Public.pdf .

Intellectual Property Office (2014) *Exceptions to Copyright: Research, UK Government*, www.gov.uk/government/uploads/system/uploads/attachment_data/file/375954/ Research.pdf.

Kahle, B. (2007) Universal Access to All Knowledge, *American Archivist*, **70** (1), 23–31.

Kahle, B. (2017) Books from 1923 to 1941 Now Liberated!, *Internet Archive Blogs*, http://blog.archive.org/2017/10/10/books-from-1923-to-1941-now-liberated.

Kremerskothen, K. (2013) Welcome the British Library to the Commons!, *Flickr Blog*, 16 December, http://blog.flickr.net/2013/12/16/welcome-the-british-library-to-the-commons.

Larivière, J. (2000) *Guidelines for Legal Deposit Legislation*, United Nations Educational, Scientific and Cultural Organization, http://unesdoc.unesco.org/images/0012/001214/121413eo.pdf.

Larsen, S. (2005) Preserving the Digital Heritage: New Legal Deposit Act in Denmark, *Alexandria: The Journal of National and International Library and Information Issues*, http://journals.sagepub.com/doi/abs/10.1177/095574900501700204.

Leetaru, K. (2017) Common Crawl and Unlocking Web Archives for Research, *Forbes*, 28 September, www.forbes.com/sites/kalevleetaru/2017/09/28/ common-crawl-and-unlocking-web-archives-for-research/#86131fc3b833.

Legal Deposit Libraries Act 2003 c.28, www.legislation.gov.uk/ukpga/2003/28/contents.

Library of Congress (2009) *WARC, Web ARChive File Format*, www.loc.gov/preservation/digital/formats/fdd/fdd000236.shtml.

McGregor, N. and Farquhar, A. (2013) The Digital Scholarship Training Programme at British Library, *Digital Humanities 2013*, http://dh2013.unl.edu/abstracts/ab-264.html.

Mahey, M. (2018) Building Library Labs Around the World – the Event and Complete Our Survey!, *Digital Scholarship blog*, https://blogs.bl.uk/digital-scholarship/2018/09/building-library-labs-around-the-world.html.

Manovich, L. (2001) *The Language of New Media*, MIT Press.

Menell, P. S. (2007) Knowledge Accessibility and Preservation Policy for the Digital Age, *Houston Law Review*, **44** (4), https://papers.ssrn.com/sol3/papers.cfm?abstract_id=999801.

Meyer, E. T., Yasseri, T. and Hale, S. (2017) Analysing the UK Web Domain and Exploring 15 Years of UK Universities on the Web. In Brügger, N. and Schroeder, R. (eds), *The Web as History: Using Web Archives to Understand the Past and Present*, UCL Press, http://discovery.ucl.ac.uk/1542998/1/The-Web-as-History.pdf.

Milligan, I. (2016) Lost in the Infinite Archive: The Promise and Pitfalls of Web Archives, *International Journal of Humanities and Arts Computing*, **10** (1), 78–94, www.euppublishing.com/doi/10.3366/ijhac.2016.0161.

National Library of Scotland (2013) *Electronic Legal Deposit*, www.nls.uk/news/press/2013/04/electronic-legal-deposit.

National Library of Scotland (2016) *National Library Opens in Glasgow*, www.nls.uk/news/press/2016/09/library-opens-at-kelvin-hall.

National Library of Scotland (2019) *Launch of Data Foundry Website – National Library of Scotland*, www.nls.uk/news/archive/2019/09/data-foundry.

Padilla, T., Allen, L., Frost, H., Potvin, S., Russey Roke, E. and Varner, S. (2019) Final Report – Always Already Computational: Collections as Data, DOI: 10.5281/zenodo.3152935.

Philip, I. (1983) *The Bodleian Library in the Seventeenth and Eighteenth Centuries*, Clarendon Press.

Pugh, S. L. (2010) The National Library of Wales and Flickr Commons, *Cultural Heritage: a UKOLN Blog for the Cultural Heritage Sector*, 26 July, http://blogs.ukoln.ac.uk/cultural-heritage/2010/07/26/the-national-library-of-wales-and-flickr-commons.

Quint, B. (2001) Don't Burn Books! Burn Librarians!! A Review of Nicholson Baker's Double Fold: Libraries and the Assault on Paper, *Searcher*, **9** (6), www.infotoday.com/searcher/jun01/voice.htm.

Rossi, A. (2012) 80 Terabytes of Archived Web Crawl Data Available for Research, *Internet Archive Blogs*, 26 October, http://blog.archive.org/2012/10/26/80-terabytes-of-archived-web-crawl-data-available-for-research.

Scholz, H. and Miles, T. (2015) From the British Library to Flickr to Europeana – 60000 Public Domain Images on the Move, *Europeana Pro*, https://pro.europeana.eu/post/from-the-british-library-to-flickr-to-europeana-60000-public-dom.

Science Europe (2018) What is cOALition S?, *Science Europe: Shaping the Future of Research*, 4 September, www.scienceeurope.org/coalition-s.

Seadle, M. (2001) Copyright in the Networked World: Digital Legal Deposit, *Library Hi Tech*, **18** (3), 299–303.

Spedding, J. (1861) *The Letters and the Life of Francis Bacon*, Longman, Green, Longman, and Roberts.

Tanner, S. (2013) The Value of Welsh Newspapers Online, *When the Data Hits the Fan: The Blog of Simon Tanner*, 28 March, http://simon-tanner.blogspot.co.uk/2013/03/the-value-of-welsh-newspapers-online.html.

The Legal Deposit Libraries (Non-Print Works) Regulations 2013 (S.I. 2013/777), www.legislation.gov.uk/uksi/2013/777/contents/made.

Townsend Gard, E. (2017) Creating a Last Twenty (L20) Collection: Implementing Section 108(h) in Libraries, Archives and Museums, *Libraries, Archives and Museums*, DOI: 10.2139/ssrn.3049158.

UK Research and Innovation (2013) *RCUK Policy on Open Access and Supporting Guidance*, www.ukri.org/files/legacy/documents/rcukopenaccesspolicy-pdf.

Warwick, C., Terras, M., Huntington, P. and Pappa, N. (2008) If You Build It Will They Come? The LAIRAH Study: Quantifying the Use of Online Resources in the Arts and Humanities, *Literary and Linguistic Computing*, **23** (1), 85–102, http://dro.dur.ac.uk/13505/1/13505.pdf?DDD11+d700tmt.

Weber, M. S. (2017) The Tumultuous History of News on the Web. In Brügger, N. and Schroeder, R. (eds), *The Web as History: Using Web Archives to Understand the Past and Present*, UCL Press, http://discovery.ucl.ac.uk/1542998/1/The-Web-as-History.pdf.

Wilkinson, J. M., Pollard, T. and Farquhar, A. (2010) British Library Dataset Programme: Supporting Research in the Library of the 21st Century, *LIBER Quarterly*, **20** (1), 94–104, DOI: 10.18352/lq.7979.

Winters, J. (2017) Coda: Web Archives for Humanities Research – Some Reflections. In Brügger, N. and Schroeder, R. (eds), *The Web as History: Using Web Archives to Understand the Past and Present*, UCL Press, 238–48.

Index